Negotiating Identities in Women's Lives

Recent Titles in
Contributions in Women's Studies

Negotiating Identities in Women's Lives

English Postcolonial and Contemporary British Novels

CHRISTINE WICK SIZEMORE

Contributions in Women's Studies,
Number 196

GREENWOOD PRESS
Westport, Connecticut • London

I-1521

Library of Congress Cataloging-in-Publication Data

Sizemore, Christine Wick.
    Negotiating identities in women's lives : English postcolonial and
contemporary British novels / Christine Wick Sizemore.
        p. cm.—(Contributions in women's studies, ISSN 0147-104X ; no. 196)
    Includes bibliographical references (p.   ) and index.
    ISBN 0-313-32163-9 (alk. paper)
    1. English fiction—20th century—History and criticism.   2. Women and
literature—Great Britain—History—20th century.   3. Women and literature—
English-speaking countries—History—20th century.   4. Literature,
Comparative—Commonwealth (English) and English.   5. Literature,
Comparative—English and Commonwealth (English).   6. English fiction—
Women authors—History and criticism.   7. Commonwealth fiction (English)—
History and criticism.   8. Postcolonialism—English-speaking countries.
9. Identity (Psychology) in literature.   10. Group identity in literature.
I. Title.   II. Series.
PR888.W6S59   2002
823'.91099287—dc21   2001058642

British Library Cataloguing in Publication Data is available.

Library of Congress Catalog Card Number: 2001058642
ISBN: 0-313-32163-9
ISSN: 0147-104X

First published in 2002

Greenwood Press, 88 Post Road West, Westport, CT 06881
An imprint of Greenwood Publishing Group, Inc.
www.greenwood.com

Printed in the United States of America

The paper used in this book complies with the
Permanent Paper Standard issued by the National
Information Standards Organization (Z39.48-1984).

10 9 8 7 6 5 4 3 2 1

For the women of my family with love and gratitude for all they have taught me about the myriad roles women play—my mother, Chris Wick; my sisters, Laura Wick, Wendy Wick Reaves, and Sandy Wick Ruggiero; and my daughter, Christi Sizemore

Contents

Acknowledgments

I would like to thank a number of my Spelman colleagues for their support and intellectual exchange. Three recent department chairs, Anne Warner, Akiba Harper, and Opal Moore, and our former provost, Glenda Price, now president of Marygrove College in Detroit, provided continual encouragement and support for this project in numerous ways. Anne Warner and Stephen Knadler gave invaluable critiques of drafts of several chapters. Candace Raven was consistently helpful (and cheerful) in solving numerous problems with machines and software and general procedures. The fourteen students in my Fall 2000 Senior Seminar were a delight to teach. Their inquiry and investigation of postcolonial women's novels complemented and extended my own.

My engagement with postcolonial theory was greatly enhanced by Feroza Jussawalla and Reed Way Dasenbrock's National Endowment for the Humanities Institute in London in the summer of 1998 on Postcolonial Literature and Theory. It was exciting to meet and hear many of the theorists and novelists I had studied. I am grateful to both directors and to my twenty-three institute colleagues for a wonderful summer of intellectual discussion, rethinking of issues, and grappling with new ideas as well as interesting explorations of London such as Buchi Emecheta's walking tour of Camden and the discovery of British/Caribbean theater at Kennington Oval.

I am grateful to Barbara Burford for taking time away from her demanding job as one of the directors of the National Health Service for an interview (published in *MaComère*) about her work that enhanced my understanding of it.

I would like to thank both Tuzyline Jita Allan and Marie Umeh for their interest in my work on African women's novels and their publishing of some of my early studies of the novels discussed here.

The annual conference on British Commonwealth and Postcolonial Studies organized by Gautam Kundu of Georgia Southern University has provided stimulating opportunities for a number of years for the exchange of ideas about postcolonial theory and literature.

I thank George Butler and Tod Myerscough of Greenwood Press for their support of my project, for answering all my numerous questions, and for shepherding my book through the publication process.

As always, I am grateful for the love and encouragement of my husband Michael and my daughter Christi and son James.

Negotiating Identities in Women's Lives

Introduction

As we move forward in the new millennium, there is a call for a new kind of global literature that will better describe the new identities the late twentieth century has produced. In "The World and the Home," Homi Bhabha says:

> Where the transmission of "national" traditions was once the major theme of a world literature, perhaps we can now suggest that transnational histories of migrants, the colonized, or political refugees—these border and frontier conditions—may be the terrains of world literature. The center of such a study would neither be the "sovereignty" of national cultures nor the "universalism" of human culture but a focus on those "freak displacements" . . . that have been caused within cultural lives of postcolonial societies. (449)

This new kind of global literature, Bhabha explains, emerges from "the interstices—the overlap and displacement of domains of difference—[where] . . . the intersubjective and collective experiences of *nationness*, community interest, or cultural value are negotiated" (*Location of Culture* 2). Bhabha says that it is in these interstices that hybridity[1] can be developed: The "interstitial passage between fixed identifications opens up the possibility of a cultural hybridity that entertains difference without an assumed or imposed hierarchy" (*Location of Culture* 4). The value of hybridity, a space of liminality or border,[2] for Bhabha is that it opens up spaces of difference without hierarchy. It opens up passageways between fixed identities. Edward Said also embraces the term *hybridity* in *Culture and Imperialism* and broadens it further, arguing that "because of empire, all cultures are involved in one another. . . . [A]ll are hybrid, heterogenous" (xxv). A focus on the work of migrants, people of diaspora, and those of mixed heritage and nationality can be a valuable entry point into a variety of global literatures. This study joins that focus by looking at contemporary women's novels of hybridity.

Bhabha's concept of a space that can promote difference without hierarchy is one that is very useful to feminist critics struggling with definitions of gender and difference. Not only is there debate about whether sexual difference is biological or performative,[3] but, as Rita Felski explains, "the experiential diversity of real women[4] mitigates against any general claims about the nature of female difference" ("Doxa of Difference" 3). After surveying a number of positions on the nature of difference, Felski concludes that the concept of hybridity offers "the most viable alternative to the current doxa of difference":

> Metaphors of hybridity [which she also calls creolization and *métissage*] . . . not only recognize differences within the subject, fracturing and complicating holistic notions of identity, but also address connections between subjects by recognizing affiliations, cross-pollinations, echoes, and repetitions, thereby unseating difference from a position of absolute privilege. Instead of endorsing a drift toward an ever greater atomization of identity, such metaphors allow us to conceive of multiple, interconnecting axes of affiliation and differentiation. (12)

Susan Stanford Friedman also thinks that the concept of hybridity "offers feminism new ways of moving beyond the exclusive focus on difference" and that "the term *hybridity* appears to have the most currency in English to reference forms of intercultural mixing" (82–83). For Friedman hybridity provides feminism with a "dialogic," a theory for "negotiation between [Pnina Werbner's] 'the Scylla of universalism and the Charybdis of differentialism'" (103). For both Felski and Friedman the advantages of hybridity theory include a way of recognizing affiliations between sites of difference and of discussing intercultural relations as well as a way of avoiding the splintering of identities into smaller and smaller units.

Although Felski and Friedman find the hybridity theory useful for feminism, both acknowledge some of the baggage of the term *hybridity* that Robert Young describes in *Colonial Desire: Hybridity in Theory, Culture and Race*. Young agrees that "heterogeneity, cultural interchange and diversity have now become the self-conscious identity of modern society" (4), but he has two concerns about the term *hybridity* itself. The first concern is that in its biological connotations *hybridity* evokes the racist "vocabulary of the Victorian extreme right" (10). Young balances that heritage, however, with the linguistic use by M.M. Bakhtin, which Young explains is the reference point used by Bhabha, Stuart Hall, Henry Louis Gates Jr. and others. In this context, Young finds the term a useful challenge to dominant discourses. Young's second concern about the term *hybridity* is that whichever "model of hybridity may be employed . . . hybridity as a cultural description will always carry with it an implicit politics of heterosexuality" (25). Laura Doan, however, does not find this limitation in the word. In a discussion of Jeanette Winterson's *Sexing the Cherry* in *The Lesbian Postmodern*, Doan argues:

> Winterson imagines that gender is socially constructed and enforced rather than inherent and, above all, that the hybrid—a third sex, a fusion of diverse strains, without seed and the strongest—illuminates the ways in which the dominant culture opts out of creatively and freely exploring boundless gender options. . . . [H]ybridization inevitably poses a dangerous challenge to the comfortable dualisms (nature/culture, natural/artificial, female/male) upon which patriarchal hegemony . . . is based. . . . The hybrid presupposes a biological precursor . . . but cultural (in this case, scientific) intervention bears the responsibility for the act of creation. (152)

For Doan and Winterson *hybrid* is a workable term for lesbian identity. Its botanical and linguistic connotations more than balance out its nineteenth-century biological heritage.

Both feminist and cultural critics have found the term *hybridity* useful in describing varying concepts of identity. Susan Stanford Friedman finds six different overlapping discourses of identity within feminism: "multiple oppression; multiple subject positions; contradictory subject positions; relationality; situationality; and hybridity" (20). Stuart Hall describes black identity as "an unstable identity, psychically, culturally and politically. It, too, is a narrative, a story, a history. Something constructed" ("Minimal Selves" 116). Diasporic identity in particular for Hall "is defined, not by essence or purity, but by the recognition of a necessary heterogeneity and diversity; by a conception of 'identity' which lives with and through, not despite difference; by *hybridity*" ("Cultural Identity and Diaspora" 402). Angela McRobbie likewise uses hybridity to define identity as continuously developing and changing:

> [S]ince full identity is never achieved, the question of the self is never resolved and fixed and is therefore always open to change, to transformation. . . . identity becomes much more fluid . . . [and] notions of full subjectivity . . . [are replaced] with fragile, "shaggy," hybrid identities. (42)

Despite the term's popularity, some theorists are still concerned that the concept is too generalized[5] and has the potential to "mask a new system of hierarchies," thus becoming an oppressive concept itself (Moore-Gilbert 194–95). Gayatri Chakravorty Spivak, for instance, warns: "Sometimes 'hybridity'—like the old 'androgyny' theory of feminism—can make us forget these differences [between 'migrant and postcolonial mixtures']" (*Outside the Teaching Machine* 243). Ella Shohat argues that one must "discriminate between the diverse modalities of hybridity, for example, forced assimilation, internalized self-rejection, political cooptation, social conformism, cultural mimicry, and creative transcendence" (110). These are important distinctions to add to discussions of hybridity. There are crucial differences, for instance, between the migrant characters in some of Buchi Emecheta's novels, who travel from Nigeria to England, and the postcolonial Indian characters in some of Anita Desai's novels who remain in the same place while observing the departure of the British and the partition of India in 1947. Equally there are important differences between the effects of slavery and the remnants of African culture in the Caribbean, which Paule Marshall describes in *Praisesong for the Widow*, and the British colonialism in Rhodesia that produced mimic men such as Babamakuru, one of Tsitsi Dangarembga's characters in *Nervous Conditions* (see Vizzard). Although these differences must be acknowledged, the problem remains of how to achieve a balance between a global theory like hybridity that threatens to submerge particular identities and the atomization of identities that Felski and Friedman describe.

Chandra Mohanty argues in favor of a transnational focus as a way of combining the local and the global.[6] For Alexander and Mohanty, transnational feminism is "comparative, relational, and historically based" (xvi). It recognizes "the relations of domination and subordination that are named and articulated through the processes of racism" and the economic forces of global capitalism (xvii). "What kind of racialized, gendered selves," they ask, "get produced at the conjuncture of the transnational and the postcolonial?" (xviii). Although they do not use the term, I would argue that the space of the conjuncture of the transnational and the postcolonial could sometimes be the interstitial space that Bhabha calls hybridity.[7] If one is careful to add the historical base and the relations of domination and subordination and avoid the danger of ahistorical "feminist bricolage" (Susan Friedman 108), the framework of hybridity provides a context in which to see similarities, differences, and relationships between stories. For Mohanty, it is narratives in particular that provide a way of balancing: "[T]he global is forged on the basis of memories and counternarratives, not on an ahistorical universalism" ("Feminist Encounters" 80).

In an argument similar to Mohanty's, Seyla Benhabib says: "[T]he new constellation formed by the coming together of global integration and apparent cultural fragmentation is the contemporary horizon against which the project of contemporary feminism must be rethought" (336). Benhabib proposes the concept of dialogic narrative as a model "for conceptualizing identity" at "personal, gender or national" levels (337).[8] The self is in dialogue with others, enmeshed in "webs of interlocution . . . webs of narrative," but creates its own life story (344). Benhabib explains that identity in this model does not imply "the fiction of a stable, frozen, and fixed subject. . . . [But it does provide some continuity] if we think of the identity of the self in time . . . in terms of an ability to make sense, to render coherent, meaningful, and viable for oneself one's shifting commitments as well as changing attachments" (347). Identity conceived as a narrative "does not mean 'sameness in time' but rather the capacity to generate meaning over time so as to hold past, present and future together" (353). Benhabib's concept of identity as a narrative works well with the concept of hybrid identity. Both include the idea of identity developing over time. Specifically, hybrid identity is a particular kind of narrative that tells stories from the interstices of culture. It includes Stuart Hall's description of black identity as "a

narrative, a story" ("Minimal Selves" 116) and Mohanty's transnational "counternarratives" ("Feminist Encounters" 80).

The particular kind of narrative used in this book to investigate
stories of identities is the novel. Patricia Yaeger, building on Bakhtin's
ideas, says that "the novel is a form women choose because its
multivoicedness allows the interruption and interrogation of the
dominant culture" (31). Most of the novels that I will examine come
out of a tradition that Radhika Mohanram and Gita Rajan call "English Postcoloniality." That is, all of the authors of these novels have
received English educations,[9] and English is one of their primary (if
not their only) languages. Yet, at the same time, these authors also
critique British culture, whether from the point of view of nationality
or race or heritage. As Mohanram and Rajan argue, many English
postcolonial texts, in "appropriating the dominator's language . . .
managed to encode subversive and problematic meanings" (4). These
women novelists come from different locations, but I am interested
in the ways that their stories and critiques overlap. What commonalities and affiliations can be found in the interstices of cultures?
Benhabib says that she senses "a new awareness afoot—a recognition of interdependence among women of different classes, cultures
and sexual orientations" (355). If we look at these different stories,
what bases for interdependence emerge?

In investigating the overlapping of these narratives, I primarily use
hybridity to refer to what Susan Stanford Friedman calls, in her
"mapping" of hybridity theory, the "intermingling of differences."[10]
In this usage, "the differences that make up the hybrid remain in play,
retaining some of their original character, although altered in the
weaving" (84). This definition of hybridity can embrace both hybridity that is "spatial and geographic," as in narratives of migration, and
hybridity that is "temporal and historical" (85–87), as in narratives
of colonialism and its aftermath.

The novels selected for this study involve both spatial and temporal hybridity, but their focus is primarily on only one of the three
political positions that Friedman outlines. These novels critique English colonialism and racism, but they do not focus solely on oppression. Neither do they analyze power only in terms of a detailed
historical discussion of a single location. Rather, they mostly describe
the "liberating" forces associated with hybridity. Friedman explains
that "this analytic mode does not suggest that hybridity is without
pain, dislocation, suffering, or oppression. Rather, this stance toward

hybridity emphasizes that within the context of power relations, hybridity performs progressive cultural work, as the force privileging genuine multiculturalism and heterogeneity" (90). In these senses of the word, the English postcolonial novels in this study reveal the stories that are told from the hybrid spaces between cultures where multicultural differences can play with and against each other. Women's issues from various cultures overlap, and the narratives reveal both the similarities between and the varieties of ways that women solve problems.

To look for these overlaps and commonalities among narratives, I use what Said in *Culture and Imperialism* has termed a "global, contrapuntal analysis . . . modelled not (as earlier notions of comparative literature were) on a symphony but rather on an atonal ensemble [that takes] . . . into account all sorts of spatial or geographical and rhetorical practices" (318). Although Said is analyzing novels from the modernist period that were embedded in a structure of imperialism, and I am looking at postcolonial and contemporary British novels, the contrapuntal method is a way of undercutting the periphery/center orientation that can threaten postcolonial analysis as well as colonial analysis. [I will follow Loomba in using *imperialism* "as the phenomenon that originates in the metropolis" and *colonialism* as its "result . . . what happens in the colonies as a consequence of imperial domination" (6–7).] Susan Stanford Friedman likewise argues for the value of "comparativist analysis": "Sharp juxtapositions of different locations often produce startling illuminations, bringing into focus the significance of geopolitical mediations of other axes of difference" (114). I will juxtapose novels that share themes but are rooted in different cultures and look for the atonalities as well as the harmonies. In particular, I will use the axis of age and the specific psychological "tensions" that often accompany various ages in women's lives. Thus I will read Margaret Atwood's *Cat's Eye*, set in Canada, against Tsitsi Dangarembga's *Nervous Conditions*, set in Zimbabwe, both stories in which girls struggle to find adult roles. I pair two novels that write against the romance plot of heterosexuality, one by Barbara Burford, whose parents emigrated to Britain from Jamaica, and one by Keri Hulme, whose heritage is both Maori and British. National identities are a theme in the works of Nigerian novelist Buchi Emecheta and Indian novelist Anita Desai. Margaret Drabble, the only English writer in the group, and Nadine Gordimer write novels of political upheaval. Paule Marshall, a writer of

Barbadian descent, and Jessica Anderson, a white Australian, write novels about older women taking journeys to discover cultural wholeness. Both Doris Lessing, under the pseudonym Jane Somers, and Joan Riley, who writes of Caribbean immigrants in London, tell stories of illness and death.

As this varied group of novelists indicates, I am using a very broad definition of postcolonial in my choice of writers. Although critics like Vijay Mishra and Bob Hodge are leery about including white settler colonies because they are not oppositional enough (289),[11] I follow Stuart Hall in his argument for an inclusive definition of the term:

> Australia and Canada, on the one hand, Nigeria, India and Jamaica on the other, are certainly not "post-colonial" *in the same way*. But this does not mean that they are not "post-colonial" *in any way*. In terms of their relation to the imperial centre, and the ways in which . . . they are "in but not of the West," they were plainly all "colonial," and are usefully designated now as "post-colonial," though the manner, timing and conditions of their colonisation and independence varied greatly. ("When Was 'The Post-Colonial?'" 246)

Both Ania Loomba in *Colonialism/Postcolonialism* and Bart Moore-Gilbert in *Postcolonial Theory* survey a number of critics who raise various objections to the term *postcolonial*.[12] For Anne McClintock, for instance, the term is "prematurely celebratory" ("Angel of Progress" 294) and does not acknowledge some of the complexities of power surrounding relationships between former colonies and their European colonizers and among themselves. Nonetheless, McClintock finds that postcolonial theory, if it takes into consideration the complex and continuing histories of a variety of colonialisms, can be useful. Therefore, she is willing not to "banish" the term if it can be used "judiciously in appropriate circumstances" (294). Ato Quayson argues that one can avoid some of the dangers of the term and add a focus on justice by thinking "of postcolonialism as a process of post-colonializing" (10). He argues that this way of thinking is crucial to understanding the contemporary world:

> Factors like multiculturalism, ethnicity, diaspora and transnationalism as they apply in the West can only be fully understood if seen in tandem with the realities of struggles in real postcolonial societies, precisely because some of these factors are actually the effects of global population and cultural flows after colonialism. The argument, then,

is to see postcolonialism not merely as a chronological marker but as an epistemological one; it focalizes a constellation of issues integral to the formation of a global order after empire. And this, it has to be noted, is not merely a sensibility for the formerly colonized. (11)

In order to structure my discussion of these postcolonial novels of hybridity, I would like to pry loose some of Erik Erikson's terminology from the rigid developmental schemas and essentialized concepts of female identity with which he has been associated and for which he has been strongly criticized. Erikson's name is most often associated with the concept of "identity crisis," which freezes "identity" as a label for Western adolescents' search for adult roles and implies the ability to achieve the very "fixed, stable" identity that Hall, McRobbie, Benhabib, and others have now so effectively deconstructed. Erikson's biographer, however, explains that Erikson himself felt that a fixed sense of identity and the "popular summaries of each of the eight stages within his developmental model betrayed a fundamental misunderstanding of what he had written" (Lawrence Friedman 221). Lawrence J. Friedman argues that as the illegitimate son of a Christian Dane and the stepson of a German Jew, Erikson himself struggled as a young man with a sense of blurred national identity, which was then exacerbated by his flight from the growing Nazi threat in Vienna and immigration to America. These personal experiences, Friedman says, created in Erikson a "desperate, sometimes depressing sense of marginality without defined personal boundaries" (104) that led directly to his later work on identity. Friedman argues that in Erikson's collaborations with cultural anthropologists and in his study of Sioux and Yurok youth, Erikson "became a critic of modernity, perhaps what we now might call a postcolonial critic" (186).

In order to understand Friedman's label, one must look at some of Erikson's lesser known and later writings where he is much more flexible and culturally aware than he seems in textbook summaries. Robert Butler, a psychiatrist and gerontologist, for instance, quotes Erikson as saying: "[I]dentity formation neither begins nor ends with adolescence: it is a lifelong development" (75–76). This definition of a developing, fluid identity fits much better with contemporary understandings of the term. The concepts I find most useful in Erikson's thought present the adult personality as continually developing in an effort to cope with the various "tasks" or "tensions" of adult life.

This aspect of Erikson's thought fits well with the structure of novels in which protagonists often change and develop throughout the course of their lives.

Erikson acknowledges Freud's stages of early childhood development[13] and then adds four "stages" or "tasks" of adult development: adolescence with its search for adult roles or "identity," young adulthood with its task of intimacy, middle age with its task of generativity, and old age with the task of ego integrity or wisdom (see, for instance, *Childhood and Society* 247–74; *Identity, Youth and Crisis* 91–141; *The Life Cycle Completed* 55–61). Although these eight stages of development have been popularized and schematized into the very "individualistic telos of developmental models" that Susan Stanford Friedman suggests that we have gone beyond (19), Erikson himself thought of his theory as much more fluid. It was the American setting and interpretation of his work, he explained to an Indian audience in 1977, that made it seem more a series of steps that must be achieved in order:

> I was somewhat shocked by the frequency with which not only the term identity, but also the other . . . psycho-social qualities ascribed by me to various stages, were widely accepted as conscious developmental "achievements." . . . [M]y emphasis in each stage on a built-in and lifelong antithesis ("identity" vs. "identity confusion") was given a kind of modern Calvinist emphasis. But beyond this, I gradually realized that the American world view, originally a composite of Biblical and political imageries depicting a promised land to be reached, in fulfilment of God's will, across some body of water, had developed into a ready space-time imagery of salvation by personal and social progress. ("Report to Vikram" 24)

Although the popularization of Erikson's theories seems to have made them into a quintessentially American combination of John Bunyan's *Pilgrim's Progress* and a Horatio Alger story, in reality Erikson's theories are much less "progress" oriented and more culturally flexible. In *Vital Involvement in Old Age* (1986), Erikson says that "the individual is never struggling only with the tension that is focal at the time. Rather, at every successive developmental stage, the individual is also increasingly engaged in the anticipation of tensions that have yet to become focal and in reexperiencing those tensions that were inadequately integrated when they were focal" (Erikson, Erikson, and Kivnick 39). Erikson's earlier word "task," which implies a potential completion, is now replaced by "tension." The "stages" overlap and vary according to the individual, the culture, and the historical time period: As Erikson said in India, "[T]he demonstration of psycho-social and psycho-historical relativity is part of our method" ("Report to Vikram" 25).

Given Erikson's interest in India and his writing of a psycho-biography of Gandhi, it is not surprising to find a strong interest in Erikson's work in India. Sudhir Kakar, an Indian student and colleague of Erikson, parallels Erikson's theories of adult development with Hindu thought. Kakar explains that

> Hindu philosophy and ethics teach that "right action" [dharma] for an individual depends on *desa*, the culture in which he is born; on *kala*, the period of historical time in which he lives; on *srama*, the efforts required of him at different stages of life; and on *gunas*, the innate psychobiological traits which are the heritage of an individual's previous lives. (*The Inner World* 37)

Kakar finds a parallel between the Hindu concept of *dharma*, which he defines as "the ground-plan of an ideal life cycle," and Erikson's model: "Like modern theories of personality the Hindu model of *asramadharma* conceptualizes human development in a succession of stages" (42) whose adult tasks parallel Erikson's: Thus Erikson's task of identity is matched with the Hindu's "knowledge of *dharma*"; the Western young adult's intimacy, with the Hindu "householder's" love shown by "the practice of *dharma*"; the Western adult's generativity, with the Hindu adult's "withdrawal" and "teaching of *dharma*"; and the similar task of wisdom, with the "realization of *dharma*" achieved by "renunciation" (43).

Although Kakar finds these parallel tasks in Hindu thought, other Indian theorists emphasize that different cultures conceptualize "stages" of life differently. B.K. Ramanujam says that in India not all of Western psychology's developmental stages of childhood and youth are recognized. He explains: "As far as our clinical experience suggests, only childhood is recognized. . . . Adolescence as a distinct phase . . . is not identified. . . . [However, in] the traditional Indian social matrix, even though adolescence as a phase was not recognized, the passage from childhood to the adult stage was guided through a series of what Erikson would call 'situations,' the ultimate goal being the establishment of an individual in his adult role" (37–38). Ramanujam notes here that the achievement of an "adult role" before one reaches the stage of what Kakar calls "householder" is also the goal of what Erikson calls the adolescent identity stage.

Although I do group the novels by age of the protagonists as a way of structuring my analysis, I am less interested in maintaining Erikson's concept of "stages," even if fluid, than I am in appropriating Erikson's vocabulary for adult development: the search for adult roles, the search for intimacy, the search for generativity, and the search for integrity or wisdom. These are the terms that I would like to combine with concepts of historical, geographical, sexual, and cultural identities. These terms, I think, are flexible enough to be folded into concepts of hybridity and postcoloniality. Intimacy Erikson at first associated only with heterosexual commitment in young adulthood, represented by marriage in many cultures and the romance plot of the Western novel, but in *Vital Involvement in Old Age*, Erikson describes intimacy as "the capacity for eventual commitment to lasting friendships and companionship in general" (Erikson, Erikson, and Kivnick 37). Generativity, an involvement with one's community and future generations, is also a value shared by many cultures. Gay Wilentz, for instance, finds "'generational continuity'—as traditionally . . . [an adult] woman's domain" in African and black diasporic cultures" (xii). The wisdom of the elderly is perhaps more valued in African and Asian than in western European cultures.

A more problematic aspect of the use of Erikson's thought in a work of feminist criticism is his "essentialized" concept of female identity, his notorious association of womanhood with "inner space," and his assertion, "Yes . . . anatomy is destiny" (*Identity, Youth and Crisis* 285).[14] Although Erikson can be shown to be flexible in terms of cultural difference, one must also ask whether this rigid definition of woman can be deconstructed. In her 1979 critique of Erikson's essentialism in his writings on womanhood and inner space, Cynthia Griffin Wolff notes that Erikson's jump "from descriptive to prescriptive—represents the source of the trouble" (362). She shows that Erikson makes a "metaphorical extension" (364) from his descriptions of young girls' play constructions to assumptions about their inner identity. She asks: "Even if we acknowledge the girls' preoccupation with inner space, can we accept Erikson's explanation of what it means? A home is an inner space. What is a board room? The stock exchange?" (365). Wolff argues that "the motif of 'inner space' [in girls' play constructions] . . . was not a key to innate 'feminine' identity; it was, instead, an instance of a recurrent and typically 'feminine' *mode of representation*" (366). The play fantasies of both girls and boys included active and passive elements; the play structures, Wolff argues, were results of socialization and represented merely "congenial mode[s] of representation" (366). Wolff's argument helps to separate Erikson's actual experiment and his descriptions of it from his dubious generalizations. Psychoanalyst Jessica Benjamin also found she could adapt Erikson's experiment in her intersubjective model of female desire:

> I would have to say that Erik Erikson was not all wrong in his intuitions about inner space, though he was wrong in some of the conclusions he drew from them. . . . [T]he idea of inner space or spatial representation of [female] desire can be associated with subjectivity only when the interior is not merely an object to be discovered or a receptacle. . . . Rather, inner space should be understood as part of a continuum that includes the space between the I and the you. (95)

Benjamin, too, thinks that Erikson can be revised and adapted for feminist analysis.

Erikson was also an influence on feminist critics who reacted strongly against him. In the 1970s and early 1980s feminist psychological theorists like Nancy Chodorow and Carol Gilligan wrote about the value of connectedness in the development of female identity in reaction to the emphasis on separation in Erikson's male-based model. Although both Chodorow and Gilligan have been criticized for using models that are too exclusively Western, postcolonial critic Anne McClintock says that although "Chodorow undoubtedly does not pay sufficient attention to cultural variations in family relations, she makes an important departure from theories of archetypal gender difference by locating different boundary experiences in the historical and hence mutable, social structures of childrearing and domestic divisions of labor" (*Imperial Leather* 319). From the viewpoint of 1986, Benjamin says that "critical feminist psychoanalytic theory . . . argue[s] that individuality is properly, ideally, a balance of separation and connectedness" (82), and developmental psychologists such as James Marcia now read Erikson that way as well,[15] but the need to challenge Erikson's theories was an important impetus to the early work of Gilligan and Chodorow. Both the modifications and the challenges to his work have been incorporated into contemporary psychology. Erikson's descriptions and vocabulary can be separated from his metaphors, and both he and the feminist theorists who reacted against him can be placed within historical, cultural, and social structures.[16] The prescriptive can be removed and the descriptive salvaged as Wolff does for school-age children in her reinterpretation of Erikson's article, and gerontology theorist Kathleen Woodward does for old age. She too says: "I have found much in developmental psychoanalysis that is useful, particularly its descriptive value. What is less persuasive . . . is its proscriptive or prescriptive stance" (*Aging and Its Discontents* 20).

Like these critics, I want to separate Erikson's descriptive language from his now outdated prescriptive pronouncements. By combining Erikson's descriptions with postcolonial theorists and cultural critics who are firmly committed to concepts of developing and changing identities and who bring in issues of social and historical structures, I think I can use some of his concepts without falling into mid-century conceptions of fixed identities. Although I am grouping characters roughly by age and following the order of Erikson's adult "stages"— intimacy, generativity, and ego integrity—I would like to emphasize, as does Woodward (*Aging and Its Discontents* 20–21) and as in fact Erikson himself does in his later works, that these are all ongoing adult themes, not ones that are "completed" or "ended" at a certain stage or age. To these themes I am adding contemporary and postcolonial concerns about sexuality, nationality, politics, and culture.

Thus, Chapter 1, "Girlhood Identities: The Search for Adulthood in Tsitsi Dangarembga's *Nervous Conditions* and Margaret Atwood's *Cat's Eye*," not only integrates the discussion of these novels with culturally matched theories such as Franz Fanon's for *Nervous Conditions* and Nancy Chodorow's for *Cat's Eye*, but also reads both novels in terms of Carol Gilligan's recent work on girls at risk who are caught between "voice and silence."

Chapter 2, "Sexual Identities: The Search for Intimacy in Barbara Burford's "The Threshing Floor" and Keri Hulme's *The Bone People*, turns away from the typical heterosexual search for intimacy in the romance plot to include lesbian and communal intimacy in Burford's novella, read in light of Judith Roof's and Teresa de Lauretis's theories, and nonsexual and communal intimacy within the Maori tradition in *The Bone People*.

Facing anxieties about nationality and diasporic identity is a necessary part of postcolonial writers, striving for generativity or generational continuity. I thus include a discussion of migrant identity from Bhabha's essay "DissemiNation" as well as Ashis Nandy's analysis of the psychological effects of British imperialism in India in Chapter 3, "National Identities: The Search for Place in Buchi Emecheta's *Kehinde* and Anita Desai's *Clear Light of Day*.

Chapter 4, "Social and Political Identities: The Search for Space," contrasts two novels with multiple protagonists—Margaret Drabble's *The Radiant Way* and Nadine Gordimer's *None to Accompany Me*. These novels, which portray the demise of liberalism, are read in the context of Bhabha's theories about "the Third Space" and Robert Young's analysis of two kinds of hybridity, the contestation between and the merging of cultures.

Chapter 5 uses Stuart Hall's definition of evolving cultural identity and Robert Butler's theories of life review in a discussion of two very different postcolonial journeys: "Cultural Identities: The Search for Integrity in Paule Marshall's *Praisesong for the Widow* and Jessica Anderson's *Tirra Lirra by the River*.

Chapter 6 engages Joan Erikson's and Kathleen Woodward's theories about aging and disability in "Facing Death: The Search for a Legacy in Joan Riley's *Waiting in the Twilight* and Doris Lessing's *The Diary of a Good Neighbour*," both novels in which the physical deterioration of approaching death is made all the more difficult by issues of class, race, and poverty.

I use the various theories in each chapter in the spirit of what Susan Stanford Friedman calls "negotiation." She says that "the *negotiation* among competing and often divisive discourses most fruitfully characterizes feminist engagement in the academy 'after' post-structuralism. *Negotiation* connotes a dialogic exchange, where . . . the hierarchy of 'theory' [is not reinforced] over 'history'" (198)—or, I would add, over narrative.

Although U.S. literature has many writers who could be placed in this migrant or hybrid tradition, this book focuses on the tradition of the contemporary British and English postcolonial novel because that was the educational focus both of women writers who grew up in Britain and those who had an English "colonial" education in a variety of former colonies.[17] As Helen Tiffin explains:

> Well into the 1970s, curricula of the English Department(s) of the University of the West Indies and Guyana, like most post-colonial universities in both the colonies of occupation and settler-invader colonies, were still dominated by the study of [English authors from] Shakespeare . . . to Emily Brontë, Dickens, George Eliot, in spite of the inclusion of some local writing. ("Plato's Cave" 149)

Thus the contemporary British novelists, the novelists from "white settler" colonies like Canada and Australia, and the novelists from formerly occupied colonies like India, Jamaica, Nigeria, and Zimbabwe all shared an exposure to the tradition of the English novel that underlies their engagement with and revision of the novel form. Mishra and Hodge concede that one can "accept that a European epic narrative mediated through the European bourgeois novel was an available discourse to the post-colonial writer [as long as one also emphasizes] . . . those very precise, historically and culturally specific distinctions that mark off post-colonial difference without constructing, in turn, a post-colonial homogeneity that cancels out its own oppositions and fractures" (280–81).

Most of the authors I have chosen not only build on the genre of the English novel, however encoded by cultural difference, but also use a realistic style. Vinay Dharwadker identifies four "overlapping types of realism" that predominate "in prose fiction across the transitional and former colonies": social realism, psychological realism, historical realism, and mythic realism (66). Buchi Emecheta, Joan Riley, Nadine Gordimer, Paule Marshall and Doris Lessing (under her Jane Somers pseudonym) all use predominantly social realism which is useful in bringing out politics and issues of oppression. Others like Barbara Burford,[18] Jessica Anderson, Tsitsi Dangarembga, and Anita Desai use predominantly psychological realism. Dharwadker calls Desai's style, for instance, a "lyrical" psychological realism (67), a term that fits Burford's and Anderson's styles as well.

Although Dharwadker says that "the ascendant mode since about 1975 has been 'magical realism'" and gives the example of Salman Rushdie (69), some of these authors fit Kwame Anthony Appiah's term "postrealist" much better, especially since the roots of magic realism lie in the Latin and South American tradition rather than in the English novelistic tradition. Appiah defines postrealism as a method that "allows its author to borrow . . . techniques of modernism: which . . . are often also the techniques of postmodernism" (433). For Atwood and Drabble, both of whom break up a linear narrative in postmodern fashion but also include a lot of detailed social realism, the term is useful. Although Hulme's novel could be classified as either "magic realism" or "mythic realism" since it uses Maori myths and dreams and seemingly miraculous healing, it nonetheless fits the "postrealist" label best since it clearly borrows its stream-of-consciousness techniques from Joyce and even situates its heroine in a Joycean kind of tower. Appiah associates the realism of such male African writers as Chinua Achebe in *Things Fall Apart* and Camara Laye in *L'Enfant Noir* with the early stages of African nationalism and anticolonialism (432). Although Dangarembga situates her female bildungsroman during the struggle for independence in Rhodesia and subtly embeds national politics in the background, she does not use realism as Achebe and Laye do. Her realism remains psychological rather than political.

All these women novelists share what Appiah calls "postcolonial writers' humanism—the concern for human suffering, for the victims of the postcolonial state [or oppression because of race or class] . . . while still rejecting the master-narratives of modernism" (438). Although Appiah does not use the word *hybridity*, he certainly evokes the idea when he says that the "lesson in the broad shape of this circulation of cultures . . . is surely that we are all already contaminated by one another" (439).

Each of the authors discussed in this book is very aware of the mixture of cultures within her own experience and writes out of that perspective, from the "interstices," to use Bhabha's term, the gaps between cultures, whether those are the spaces of hybridity, migrancy, postcoloniality, or marginality. Barbara Burford, Anita Desai, and Keri Hulme all discuss their varied ethnic and national heritages. Barbara Burford's father is Jewish, and her mother is part Scot, part black. She was born in Jamaica but grew up in Britain. Anita Desai's mother was German and her father Bengali. She grew up in what she describes as "old Delhi" when "it was still a capital of the British empire . . . a curious world . . . made up of all these different fragments . . . the British element . . . the Islamic element . . . the Hindu element. . . . I went to . . . a mission school . . . [and] fell in love with English literature" ("Interview" 171). Keri Hulme is a New Zealander with Scottish, English, and Maori ancestry. As her novel with its interspersed Maori words illustrates, she wants to bring her Maori and her "Pakeha" heritage together.

Joan Riley, born in Jamaica, and Buchi Emecheta, born in Nigeria, are immigrants. They came to Britain as young adults and live there, but they visit their native lands and have relatives there. Both have written of the racism they experienced in Britain. Paule Marshall was born in New York, but as Dorothy Denniston explains, she "grew up in a tightly structured West Indian–American community listening to stories about 'home' (Barbados). . . . [The two-year stay in

Barbados during her childhood instilled] within her the value of her Barbadian ethnicity as different from her African-American identity" (xii). Joyce Pettis explains that in the U.S. there was a split between the African Americans and the Afro-Caribbeans: Both "groups felt the racism of the dominant culture and reacted, the Afro-Caribbeans by distancing themselves from other blacks" (29). Regardless of her actual birthplace, Paule Marshall's predominant identity was thus like Riley's and Burford's, that of an Afro-Caribbean immigrant. Doris Lessing, who spent twenty-five years of her young life in Rhodesia, has been described as the opposite of an immigrant, an exile. Judith Kegan Gardiner calls her "a colonial in exile" whose work is characterized by a "fruitful unsettledness that makes . . .[such writers] simultaneously inheritors and antagonists to imperialism. . . . [T]he English literary tradition is the reassuring heritage of a mother tongue, but it is also somewhat alien" (13). As Lessing recounts in *African Laughter*, she was labeled a "prohibited immigrant" by the white colonial government in Rhodesia and, except for one brief visit in 1956, was prevented from returning until Zimbabwe's independence. Still, as Anthony Chennells and Debrah Raschke argue, even in Lessing's novels set in England and in her science fiction, the "postcolonial is indeed never far from the surface" (3).

The rest of the writers were born and mostly remained in a single nation, but through either colonialism or politics, they remain estranged from a comfortable sense of national identity. Tsitsi Dangarembga grew up under the colonial government of Rhodesia and portrays the damaging effects of imperialism on her people in *Nervous Conditions*. Nadine Gordimer, born in South Africa of a Lithuanian Jewish father and an English Jewish mother, has spent her career writing against apartheid. Margaret Atwood and Jessica Anderson are representative of the "white settler" countries of Canada and Australia. Their experiences were very different from that of the African authors, but they are aware of the differences between their nations and the "mother country," as Atwood conveys in her description of girls' education in the 1950s and Anderson conveys by her title, borrowed from Tennyson, and her story of a journey back to England. Although Margaret Drabble is English and not postcolonial, she shares with the other authors a sense of distance from the dominant culture that comes from both her feminism and the Quaker tradition in which she was raised. All three of her protagonists in *The Radiant Way* are described as having "a sense of being on the margins of English life . . . of being outsiders, looking in from a cold street through a lighted window into a warm lit room that later might prove to be their own. Removed from the mainstream by a mad mother, by a deviant ideology, by refugee status and the warsickness of Middle Europe" (85).

Although all these authors have spent time in warm rooms in major metropolises, parts of their identities are based in memories of various kinds of hybrid, migrant, or marginal experiences that they bring to their novels and their portrayals of women of different ages whose counternarratives bring new insights on women's search to illuminate the spaces in which they find themselves.

Chapter 1

Girlhood Identities: The Search for Adulthood in Tsitsi Dangarembga's *Nervous Conditions* and Margaret Atwood's *Cat's Eye*

The female bildungsroman, the story of young girls' search for adult roles amid the conflicting demands of parents, peers, culture, and ethnic and political traditions, is a familiar form in many cultures.[1] From among these many stories, I have paired two novels that tell the story not just of a single girl but of two girls, one who manages to negotiate a way to adulthood between conflicting ideologies and one who is caught by these ideologies and driven into mental illness. I read together two novels, written at the same time but from very different cultures, Tsitsi Dangarembga's *Nervous Conditions* (1988), set in Zimbabwe, and Margaret Atwood's *Cat's Eye* (1988), set in Canada. Both these novels complicate the bildungsroman pattern not only by telling the story of two girls but also by interweaving an older retrospective narrative voice with that of the protagonist.[2] The older adult voices of the protagonists of each novel, Tambu in *Nervous Conditions* and Elaine in *Cat's Eye*, combine with the young girls' voices to describe how both Tambu and Elaine manage to find a path to adulthood that allows them to survive both political and psychological danger. The adult women's voices, as they reappear throughout the novels, are reminders that the two protagonists have established an identity of their own that is not foreclosed by the rigid gender patterns of the ethnic and historical culture in which they live. The story of loss, however, of the two girls who succumb to these forces always echoes in the background of the stories of success.

Reading these two novels together highlights more submerged threads of narrative that illustrate the nature of the threat to young girls in each culture. The dangers of imperialism and the insidiousness of British colonial education for a young impressionable African girl are major themes in *Nervous Conditions*. The political themes of the relationship of a white settler colony to Britain and the Canadian education of the 1950s that focuses on the "pink spaces" of British imperialism on the map in *Cat's Eye* are brought out by the juxtaposition. Likewise, Atwood's use of patterns of character interaction that reflect feminist theories of female psychological development draw attention to similar patterns in Dangarembga's novel.[3] Since Atwood got an A.M. from Radcliffe in 1962 and did postgraduate study at Harvard in 1962–63 and 1965–67, it is not surprising that her novel has many parallels to feminist theories about girlhood development such as those by Carol Gilligan, who also received an A.M. from Radcliffe in 1961 and studied for her Ph.D at Harvard from 1961 to 1964. One of the psychologists who worked with Gilligan, Lyn Mikel Brown, has singled out *Cat's Eye* as being one of the best representations in fiction of the threats to adolescent girls that she has found in extensive interviews.[4] Another of Gilligan's colleagues who studied "girls at risk" in American schools describes their lives as being situated in "a territory between voice and silence" (Taylor, Gilligan, and Sullivan 202). Gilligan and her colleagues have found that there is no safe strategy for many adolescent girls: "Having a 'big mouth' often got them into trouble, but silence, the slow slipping into a kind of invisible isolation, was also devastating" (Taylor, Gilligan, and Sullivan 3). In an interview with Rosemary Marangoly George and Helen Scott, Dangarembga describes a pattern in women's lives in Zimbabwe that is strikingly similar: "[T]hose are the two alternatives: either you could just sit on the mountain [i.e., remain silent] or you risk self-destruction" from standing up to powerful cultural forces ("Interview" 313–14). Both Dangarembga and Atwood describe loud-mouthed girls who stand up to cultural forces and are destroyed by them.

The two girls who survive in each novel use a very different method to try to reach a voice of their own without being silenced or driven into mental illness by the interlocking forces of the ethnic and gender cultures and colonialism. The force of the various ideologies with which each must cope, of course, varies as a result of two very different kinds of colonialism, the race-based imperialism of British control of Rhodesia and the white settler dominion of Canada, "Britain's last North American 'possession'" (Nicholson 1). In each case, although the balance and intensity are different, colonialism and the gender culture are intertwined. Chandra Mohanty argues that there are "multiple, fluid structures of domination which intersect to locate women differently at particular historical conjunctures" ("Introduction: Cartographies of Struggle" 13). British imperialism is an overt and powerful force in Tsitsi Dangarembga's novel *Nervous Conditions*. Dangarembga's title comes from Sartre's preface to Franz Fanon's *Wretched of the Earth*: "The status of 'native' is a nervous condition introduced and maintained by the settler among colonized people *with their consent*" (20). As Sartre's italicized words make clear, it is the internalization of colonialism and racist denigration that is, as Fanon explains, the most damaging.[5] Historian Elizabeth Schmidt attests to interaction of indigenous patriarchy and British imperialism in the early years of the British domination of Rhodesia:

> [I]ndigenous and European structures of patriarchal control reinforced and transformed one another, evolving into new structures and forms of domination. The control of women's and children's labor by older African men was central to the establishment and consolidation of colonial rule in Southern Rhodesia. (734)

Atwood describes Canada in 1956 as "a recently postcolonial country" ("The Writer: A New Canadian Life-Form" 39). In *Cat's Eye* the postcolonial British influence is intertwined and complicit with the rigid North American gender culture of the 1950s. Even the successful girls cannot subvert these powerful cultural ideologies, but they can negotiate their way between them. Tambu says in *Nervous Conditions*, "If you were clever, you slipped through any loophole you could find" (179). Elaine says in *Cat's Eye* that "the trick with these silent words [that denigrate women] is to walk in the spaces between them, turn sideways in your head, evade" (261).

Nervous Conditions, the first novel by a black Zimbabwean woman to have been published in English (Dangarembga, "Women Write" 105), is the story of two Zimbabwean cousins, Tambudzai (or

Tambu, as her family calls her) and Nyasha Sigauke, who must find a meaningful female identity amid the threatening and conflicting ideologies of British colonialism and Shona traditions. Behind the seemingly straightforward pattern of young girls growing up lie the politics of colonial Rhodesia in the late 1960s and early 1970s. They are only briefly mentioned at three different points in the novel, but, as Charles Sugnet argues, "there may be a complex, partly subterranean relationship between . . . [the national liberation struggle] and the struggles of the young Tambudzai against the immediate manifestations of patriarchy in her life" (34). Jeremiah, Tambu's father, is a weak, unambitious, and uneducated man whose lack of achievement Tambu's grandmother attributes to his sufferings under colonialism, which she calls the "evil wizards' spell" (50). Tambu's uncle, Babamukuru, the head of the family, manages to break this spell but only by becoming what Franz Fanon describes in *The Wretched of the Earth* as a member of "a national bourgeoisie," which is "literally . . . good for nothing" (175–76). Tambu's task is to find a path to adulthood by using the British colonial education system to maneuver out of poverty and Shona patriarchy without being either assimilated or destroyed by colonialism.

At the opening of the novel, Tambu is represented as a resilient and self-reliant young girl. She is not unlike the American girls studied by Gilligan who "prior to adolescence . . . demonstrate a strong sense of self, an ability to know and voice their feelings and thoughts and to give authority to their experience" (Taylor, Gilligan, and Sullivan 23). As a young girl Tambu tackles the patriarchal values of her family straight on. The opening words of the novel are: "I was not sorry when my brother died" (1).[6] When Tambu discovers that her brother Nhamo has been stealing the mealies that she is growing to pay for her local school fees, she loses all respect for him. For Nhamo, earning his friends' loyalty by giving them mealies is more important than his sister's going to school. In Tambu's Shona family, traditional gender codes are enforced even by young boys. Tambu is literally silenced by her brother: "I could no longer bring myself to speak to my brother" (50). More seriously, his endangering her education threatens to push her into the long-term silence of traditional Shona womanhood.[7]

In spite of her brother's and father's efforts to drive her into silence, Tambu has enough support from the women of her family to maintain her belief in her ability to achieve. Tambu's mother emphasizes that this "business of womanhood is a heavy burden. . . . When there are sacrifices to be made, you are the one who has to make them" (16), but she nonetheless supports Tambu first in her request for seed to grow the maize and then in Tambu's request to go to Umtali to sell the mealies. Tambu's mother herself is worn down by poverty and childbearing, and she only manages to stand up to her husband Jeremiah's prohibitions for Tambu by complaining about her: "The girl must have a chance to do something for herself, to fail for herself. . . . She is wilful and headstrong" (24). Nonetheless, she gains Jeremiah's permission to let Tambu go to Umtali. In addition to her mother, Tambu is supported by her paternal grandmother who teaches her how to grow food and gives her the land that enables Tambu to grow her own mealies. Tambu's teacher, Mr. Matimba, seems to stand outside Shona traditions in his belief in educating girls. He is the one who takes her to Umtali and shows Tambu how to sell her mealies to whites, how to use the "colonialist's pity and power" (Creamer 352) to advance herself.[8] With the support of the women in her family, however subdued, Tambu is learning how to map her way between ideologies and to create a safe space where she can grow and be educated. When her brother dies and her uncle designates her as the one from her family of remaining girls to go to his mission school, Tambu is thrilled to accompany him.

Although Tambu fights against the patriarchal Shona tradition of her family and manages to separate herself completely from both parents, it is Tambu's ties to Shona culture that allow her to survive and not be overwhelmed. She knows how to relate to the other African girls at the mission school. She is sincerely grateful to her aunt and uncle and can show it because she knows the appropriate manners a grateful and demure female relative must have. As Juliana Nfah-Abbenyi explains, Tambu's "knowledge of her roots, history, and culture . . . create[s] a balance for her when she goes to the 'whiteman's' school" (65). Tambu's connection to the larger family is important to her. When her aunt and uncle, Maiguru and Babamukuru, first return home from England, Tambu is proud of her role in the family and her ability to cook[9] for the guests:

> Chatting to aunts and cousins as we waited for the *sadza* [the corn-meal staple of the Shona diet] to thicken . . . I stopped feeling excluded. . . . Exclusion held dreadful horrors for me at that time because it suggested superfluity. Exclusion whispered that my existence was not necessary. (39–40)

Gilligan also warns of the dangers of exclusion: "Psychological health and development . . . are grounded in one's relationship with self and others. Too great a loss of relationship poses a serious threat to healthy development" (Taylor, Gilligan, and Sullivan 45). Although Tambu feels connected to her family when young, there is the psychological risk for her of loss of connection as she pursues a colonial education. Tambu's mother is particularly afraid of Tambu's being assimilated into British culture: "[Y]ou couldn't expect the ancestors to stomach so much Englishness" (203). Tambu does sacrifice her closeness to her mother in order to escape poverty, but she placates her ancestors by maintaining her cultural connections.

Tambu's grounding in an identity as a "good Shona girl" allows her to embrace a colonial education, "my reincarnation" (92), without losing connection. She is able to reach out to be friends with her cousin, Nyasha, and to love her even if she did not approve of all her actions. Tambu is shocked at much of Nyasha's "English" behavior, her flirting with boys, her smoking, her lack of tact in dealing with her parents, but she learns from Nyasha. When Nyasha fights with her father, Tambu secretly sympathizes with her, but Tambu herself reverts back to "the image of the grateful poor female relative. . . . It mapped clearly the ways I could or could not go, and by keeping within those boundaries I was able to avoid the mazes of self-confrontation" (116).

It is only when Babamukuru himself violates those cultural boundaries by demanding a Christian wedding for Tambu's parents[10] that Tambu confronts him and refuses to participate. Tambu is able to go beyond the safe boundaries of "the grateful poor female relative" because she takes a stand against superimposing inappropriate Western religious ideas upon Shona marriage traditions. Tambu's willingness to take a stand and her respect for Shona traditions imply that Tambu will escape the assimilation that Nyasha warns her against when Tambu wins a place at the Roman Catholic convent school: "It would be a marvellous opportunity," Nyasha sneers, "to forget who you were, what you were and why you were that. The process, she said, was called assimilation" (178–79). Tambu, however, is confident that she will remember: "How could I possibly forget my brother and the mealies, my mother and the latrine and the wedding? These were all evidence of the burdens my mother had succumbed to. Going to the convent was a chance to lighten those burdens" (179). By taking advantage of a convent education, just as she had taken advantage of the white woman's money for her mealies as a child,

Tambu has a chance to escape the first two elements of what Uwakweh calls "the triple levels of entrapment": "poverty [and] the weight of womanhood." The memory of who she is and the telling of her own story and the stories of her family give Tambu a chance also to escape the third level, the "Englishness" (Uwakweh 79) that both Tambu's mother and Nyasha so fear. By claiming an identity grounded in Shona traditions and by claiming a narrative voice, Tambu finds a pathway between patriarchy and colonialism, between disconnection and assimilation, between voice and silence.

Nyasha is not so fortunate. When Babamukuru and Maiguru win scholarships, they take their two children to Britain against the advice of the children's grandmother. When they return home, Tambu is shocked at Nyasha's indecent English dress and her refusal to speak Shona. Nyasha has no understanding of Shona traditions or even of the manners that a culture coping with scarcity requires. On one visit, Tambu reports, Nyasha "behaved very badly indeed" (52). Nyasha first said that she would have milk for lunch but then helped herself to vegetables as well. At school Nyasha does not have many friends because the other Shona girls perceive her as acting "white." Her casual interaction with boys is viewed by them as "loose" behavior. Nyasha is, however, politically sophisticated; she has "an egalitarian nature and had taken seriously the lessons about oppression and discrimination" (63) that she had learned while she was in England. She is outspoken, but she has no connections to protect her when she does speak out. Taylor and Gilligan found the same danger in their study of American girls at risk. Voice alone without connection can be as dangerous as silence:

> Efforts to be strong, self-reliant, and outspoken can be reasonable and effective survival strategies in a difficult, and sometimes hostile environment. These efforts can cease to be adaptive, however, when they move to a position that precipitates disconnections from others, covering over vulnerabilities and the desire for relatedness. (Taylor, Gilligan, and Sullivan 68)

Nyasha is outspoken in her critique of colonialism, but she has no other culture with which to connect.

Nyasha's disconnection from Shona culture and the larger family also leaves her at the mercy of her own nuclear family, particularly her parents, Babamukuru and Maiguru.[11] Both of them, in spite of their excellent education, have precarious identities. Sue Thomas argues that Babamukuru's "bad nerves" are a "common symptom of male hysteria" resulting in his case from the effects of colonization (29). Babamukuru avoids becoming one of the worst of Fanon's "native bourgeoisie," however, because he maintains his ties to his larger family and takes seriously his position as family patriarch. Although this role works well for him, it works against Nyasha because he expects Nyasha to behave as a traditional Shona girl even though she has had no connection to the culture. Her mother Maiguru, although educated and working, is "hysterically over compliant with Shona patriarchal expectations" (Thomas 29). Education alone does not allow Maiguru either to support Nyasha or to function as a role model for her. Tambu observes Nyasha's problems with both her parents. Even though Tambu admires Nyasha's outspokenness, she worries about Nyasha's lack of respect for both her mother and her father. Tambu is appalled when Nyasha goads her father until he strikes her and calls her a "whore" (114). Tambu recognizes with shock that for all her outspokenness Nyasha is "a victim of her femaleness. . . . The victimisation, I saw, was universal" (115). Nyasha, for all her insight and bravery and education, has even fewer resources than Tambu. Nyasha is alone. She lapses into silence trying her "best not to antagonise" her father (196), but her anger and her feelings of being trapped lead to anorexia nervosa and bulimia. The first psychiatrist that she sees dismisses her, saying that "Africans did not suffer in the way we had described" (201).[12] Finally, another psychiatrist puts Nyasha in a clinic, but "Nyasha's progress was still in the balance, and so, as a result," Tambu recognizes, "was mine" (202). By claiming both her Shona heritage and a British education, Tambu has negotiated an identity and found a potential space between voice and silence that Nyasha has not, but Tambu remains connected to Nyasha, and Nyasha's story is part of her own.

Margaret Atwood's *Cat's Eye* is also the story of two girls, Elaine Risley and her best friend, Cordelia. Like Tambu, Elaine is at first self-reliant and resilient because the first eight years of her life were spent outside of the dominant culture. Since her father researches insect infestations, her early life in the 1940s is spent camping out and playing with her brother.[13] It is only when her father becomes a professor in Toronto that Elaine gets caught in the gender ideology of 1950s Canada. It is more subtle than the gender ideology of the Shona because, as Molly Hite argues, the gender systems in *Cat's Eye* are policed by the women themselves. Like Tambu, Elaine also has a brother who dies, but Stephen dies as an adult at the hands of terrorists. His death does not benefit Elaine, as Nhamo's does Tambu, but rather "replays the gender-enforcing torture of the nine-year-old Elaine at the hands of her purported friends" (Hite 136). Hite suggests that the "recurrence of such incidents" of torture "underscores the political implications of conventionally personal events" (136). Like *Nervous Conditions*, *Cat's Eye* seems to be primarily a personal novel, but gender and colonial politics lie behind the seemingly private stories.

Although one might at first dismiss Canada's dominion status and relationship to Great Britain as not being significant in the novel,[14] Canada's political position was in fact intertwined with the gender ideology of the day. Elaine and Stephen are sent to Queen Mary Public School in Toronto. Elaine's classroom is adorned with a large photo of King George and Queen Mary, but the school is rigidly segregated by gender with separate doors for girls and boys. This culture is new to Elaine. Elaine's first friend, Carol Campbell, describes the difference between the Risley household and her own in colonial terms. Carol thinks the scarcity of furniture and Elaine's boyish clothes are "exotic specialties. . . . It's as if she's reporting on the antics of some primitive tribe" (54). Elaine realizes when she plays with Carol and Grace Smeath cutting out pictures of "ladies' household items" from *Eaton's Catalogue* that "there's a whole world of girls and their doings that has been unknown to me" (59). The association of colonial status and the proper behavior of girls is reinforced in school by their teacher, Miss Lumley, who teaches them "to name all the pink parts of the map" (86) and shows them clippings of "Princess Elizabeth and Princess Margaret Rose, in Girl Guide uniforms, making radio and other speeches during the Blitz. This is what we should be like, Miss Lumley implies" (87). The clippings about the two princesses as role models give a new shade of meaning to the traditional pink places on the map that mark the British Empire. Miss Lumley vividly describes the dangers of being outside British civilization:

In countries that are not the British Empire, they cut out children's tongues, especially those of boys. Before the British Empire there were no railroads or postal services in India, and Africa was full of tribal warfare, with spears, and had no proper clothing. The Indians in Canada did not have the wheel or telephones, and ate the hearts of their enemies. (86)

Male outsiders are tortured and silenced, but females could possibly pass as insiders if they wore the proper girl guide uniforms and behaved like princesses.

Elaine's problem is that she knows very well that she is not an insider. Every morning they sing "*Rule Britannia . . . Britons never, never, never shall be slaves*," but Elaine thinks, "[W]e aren't real Britons, because we are also Canadians" (86). Furthermore, Elaine already knows that she does not wear the proper clothes, and the rumor is that Miss Lumley does not either. Some girls report that Miss Lumley wears "heavy navy-blue wool" bloomers to and from school: "The aura of Miss Lumley's dark, mysterious, repulsive bloomers clings around her and colors the air in which she moves. It makes her more terrifying" (84). For Elaine

> the flags, the pitch pipe songs, the British Empire and the princesses, the war orphans, even the strappings—are superimposed against the ominous navy-blue background of Miss Lumley's invisible bloomers. . . . They're sacrosanct, at the same time holy and deeply shameful. Whatever is wrong with them may be wrong with me also, because although Miss Lumley is not what anyone thinks of as a girl, she is also not a boy. When the brass handbell clangs and we line up outside our GIRLS door, whatever category we are in also includes her. (87–88)

The status of Miss Lumley's bloomers is unstable and thus threatening. Are they shameful merely because they are the underclothing of an adult female, or are they shameful because they seem to cross gender categories and are close to men's clothing? Whatever their status, it is clear that the person enforcing the politics of empire and the gender codes is herself in danger of not achieving them. This is what makes her so fierce and terrifying. Elaine is in double jeopardy; she is a Canadian and not a Briton and thus can be enslaved and silenced for her political outsider status. Second, she is female but does not wear the proper uniform. Her gender status is also unclear, and she is at an age in which she desperately wants to define both gender and adulthood. She senses her precarious position.

Ironically, Elaine is silenced and tortured in her preteen years, but not by colonists or savages or even males; she is silenced from within her gender group by her best friends. Hite points out that in *Cat's Eye* it is Elaine's friends who teach her how to turn a "mechanism of blaming" on herself (144), a method that is even more effective than Miss Lumley's in silencing women. In *Cat's Eye* brothers do not need to put women down; girls have learned to do it to each other. For Elaine the effectiveness of the torture is that it is at the very site of connection that exclusion occurs.

The psychoanalytic theories of Nancy Chodorow offer useful explanations for Elaine's dependence on her friends in spite of their cruelty. Although Elaine's mother does not participate in the rigid gender categories of the 1950s and could potentially be a model for Elaine, Elaine's need to differentiate herself from her mother precludes her reaching out to her mother for connection. Chodorow explains that girls do not "give up . . . their preoedipal and oedipal attachment to their mother"; they engage "in an ambivalent struggle for a sense of separateness and independence"[15] (*Reproduction* 168). Following Helen Deutsch, Chodorow suggests that one solution that a girl often uses to achieve separation from her mother is "to find a 'best friend'. . . with whom she shares everything. . . . Her friendship permits her to continue to experience merging, while at the same time denying feelings of merging with her mother" (137–38). As a young girl Elaine chooses her friends over her mother. It is not until adulthood when Elaine paints her mother in a double triptych that Elaine comes to terms with her mother. Elaine's painting, *Pressure Cooker*, first depicts Elaine's mother in a realistic drawing in a 1940s dress, then a magazine cut-out collage, and then a faded white-on-white figure. The bottom half goes in the other direction from the white-on-white figure to the magazine collage to a realistic picture of her mother in slacks and a man's jacket cooking over a campfire (Atwood, *Cat's Eye* 167). In this painting, Elaine demonstrates that she has both separated from her mother and separated herself from the gender culture of the women's magazines. She can now appreciate her mother's difference. As a young girl searching for an identity within her own culture, however, that difference was too threatening.

Chodorow's theories are also useful in analyzing the structure of the friendship of Elaine, Cordelia, Grace, and Carol. According to Chodorow, not only does a girl emerge from the oedipal period with greater "empathy" than a boy, "with a stronger basis for experiencing another's needs or feelings as one's own" (*Reproduction* 167); but also, since a girl does not cut herself off from her mother, she merely adds her father to her inner world of primary objects—she "defines herself . . . in a relational triangle" (167). Although Chodorow does not link these inner relational triangles to girlhood friendships,

Atwood does. A triangle is basically unstable, and thus girls in groups are often preoccupied with who is "in" and who is "out" or excluded. Gilligan, in applying some of Chodorow's theories to girls' development, notes that "female gender identity is threatened by separation" (8). Although a girl has to be careful not to be engulfed by the mother figure, she still needs connection and relationship. Atwood shows how Elaine is enmeshed in triangles within her friendship group as first one and then the other of the friends is put "outside" the group. Cordelia is at the pinnacle of the triangle, and Grace, Carol, and Elaine vie for the other two places. Sometimes "Cordelia decides that it's Carol's turn to be improved. I am invited to join Grace and Cordelia as they walk ahead on the way home from school, with Carol trailing behind, and to think of things Carol has done wrong. . . . But these times don't last long" (*Cat's Eye* 133). Usually Elaine is the one left out, the one the others are trying to improve:

> "Don't hunch over," says Cordelia. "Don't move your arms like that." . . . With enemies you can feel hatred, and anger. But Cordelia is my friend. She likes me, she wants to help me, they all do. They are my friends, my girl friends, my best friends. I have never had any before and I'm terrified of losing them. (131–32)

Elaine submits to psychic torture and exclusion because she is afraid of being disowned, of being sent out of her universe of girlhood into a black hole such as the ones her budding physicist brother tells her about. Ironically, that is precisely where her "friends" put her, but she does not "tell." She maintains the code of silence, which she hopes will keep her in relationship. In her adult narrative voice Elaine comments: "Little girls are cute and small only to adults. To one another they are not cute. They are life-sized" (129).

Elaine is not only silenced by her best friends; she is literally buried by them. Elaine is dressed in black and put in a deep hole in the backyard to pretend she is Mary Queen of Scots, but when the other girls put boards over the hole and leave her, Elaine realizes that it is no longer a game. Elaine feels acutely the darkness and terror of the hole. That time the girls come back and get her out, but the torture continues. Like Mary Queen of Scots, the Celtic outsider and Roman Catholic, no one can save Elaine. Her own family is powerless against the system of gender ideology that none of them understand. Although Elaine never tells her own family, she learns to her shock that Mrs. Smeath knows all that is going on. "'It's God's punishment,' says

Mrs. Smeath. 'It serves her right'" (199). The adult women like Mrs. Smeath are caught within the gender codes of their day, but they also enforce them. Elaine looks desperately for someone to save her. When Princess Elizabeth comes to town, Elaine thinks that if she can only get Princess Elizabeth's car to stop, somehow things will magically change. The empire too, however, enforces gender codes. Princess Elizabeth wears "a plain suit and gloves" and "a ladies' hat" (176). The "car with the pale glove coming out the window" (178) drives by and leaves Elaine standing motionless on a hill of mud. Princess Elizabeth could no more have saved Elaine than Queen Elizabeth I could have saved her cousin Mary Queen of Scots. There is no simple political process that can save those who threaten either power or gender ideologies.

Elaine finally manages to save herself from the second "hole" her friends send her to, one that might well have ended in permanent burial in the icy dark water of the ravine. Cordelia throws Elaine's hat into the ravine because Grace claims Elaine laughed when Cordelia fell down in the snow. Cordelia tells Elaine that if she goes into the ravine to retrieve her hat, she will be forgiven. The ravine is dangerous on many levels, both mythic and real. Carol tells Elaine when they first meet that the ravine is a place where "shadowy, nameless" men ravish young girls (53). Later "Cordelia says that because the stream [in the ravine] flows right out of the cemetery it's made of dissolved dead people" (81). The stream literally almost kills Elaine when she breaks through the ice, and all her clothes get wet in the freezing Canadian night. It is only Elaine's vision of the Virgin Mary, the Virgin of Lost Things, that saves her. In Elaine's vision, the Virgin Mary speaks to her: "*You can go home now*" (209). Hearing these words, Elaine manages to pull herself out of her frozen lethargy and start to walk home.

Earlier when Elaine is disillusioned by Mrs. Smeath's God, she starts to pray to the Virgin Mary, but her prayers are "wordless." Elaine explains, "I haven't learned the words for her" (203). Martha Sharpe argues that it is precisely this wordlessness that saves Elaine, who finally achieves "individuation through her imaginative vision" (Sharpe 181). It is safe for Elaine to go home now, as the Virgin Mary tells her, because Elaine has defined herself as separate from her mother, and she has demonstrated the courage to reject her friends' taunts. She feels secure enough within herself to accept herself as an outsider, someone with a particular vision, and recognize that connection with her friends has been no protection from terror: "I can hear the hatred, but also the need. They need me for this, and I no longer need them" (214). It is Elaine's "imaginative vision" that gives her a way out from the ravine and a way to slip between the dual threats of engulfment by mother and destruction by friends.

Elaine's imaginative vision is also the source of her identity as a painter. Hite argues that "as a painter she occupies a position usually reserved for the dominant class of men in a patriarchal system: she can disengage seeing from being seen" (140). As a painter Elaine is no longer the object of a gaze but one who sees. It is as a painter that Elaine can retrieve the "lost things" of this period of her life. She can paint Mrs. Smeath for the "Bad Mother" (Ingersoll 21–22) that she is. She can paint her vision of the Virgin Mary in her black robe hovering above the ravine and holding the "talismanic cat's eye marble" (McCombs 10).[16] After accepting herself in her dual role as outsider and seer, someone who sees between ideologies, Elaine can pay tribute in another painting, *Three Muses*, to three outsiders in her life, Mrs. Finestein, her Jewish neighbor, Mr. Banerji, her father's Indian graduate assistant, and Miss Stuart, her Scottish teacher.

Now that she has had her vision, Elaine can slip sideways not only through the colonial, or dominion, codes of her day but also through the rigid gender codes. In high school Elaine is popular because she can relate to boys who "must not be startled by too many words" (260). She knows that the words that boys apply to girls "*stunned broad, dog, bag,* and *bitch* . . . are another version of pickled ox eyes and snot eating. . . . The trick with these silent words is to walk in the spaces between them, turn sideways in your head, evade" (261). Elaine cannot dismantle the gender codes of her culture, but she has learned how to walk in the spaces between the silent, and silencing, words.

Having learned this method of evasion, Elaine recognizes that she and Cordelia have "changed places" (249). Elaine is comfortable in the way she has defined gender identity for herself, but Cordelia, worrying now about boys, loses her girlhood power and becomes like one of the adolescents Gilligan studied who are afraid that they will "jeopardize their chances" (Taylor, Gilligan, and Sullivan 3). Elaine can challenge the system both verbally and in her paintings: "I've come to enjoy the risk, the sensation of vertigo when I realize that I've shot right over the border of the socially acceptable, that I'm walking on thin ice" (258). Elaine has learned that if she breaks the ice, she can pull herself back. Cordelia, however, falls into mental illness. She moves from the enforcer of codes to the victim of them.[17]

Elaine last sees her in "a discreet private loony bin. A rest home" (388). Elaine refuses to get Cordelia out of the home and take responsibility for her. Elaine can save herself, but she cannot save Cordelia.

Elaine has one last vision of Cordelia as a young girl on the path above the ravine. Elaine feels "the same knowledge of my own wrongness, awkwardness, weakness; the same wish to be loved; the same loneliness; the same fear. But these are not my own emotions any more. They are Cordelia's; as they always were" (459). She says to Cordelia the same words that were said to her: "*It's all right. . . . You can go home now*" (459). But it is too late for Cordelia.

In Dangarembga's novel the dangers of British colonialism and Shona patriarchy are overt, if hard to avoid. By maintaining her belief in herself and her connection to extended family and Shona traditions and by working hard both at home and in school, Tambu finds a way between the two ideologies. She manages to pit one against the other and find a "loophole" between the two. She uses the British colonial education system to escape poverty and Shona patriarchy; she uses her Shona traditions and connections to avoid being assimilated into colonialism. In Atwood's novel, the workings of colonialism and patriarchy are more subtle and intertwined. The dangers of the ideologies penetrate the very connectedness that girls usually use to avoid those dangers. Elaine suffers torment and silencing at the hands of her best friends but finally finds a vision and an adult role as a painter that allows her to find a place for herself and a way to slip between the cruel words and realities of gender ideology.

Because Atwood's novel extends to middle age, we know Elaine has found a way out. Dangarembga's novel ends as Tambu enters the convent school. Since Tambu's "progress" is linked to Nyasha's, we do not know for sure that Tambu will survive, but we can see the path between competing ideologies that Tambu has discovered. In many cultures, however, there is no such path for a number of girls. Cordelia and Nyasha and some of Gilligan's "girls at risk" remind us that whatever the culture, girls can be caught between voice and silence.

Chapter 2

Sexual Identities: The Search for Intimacy in Barbara Burford's "The Threshing Floor" and Keri Hulme's *The Bone People*

One of the dominant plots in Western novels has been women's search for intimacy that in the typical romance plot leads to marriage. Since this plot is so well known, I have chosen novels that "break this sequence" and "write beyond" the "cultural conventions of [the Western] narrative" (DuPlessis 31, 1) to explore intimacy in different ways. I thus have paired Barbara Burford's story of a lesbian relationship in "The Threshing Floor" (1986) with Keri Hulme's portrayal of the nonsexual, non-blood-related intimacy of a man, woman, and child in *The Bone People* (1983).[1] Both of these novels are also "kunstlerromane,"[2] stories of women artists whose work has been blocked by grief and isolation. They are vivid fictional representations of Audre Lorde's assertion in "Uses of the Erotic" that artistic work has its roots in the erotic: "[E]ros . . . [is] the personification of love in all its aspects—born of Chaos, and personifying creative power and harmony. When I speak of the erotic, then, I speak of it as an assertion of the lifeforce of women; of that creative energy empowered" (55). For Lorde, love and work are so interconnected that one cannot access one's creative abilities if love is blocked. Both

"The Threshing Floor" and *The Bone People* tell the story of the painful opening up to intimacy[3] and the return to creativity.

Interwoven with the search for intimacy and creativity in these postcolonial novels is a third narrative strand, that of the two protagonists' search to understand their mixed-race, ethnic identity, their biological "hybridity," and to forgive the pain and loss that have been embedded in that heritage. In "The Threshing Floor" Burford explores the pain of racism in Britain in her depiction of Hannah Claremont whose white mother deserted her at birth.[4] Keri Hulme's character Kerewin Holmes,[5] who, like Hulme herself, is one-eighth Maori and the rest "Pakeha" or European ancestry,[6] experiences the difficulties of the postcolonial who is in danger of losing her culture through assimilation. Burford tells the story of an artist recovering from the death of her white lesbian partner and reestablishing relationships with both her white and black women partners at her glass-blowing collective. In Hulme's novel Kerewin can recover her artistic ability only by reconnecting both with her ancestors and with a young child and his Maori foster father. In both works it is the acceptance and recovery of ethnic heritage and the forgiveness of wrongs that allow the protagonists to open up to intimacy. Once the protagonists have let go of their grief and isolation, they can rediscover that "resource within each of us that lies in a deeply female and spiritual plan, firmly rooted in the power of our unexpressed or unrecognized feeling" (Lorde 53). In reestablishing the intimacy of close, committed relationships, each heroine gains access once again to her artistic identity.

Although Burford uses a traditional realistic, if lyrical, style in "The Threshing Floor," the lesbian plot itself, as a number of critics have argued, and particularly a plot that examines the intersections of racial and sexual identity, is an effective way of opening up new narrative sequences. Marilyn Falwell argues that "the lesbian subject appears as a powerful discursive and political tool for challenging the asymmetrical gender codes in the narrative" (17). Teresa de Lauretis explains that one reason why "the figure of the lesbian in contemporary feminist discourse" is so valuable and capable of disrupting traditional plots is that she "represents the possibility of female subject *and* desire: she can seduce and be seduced, but without losing her status as subject" (156). For a black lesbian these positions become more complex because, as Heidi Mirza reminds her readers, "as black women . . . our eroticized, exoticized bodies have become objects of desire. They preoccupy and obsess the white gaze" (17). In *Talking Black: Lesbians of African and Asian Descent Speak Out*, Linda Bellos confirms that the "myths and stereotypes about Black sexuality in the predominantly heterosexual world were alive and well and living within the lesbian community" (56). On the one hand, the lesbian can be both subject and the one who desires, as de Lauretis argues, but for black lesbians there is always the social danger of being driven back into an object position, as Mirza and Bellos warn.

Burford explores both these positions in "The Threshing Floor," which opens with a lyrical portrayal of the desiring subject, stricken now by grief. Burford's novella draws in a number of potential readers, even those who have little knowledge of lesbian themes, because most readers can sympathize with the grief that Hannah Claremont feels as she awakens from sleep and reaches out for her lover of twelve years, only to remember that Jenny Harrison has recently died from cancer. Passages from the funeral service and phrases from Jenny's poems echo through Hannah's mind as she listens to the rain and experiences again the rawness of grief. Hannah has been comfortable both with her lesbian identity and with her cross-race relationship; she has achieved artistic excellence as a glassblower, but Jenny's death has left her emotionally vulnerable once again. In the elegiac opening chapter of her memory of her relationship with Jenny, Hannah is in a subject position, capable of desiring and responding to desire. That tone gives way to social realism in the second chapter in which Hannah must cope with the social complexities of being made the exotic object of desire.

Before exploring the complexities of relationships within the group of women artists, Burford illustrates the black lesbian as an object of white desire in an isolated event. When Hannah returns to the home that she and Jenny shared after doing some errands, she finds Heather Hartley, the wife of Jenny's editor, waiting for her. Heather, or "Blue" as Hannah calls her, is white, married, forty years old, and pregnant. She seemingly has come to console Hannah, but she starts talking instead about how jealous she had been of Jenny. Hannah hears her with surprise, thinking, "Such depth of emotion could surely not go unreciprocated," but she immediately draws back: "[I]t won't come from me. The familiar public armour of clear, cool, eternally malleable glass, surrounded her" ("The Threshing Floor" 93). Hannah protects herself with an image drawn from her art, the outer glass casing that surrounds a piece of blown glass. Then she confronts Heather, communicating emphatically that she is not interested in becoming someone's object: "Come off it, Blue! . . . You enjoy flirting with me. Especially when there are people around that you wanted to scandalize. I was the moral outrage status symbol to end all status symbols" (96). Burford explains in an interview:

> if you are into lion hunting, Hannah would be a really big one.
> . . . Heather sees Hannah as stylish and experienced, a real catch, not
> the emotional mess that she really is. ("When Everything Else Is Done
> and Dusted" 30)

With Jenny, Hannah had a mutual relationship, one between two subjects. Although Hannah feels a surge of purely physical attraction to Heather, she will not allow herself to be made into an object by Heather. She makes Heather a cup of tea and drives her home.

Burford also explores cross-race relationships in mother-daughter connections and raises the issue of whether lesbian love has its source in mother-daughter relationships. In 1981 Catherine Stimpson suggested that a "mother waits at the heart of the labyrinth of some lesbian texts. . . . Of course lesbianism is far more than a matter of mother/daughter affairs, but the new texts suggest that one of its satisfactions is a return to primal origins, to primal loves, when female/female, not male-female, relationships structured the world" (256–57).[7] In 1991, Judith Roof revises that idea, saying that the "absence of a biological mother in a remarkable number of lesbian novels . . . denies from the start the nostalgic wish and maternal fulfillment" of some contemporary theories of mothering (108). Teresa de Lauretis adds that "the place of the mother [in many lesbian novels] is empty, or rather, structured by an absence" (200). This maternal absence and emptiness echo strongly in "The Threshing Floor" where the emptiness is linked to the white mother's rejection[8] of her black child. Hannah's mother put Hannah in a children's home and refused to let her be adopted. Early in her relationship with Jenny, Hannah realizes that Jenny worries about whether "Hannah might love her mainly because, however, unconsciously, she saw in Jenny the white mother who had abandoned her into care at birth" (104). After an altercation with her own racist mother, Jenny says to Hannah: "I love you. I will *not* be a mother to you. . . . I won't say stop searching for a mother. But I will say this, my love: you've been a good mother to yourself up to now, it's something you should think about" (112). Jenny very consciously separates out their lesbian relationship from Hannah's and her own relationship, or lack of relationship to their mothers. Hannah must deal with the pain of maternal absence in her life, made worse by its roots in racial prejudice and rejection, but as Jenny reminds her, Hannah has dealt with that pain and grown beyond it. Burford comments on the importance of facing the problems of intimate cross-race relationships:[9]

> "How do you relate as a black woman to a white colleague, to a white lover, to a white husband, to a child that is part white, to a father that is white?" You can't enghetto yourself, and you can't create a quasi "we-are-one" feeling. You have to face up to all the history that both sides bring. For Hannah a white woman . . . was the greatest source of her pain, and continues to be so in terms of Jenny's mother, but also in Jenny herself a source of healing. ("When Everything Else Is Done and Dusted" 30)

In coping with Heather's attempts to objectify her and her feelings of grief and loss, Hannah turns to a black couple, Elaine, her friend from art school, and her husband Roy. Unlike Heather, Elaine has not rushed to Hannah's side but waited for her to call. More shaken by Heather's advances than she wants to admit, Hannah realizes after she drops Heather off that she cannot drive home. She calls Elaine, who comes to rescue her. Although Hannah feels regret that she was never able to celebrate her love for Jenny publicly, as Elaine and Roy can, Hannah receives healing in her conversations with them and can think about both her own white mother's abandonment of her and her true love for Jenny in the comforting environment of her black friends' acceptance of her as a suffering black woman.

After her visit with Elaine and Roy, Hannah is able to proofread Jenny's last volume of poetry and think about a return to her own work. Burford links the title of her collection and of this story to the theme of women's work in a harvest image. "The Threshing Floor" is what Jenny called the room in their cottage where she writes her poetry. Hannah uses the term to apply to her glassblowing studio as well. Burford explains that a threshing floor is an appropriate image of women's work:

> "It's grown, but somebody's got to thresh it, . . . to separate the wheat from the chaff, . . . to take the risk of throwing it up in the air after you've threshed it to let it winnow." . . . The fact that a threshing floor is often used as a dancing floor as well is an important part of the metaphor. ("When Everything Else Is Done and Dusted" 28)

The idea of threshing involves physical work, partnership, risk, and even the joy of dancing. All these elements are linked in Hannah's craft of glassblowing.

Burford clearly uses Lorde's ideas in her linking of work with erotic feelings. Burford says that Lorde is one of her favorite African American authors and that she was especially honored to be asked to launch Lorde's *Cancer Journal* for her in Britain ("When Everything Else Is Done and Dusted" 32). When Hannah returns to the glassblowing workshop, both erotic and spiritual feelings begin to surface:

> Walking into the darkened workshop was like being earthed again. . . . [She] listened to the croon of the furnace. . . . It was hot, but nothing of course to later in the day when the furnace and the *glory hole* would be open. . . .[She felt] something loosen and begin to flow within her, much like the molten glass in the tank furnace, pregnant with wild possibilities. This was *her* Threshing Floor, where she laboured hard to create form, beauty—and . . . spiritual sustenance out of the raw materials around her.
>
> At last, she could begin to see her avoidance of the studio since Jenny's death, for what it was. Guilt. Why should she still be able to create, when Jenny no longer could? Emotional and creative *Suttee*. Except that she had shut herself *away* from the fires out of which she birthed her fancies. (116–17)

Mixed with her guilt is a fear that she really had buried her creative power with Jenny as "a suitable gravegift, like the precious artifacts surrounding some dead princess in her sarcophagus," that "she would not be able to tap the deep grief-silted wellspring of her creativity" (142).

Hannah's four partners and the three apprentices at Cantii Glass are glad to see her again, and they ultimately form the community that will restore her creative power, but first she must work through various complications in the relationships that her absence and absorption in her grief have caused. Lynn Harne praises this aspect of Burford's work in "Beyond Sex and Romance? Lesbian Relationships in Contemporary Fiction:"

> Burford stresses that in order for women to be able to work together on common projects, conflicts brought about by personal friendships and differences of inequality have to be recognised and addressed. . . . [S]he brilliantly illustrates the resentments common to a number of women's collectives, where inequalities created by racism, differ-

ences in income and expertise fail to be recognised. Her idea of community between women is one that is both fragile and precarious, and where a sense of unity can be attained only through the hard work of . . . trying to resolve power differences and working through conflicts. (138)

For Harne it is one of Burford's strengths as a lesbian novelist that she depicts not only a sexual relationship between two women but also relationships within a community of women that form a basis for intimacy.

The art of glassblowing becomes a symbol of creativity's rootedness in community. Unlike painting or writing, it cannot be done alone; it does not require clients like architecture or audiences like music, but it does require a small group of people to work together to help each other blow the glass and afford the expense of the furnace. Burford describes the relationship between the glassblower and her helper as a dance, the same idea she linked to the image of the threshing floor. The craft of glassblowing requires physical strength, balance, and an intricate relationship between the artist and helper that is very much a dance involving not only physical agility and response to a partner's needs but careful attention to a glassblower's choice of color and shape. Burford says that she knew a little about glassblowing when she chose it as her protagonist's art since she was taught to do scientific glassblowing to produce her own pipettes during her training in medical research, but she sought out artistic glassblowers to learn about the craft. She spent a day at the London Glassblowing Workshop[10] watching the process:

Luckily I have a photographic memory. . . . I just listened . . . and watched them very acutely. It's a dance, isn't it? ("When Everything Else Is Done and Dusted" 29)

Given the intimacy needed between glassblower and helper, it is not surprising that the first problem in relationships that Hannah has to face is with one of the apprentices with whom Hannah has worked most closely. Burford, as Harne notes above, describes multiple social and economic inequalities in women's relationships very sensitively. Although Hannah has suffered from racial prejudice in a number of ways and is aware of the social judgments about her sexual identity, she is nonetheless one of the five partners of Cantii Glass, all of whom made the initial financial investments and make all the decisions about the workshop. Nikki, one of the most talented apprentices, worked closely with Hannah. She is white but poor. She lives ten miles from the workshop, and the bus service is erratic, so Hannah had been driving her home. When Jenny became increasingly ill and Hannah had less time, Hannah had been paying for Nikki's bus fare but said the money came from petty cash to save Nikki's pride. When Jenny was dying, Hannah left work completely and forgot to tell either Nikki or her partners about her arrangement. The other partners were astonished and critical when Nikki asked for petty cash after Hannah left. As Burford comments: "I wanted it to be clear that Hannah isn't some perfect person. In many ways she's . . . terribly egocentric. . . . After a long period of really dreadful life, Jenny surrounded her with . . . attention and consideration . . . and she's forgotten a lot" ("When Everything Else is Done and Dusted" 29). When Hannah remembers after Nikki's cool reception, she apologizes to Nikki and even praises Nikki's new style of glassblowing, but one apology doesn't solve the problem. Nikki points out that Hannah never noticed that Nikki in her admiration had been trying to imitate Hannah's style. Nikki blurts out: "You never even *noticed* that I loved you. . . . [Since I'm not one of your partners], I didn't have anything to offer" (123). Wary of being considered an exotic love object, Hannah ignores the issues of power imbalance and never even considers that this statement could merely reflect a student's idolization of her teacher. Hannah cuts Nikki off, saying, "Loving someone doesn't put them under any obligation to you" (124).

This issue of the economic and power imbalances between the five partners and the apprentices of Cantii Glass goes beyond just Hannah's and Nikki's relationship. Although Nikki is the one to send a "customized, personalized thundercloud" (125) to the partners' meeting, complaining about Hannah's exploitation of her feelings, the other apprentices have complaints as well. Although all the women have feminist principles and share the ideal of "craftswomen" working together on an equal basis (151), the group has become "stratified" (127), as Hannah now recognizes with the five partners making the decisions and informing the apprentices. Caro, the one black apprentice, "facetiously called" the partners *The Pilgrim Mothers* (168). It is only after many meetings that they are able to sort out both the emotional "ripples" (139) that Jenny's death and Hannah's absence have caused and economic and decision-making inequities. The five partners finally listen to the apprentices and hear their needs. They work out a profit-sharing scheme that will allow the partners to be paid back for their investments and yet allow the apprentices to benefit. They work out more time for Nikki, the most talented glassblower of the three, to practice her art with Hannah as her helper, a chance for Caro to work part-time and enroll in the business courses she's been wanting to take, and for Sandra, the newest apprentice who is afraid of the furnace, to learn to make jewelry over a Bunsen burner as well as sell their work in the gallery. They recreate their intimacy as a working collective by listening to each other and meeting the needs of individuals. They address the power and economic imbalances as a group.

It is after working through these relationships that Hannah is able to return to her art. The furnace at first sounds "dangerous" to her, "as if wild animals dwelt inside, waiting to feed on her fear and failure" (142), but then Hannah has a vision of swifts flying through a "fresh washed morning sky" (145), and she feels within herself "that almost sexual, certainly erotic, huge welling strongness at her core" (142). Nikki is able to relax and laugh with her again and join the intense dance of glassblowing. Hannah

> worked absorbedly, rolling the parison in the powered blue on the marver plate, then heating it in the Glory Hole to fuse the colour into the glass . . . aware of the song of the furnace, the beautifully weighted swing of the loaded iron. . . . By the time that she had approached the Glory Hole, Nikki was there to take the iron from her, resting it on the yoke and slowly rotating it, while she watched intently as Hannah prepared the first trails of colour that she would be adding. The next time through Nikki would know exactly how Hannah wanted them prepared, her visual memory for colour was acute. (145)

It is during this glassblowing that another black woman, Marah Cummings, comes into the workshop, and Hannah finds not only that she can return to her work and her art but that work has allowed her to open up her feelings again, to remove the protective glass casing from around her. That emotion, in turn, reaches back to her art. The next day, as all the women of Cantii Glass huddle companionably around the furnace to look at Hannah's new work, they acknowledge the power of the second bowl: Hannah "reached for the second bowl, the one made in Marah's presence. . . . Where the first bowl had been beautiful, this one sang. Filling with light as she turned it slowly in the silence, the joyous dance of the swifts through the liquid blue morning, a symphony of light and colour" (165).

All the complexities of Hannah's relationships are not solved merely because she meets a black woman, however. There are a number of intrarace tensions and issues that Hannah must face as well. Marah Cummings is a friend of Caro's, the only other black woman at Cantii Glass. Before Hannah can get to know Marah, she first must heal her relationship with Caro. Caro is genuinely glad to see Hannah, but she finally admits that she felt very hurt that Hannah would not share her grief with her. Caro says to her: "You're very good at making people feel they are important to you, but you're also bloody good at ignoring them when something else comes up" (136). Hannah realizes the truth of this accusation, thinking that "there had been no room for anything but the hugeness of missing Jenny" (138). Hannah and Caro reestablish their friendship, and Hannah promises to go to "MacDonalds" (138) with Caro and Caro's daughter Zhora. These emotional issues are easier to resolve than the underlying economic and power issues, however. When Caro has to leave a contentious meeting early because she has to pick up her babysitter, Hannah claims she's on Caro's side. Caro responds bitterly:

> "My side! How can you be on my side? Because we're the same colour? Let me tell you something, Hannah. You don't live in the real world. *I'm* the only one on my side. When a woman is on her own with a child, she doesn't have time for wellwishers and the right politics. You don't have any idea, you really don't." (170)

Color alone does not provide solidarity. As the only single mother in the group, Caro has needs the others do not. She needs to have her own specific issue of time as well as economics addressed in order to remain at the glassworks. Eventually through many meetings of the whole group, these issues are resolved for Caro, and she agrees to stay, but they are issues that must be handled structurally within the whole group. Hannah alone cannot solve them.

One last issue remains between Caro and Hannah. Caro sees that Hannah is attracted to Marah Cummings, but she also knows that Marah is coming out of a difficult divorce and wants to have a child. Caro thinks Hannah should not allow Marah to get involved with her because it might preclude Marah's having a child. Burford notes the parallels between black women's infertility and lesbianism:

> Another [important] issue . . . was the fact that Marah couldn't have children. . . . [A]ssumptions about black sexuality and black fertility

... make ... it very hard for a black woman who can't have children to actually voice that. For a black woman ... lesbian, it's even harder because it's "a white woman's disease." ("When Everything Else Is Done and Dusted" 30)

Although Caro accepts Hannah's sexuality, she is distrustful of Hannah's transferring this "white woman's disease" to another black woman. Finally, Hannah confronts Caro: "I am not an emotional vandal, neither am I some sort of predatory stereotype. I care a great deal for you, Caro, but I will not be dictated to, or guilt-tripped by you" (188). Caro finally accepts Hannah's position and wants to remain friends with both of them.

It is the artist in both Hannah and Marah that draws them to each other. Hannah accepts a casual offer from Marah to have dinner at her house. Hannah is amazed at Marah's weaving: "[T]he vibrancy, the sense of colour, the sheer singing joy of ... [the tapestries] were the final pieces of the puzzle that this woman presented" (177). Marah finally admits that she has admired Hannah's art for a long time, that she has owned one of Hannah's bowls since the very beginnings of Cantii Glass. Marah tells Hannah that she is in love with her; she still wants children, but she suggests that she could use a donor or adopt a child. Hannah feels ready to open up her life to another woman. Although the novella ends with this possibility of a new relationship, Harne overstates the case when she says that "it is still romantic love which wins out" (140). When Hannah and Marah go on a picnic, both want an exclusive romantic afternoon on one level, but both realize how much Zhora would enjoy an afternoon in the country, so they invite Zhora and Caro to come along. Any new relationship between Hannah and Marah would be grounded in their community of black women friends, in Hannah's work community of Cantii Glass, and in the larger artistic community to which both women belong. Hannah and Marah have declared their love for each other and have the possibility of an intimate sexual relationship, but the ethical concerns and commitments to larger groups undergird their relationship.

Commitments to larger groups are also an important part of the revision of the romance plot in Keri Hulme's novel, *The Bone People*, about a woman artist in postcolonial New Zealand. In this work Keri Hulme deconstructs not only the romance plot but the realist novel and traditional attitudes toward race and gender as well. Critics

describe *The Bone People* as a novel that "breaks literary boundaries
... and flout[s] gender stereotypes" (Hughes 57), as a "post-
modernist" novel that shifts between "Realist" and "Symbolic
modes" in a "double spiral" structure and dismantles gender bina-
ries (Covi 222–25), and as a work that decenters the narrative and
undermines the "unitary voice of authority" with its interspersion of
Maori words and shifting points of view (Dever 25). Chris Prentice
says that in "refusing the binary Maori-Pakeha racial dichotomy, Keri
Hulme enacts, and Kerewin embodies, a rejection of 'either-or' in
racial identity or affiliation" (71). Hulme says of her own combination of Maori, Scottish, and Lancashire English ancestry in a 1989
talk: [I]t's bloody difficult when you have your own relations at one
another's throats, because one lot happens to be Pakeha and the other
lot happen to be Maori. My commitment is to my people and to my
tribe, but they happen to be on both sides of the fence" (Hulme and
Turcotte 149). In an interview with Andrew Peek, Hulme comments:
"[A]s a person who is intrinsically a mongrel you can never be fully
committed to one way alone. Now I'll throw again and again to my
Maori side, but there is no way honestly I can say that I will totally
ignore or exclude . . . all the joys and benefits of the Pakeha side of
things" (3).

In her exploration of this "mongrel condition" with the lingering
effects of racism and colonialism and a woman's fear of intimacy and
connection, Hulme has created a tour de force, a postrealist novel
that took twelve years to write and was rejected by three publishers
before being published by Spiral Press, a women's collective, and
winning the Booker Prize in 1985. Hulme describes her motivation
for writing the novel as rooted in her desire to bring the two sides
of her family together. She says she wanted

> to show particularly my relations on my father's side, who are purely
> of English stock and very English still, that there are wonderful riches
> on the Maori side of things. I also wanted to show, despite the ways
> in which that side of New Zealand life has been corrupted and dam-
> aged, how vital, how very potent it still was. (Bryson 132)

Although the novel does show how the Maori values of relationships
and the honoring of ancestors can heal an overdose of English individu-
alism, Hulme does not imply that a solution is easy or without suffering. The novel vividly depicts the damage of colonialism a well as hope
for healing in a nonsexual and nonbiological family relationship.

The novel's departure from traditional forms is evident in its prologue, "The End at the Beginning," whose four short prose poems and three disconnected narrative passages set up the double spiral structure. The prose poems describe three characters, two "he's" and a "she," who, the fourth section says, are connected in a unique way: "Even paired, any pairing, they would have been nothing more than people by themselves. But all together . . . they are the instruments of change" (4). This mood shifts abruptly in the three ominous narrative fragments about a boat wreck and drownings, the death of a mother and child, and a seemingly less threatening description of the building of a tower, but the voice that emerges is one submerged in despair and haunted by "secrets that . . . chilled and chuckled in the marrow of her bones" (7). Her tower becomes an "abyss," a "prison" (7). In the first chapter after the prologue, the narrative shifts into a realistic style, and it becomes clear that this voice is that of Kerewin Holmes.

Kerewin's voice, as Judith Dale points out, dominates the first three-fourths of the book, where her "inner-consciousness" alternates with her "outer response to what's going on" (416). Hulme admits that of the three Kerewin is "my touchstone character" (Hulme and Turcotte 140). As the reader moves into the realistic section, Kerewin's dilemma begins to emerge. Homi Bhabha's description of "a contested cultural territory . . . [whose] people must be thought in double-time" ("DissemiNation" 297) fits well Kerewin's postcolonial space where she feels the contested heritage within her own body: "[B]y blood, flesh and inheritance, I am but an eighth Maori, by heart, spirit, and inclination, I feel all Maori. Or . . . I used to. Now it feels like the best part of me has got lost in the way I live" (*The Bone People* 62). Kerewin's problem is that her experience of adulthood has all been in Pakeha terms. In spite of all her achievements, Kerewin feels that the "best part" of her has been lost.

In terms of Western psychological development, Kerewin has successfully separated from her family and individuated. In fact, she has totally broken away from her family and achieved a successful identity as an artist. She has no financial worries because she won a lottery. With the lottery money she has built herself a Joycean tower and has a self-sufficient lifestyle in which she grows her own herbs and vegetables and catches fish. Kerewin has already attained what Carol Gilligan describes as the typical life pattern of white Western males for whom "the road to mid-life salvation runs through either achievement or separation" (152). Kerewin has realized both, but she is unhappy. No sooner does she complete her tower than she feels blocked as an artist.

At this point in her life, Kerewin lacks not individuation but intimacy and community. The actual events of Kerewin's conflict with her family are never narrated, only her sense of loss and loneliness. She only says that she lost her temper and that the ensuing argument was never reconciled. Kerewin has not only lost her family, however; she's lost her connection to her Maori side. She is typical of many Maori in that initially she seems completely assimilated. As Patrick Morrow warns, "[A]ssimilation can eliminate minorities, and one aspect about the Maori that virtually everyone agrees upon is that they have been uncommonly successful at getting themselves assimilated" (92). Hulme spells out Morrow's ironic "successful" in Kerewin's artistic block: "Estranged from my family, bereft of my art, hollow of soul," Kerewin feels "parched, cracked" (*The Bone People* 289).

In addition to probing contested ethnic and cultural territory and definitions of success, Hulme also subverts gender categories and the romance plot. Hulme says of Kerewin: "[S]he's doing things which in New Zealand society are still considered to be masculine, or part of the masculine role. Being extraordinarily skilled in fighting, being able to drink anyone under the table, taking on the male ethos in its own terms, being financially independent and able to take care of herself physically" (quoted by Jones 38). Likewise, Joe, Kerewin's friend whom she first overhears swearing in a bar, is described by Hulme as also having "a lot of gentle, sensitive, nurturing so-called female traits. I deliberately set out, in the character of Joe, to turn sexual stereotype on its head" (quoted by Jones 39). Hulme not only dismantles conventional gender behavior but sexuality itself in the character of Kerewin. She says to Joe that she is a virgin and that furthermore she has not experienced sexual attraction: "I've never been attracted to men. Or women.[11] Or anything else. . . . [W]hile I have an apparently normal female body, I don't have any sexual urge or appetite. I think I am a neuter" (*The Bone People* 266).

Hulme does not see the solution to isolation in terms of intimacy with a single partner. Hulme does, however, acknowledge the power of sexuality in Maori myth: "[W]e believe the world is partly run, indeed generated, by sexual energy. . . . [S]exuality is an enormously potent force, one way or the other; repress it and you're in trouble. Let it loose too much, you are in trouble" (Hulme and Turcotte 154).

Hulme uses sexuality in Joe's dreams and in Maori mythology when Joe begins to grieve for his dead wife and learns to let her go, but overall her novel is focused on a radical revision of the definition of the family and of the marriage plot, and so sexuality plays a lesser role.

Kerewin's isolation is initially disrupted by Simon, a mute child, who reverses the racial tradition of both *Robinson Crusoe*[12] and English imperialism. Simon, whom Joe rescued from the boat wreck and is raising as his son, is of Irish descent. He loses his sandal and leaves a footprint in the sand, thereby evoking Crusoe's Friday, on his way to Kerewin's tower. In a letter to Dale, Hulme identifies Simon "as the Celtic 'marvellous stranger' or 'marvellous child' (Aifa's and Cuchulain's son Connla, or Arianrhod's child Dylan from the *Mabinogion*)" (Dale 427–28). Kerewin's experience of Simon, however, is grounded in realism, not the marvelous, because he is a delightful but needy child who, Kerewin eventually discovers, is being badly beaten[13] by his loving but hurt foster father, Joe Gillayley. Gillayley and Simon represent the complexities of postcolonial relationships. Gillayley, who is half Maori, is damaged by the colonial attitudes toward Maoris that he has absorbed and tried to compensate for, by the death of his wife and infant son in a flu epidemic, and by the alcoholism that he uses to deaden his pain. He is a victim but also a victimizer. The clearest "victim" of the novel is Simon, the European; but he is not just any European, he is an Irish child, despised historically by the English imperialists[14] and, in the novel, within his own Celtic heritage as well by his aristocratic grandfather because of his drug-addicted father. With these characters, Hulme deconstructs a simple binary division between European colonizer and Polynesian victim. Hulme's plan for Kerewin's healing does involve the use of Maori culture, but she does not propose a simple return to one's roots as a solution to the hybridity of the postcolonial condition.

Kerewin gradually allows herself to come out of isolation and be drawn into the complex relationship between foster father and son, but when she discovers a problem, she still relies on the traditionally masculine solution of a physical fight. When Simon first arrives, Kerewin removes the splinter from his foot and begrudgingly lets him stay for dinner. Gradually she lets Simon and Joe Gillayley befriend her, and they share drinks and meals. She even invites them to go on a vacation with her to her small seaside cabin, or "bach," on the southern tip of New Zealand near the Stewart Islands. It is just before this trip when Simon, who is somewhere between six and eight years old, gets drunk at Kerewin's tower. As Kerewin scolds him and puts him in a cold shower, she discovers Simon's scars and infected sores from the savage beatings Joe has given him. Kerewin at first does not confront Joe with this abuse, but finally she feels compelled to act when she sees that Joe is ready to hit his child again. Kerewin, who has spent a year in Japan studying aikido, easily beats Joe in a fight on the beach. In this fight Kerewin illustrates that she can win using masculine values. Suzette Henke notes that "Kerewin amalgamates an anti-heroic subject-position with traditionally masculine characteristics of bravery, courage, self-sufficiency, and gallantry in the face of abusive patriarchal authority" (90).

Kerewin, however, is not proud of winning the fight. She realizes that she has not lived up to the principles of aikido. She explains to Joe that one is supposed to use aikido to unify the body, mind, and spirit, not just to beat one's opponents. Kerewin realizes that by assuming the role of the "ultimate warring barbarian" (*The Bone People* 199), she has abused the principles of aikido. Even if Kerewin recognizes her failure to achieve the ideal of unification, however, her winning of the fight has a potentially positive effect for Simon. Joe makes a pact with Kerewin that he will never again beat Simon unless she agrees. Unfortunately, Kerewin experiences a fit of anger at Simon after Simon has kicked in her guitar in his frustration at not being able to tell about seeing the death of an old man. When Kerewin tacitly agrees to Joe's "disciplining" Simon, Joe beats Simon so badly that Simon is hospitalized, and Joe is sent to prison. Joe is forced to expiate his guilt by prison and by a period of initiation with a Maori elder. Simon is put in a foster home. Kerewin is left, once again, alone, but this time ridden with guilt and sorrow. Furthermore, her tower home is struck by lightning and burns to the ground.

In her agony over the knowledge of her complicity in Simon's beating and Joe's suffering, Kerewin has begun to open herself up to the feelings of others, and in her pain, her artistic ability returns. She creates a sculpture of the three of them, a tricephalos, which she fires with what was left of the wood that once made up her tower. When Simon runs away from the foster home and comes to the burned-out tower, it is this sculpture that expresses the love he knows exists between the three of them and gives him hope of reunion. The firing of the clay statue is foreshadowed by the one item Simon has with him after the boat wreck: a rosary with a signet ring embossed with a phoenix, that ancient Egyptian bird that rose again from the funeral pyre.[15] But before Kerewin can reunite with Joe and Simon, she must go through her own purgation and rebirth. Kerewin's purgation and expiation take the form of a journey and a battle with illness. Since Kerewin's problem is not only guilt but also isolation and separation, the journey she is forced to undergo is homeopathic. She is forced to face the most extreme form of separation and isolation, an encounter with death.

For Kerewin in particular, illness and the approach of death are completely isolating. Since Joe is in prison, Simon is in a foster home, and Kerewin is determined not to contact her family, she experiences a complete loss of community. Hulme sees the loss of family as especially debilitating because the loss of family means the loss of ancestors. Hulme said in an interview that if "you take away your ancestry, you are . . . nothing—you're a slender kind of skeleton" ("An Interview" 3). Kerewin must literally be reduced to skin and bones, almost to a skeleton, before she can realize her need for her family and her ancestors, the Maori people. These ancestors join with Joe, who breaks his arm, and Simon, who has had many broken bones, to become the "bone people." The title is a statement both of the suffering that the characters must go through and of the unity that comes from acknowledging community and ancestry.

When Kerewin first fought Joe, she doubled up in pain after the fight, although Joe had not been fast enough to fight back. She thinks at first that the pain was a pulled muscle as a result of her misusing aikido, but when the pain continues and she feels a hard growth in her stomach, she realizes that she is sick. Pakeha doctors think she might have stomach cancer, but she refuses tests and treatment. One of the doctors admits that although her symptoms match those of carcinoma, there is a possibility that they could be psychosomatic. Kerewin thinks the pain is probably cancer, but she takes only painkillers, her own herbs, and some potent mushrooms. She goes to her family's small beach shack to await death.

One can read Kerewin's encounter with illness realistically as the resolution of a psychologically induced illness or in terms of magic realism and myth in which a real disease is miraculously cured by the intervention of a spirit or an ancestor. Kerewin buys food and whiskey and goes down to the bach alone to wait. She plays her guitar, walks on the beach, and copes with the pain as best she can, but she loses weight and begins to suffer increasingly. As Covi says, Kerewin's "rebirth entails a temporary abandoning of language and immersion in the body" (230). Kerewin has to feel her vulnerability physically before she can let go of her self-sufficiency and experience vulnerability mentally and spiritually. In the grips of physical pain and intense loneliness, Kerewin analyzes her own condition: "Mentally I am almost drowned. . . . Spiritually, I still hope . . . idiot Holmes. . . . Why hope?" (*The Bone People* 412). Eventually she is bedridden, and the drugs she takes for the pain give her vivid nightmares; she dreams that Simon and Joe are decaying, that her family stand around with spears tormenting and mocking her.

As she seems to be dying, she experiences a vision, perhaps inspired by the potent mushrooms and painkillers, or a visitation, perhaps of an ancient ancestor who decides that Kerewin is now ready for a new value system. The visitor is a strange figure of "indeterminate sex [and] . . . race" with a "massive burnscar . . . twisted by pink keloid tissue" (424) who gives Kerewin a sour-tasting drink. Susie O'Brien, who suggests a realistic interpretation of the visitor, argues that "the mysterious visitor's key role is to provide Kerewin with the spiritual sustenance she has just demonstrated her readiness to receive" (88). Kerewin sleeps, and when she awakens, her pain and the growth in her stomach are gone. She manages to eat and clean her soiled clothes. She dreams again, but this time the dream is positive: "The light bursts into bright blue daylight. . . . [S]trangely clad people, with golden eyes, brown skin . . . touch and caress [her] with excited yet gentle hands. . . . She diminishes to bones and the bones sink into the earth which . . . is clothed in beauty" (428). Kerewin recognizes this dream as a connection back to her ancestors, the bone people. In the dream her bones mingle with her ancestors' bones and the earth itself. She has overcome both illness and isolation.

After experiencing healing and this connection to her ancestors, Kerewin is ready to return to her people and act on the values of community that she has learned during her battle with illness. She initiates the rebuilding of a traditional Maori gathering place, a "marae." Finally, she goes back to the site of the tower and decides to rebuild a home, not a lonely tower this time but a spiral-shaped building, a "round shell house [that] holds them all in its spiralling embrace" (442). Like the phoenix, the spiral is a symbol of rebirth, but it comes from Maori tradition: The double spirals that occur so often in Maori carvings were modeled on "uncurling fernfronds" (45), a traditional Maori symbol of renewal and rebirth.

Kerewin labels the intimacy that is enabled by her spiral home and Maori values "commensalism." Kerewin first uses the word in a note to Joe that she sent just before he was let out of prison:

> But if I exist this coming Christ Mass, rejoin me at the Tower, eh? O the groaning table of cheer . . . speaking of tables [mensa is Latin for table], does commensalism appeal to you as an upright vertebrate? Common quarters wherein we circulate like corpuscles in one blood stream, joining (I won't say like clots) for food and drink and discussion. (383)

This is not a merging, like clots, but an eating together, a sharing of space and food, an acknowledgment that people of many different heritages are all "corpuscles in a single bloodstream." The metaphor drawn from the body has stretched to become a metaphor for a nonbiological family. As Hamelin comments: "Hulme creates new love relationships which go beyond labels such as sexual union, parents and family" (109). As Simon thinks to himself of the three of them: "Not family, not whanau [Maori word for extended family]. . . . [T]here aren't words for us yet" (*The Bone People* 395). Simon, the mute Irish boy, a Pakeha child from a culture that also experienced colonization, a European child who personally suffered the effects of postcolonial violence but who can forgive those he loves, has always understood commensalism. When the police find Simon after he runs away from the foster home, they approach Kerewin about adoption. Kerewin rejoices to herself: "It made me want to dance. It made me want to weep. It made rebuilding so bloody pointed and poignant and REAL. Commensalism—right on" (434).

In spite of what he has done, commensalism also includes Joe, the half Maori man, abused himself as a child, who also abused Simon, but is the one Simon loves most. It includes Kerewin's formerly estranged family. Joe invites them to the opening of Kerewin's new spiral house, and they are reconciled with her. As Susan Ash says,

Kerewin "undergoes a literal and symbolic journey and acquires the strength to return to society with the gift of her new knowledge: the paramount importance of bridging human alienation and establishing community" (124). The community is not an exclusively Maori community, nor is Kerewin's new reestablishment of relationships restricted only to a love relationship with Joe or even a nuclear family of herself, Joe, and Simon. Kerewin recovers the Maori values of community, but she broadens them to include not just family and not just Maoris but a hybrid, inclusive community.

Although Kerewin does not have to experience sexuality to achieve intimacy and a return to art, she does connect with an aspect of the erotic that Lorde sees as equally important: spirituality. Spirituality, for Lorde, is part of that "resource" that lies "within each of us . . . firmly rooted in the power of our unexpressed or unrecognized feeling" (Lorde 53). Kerewin has known that she was full of "god-hunger" (*The Bone People* 261) and in need of "the numinous" (329), but she cannot open herself up to the spiritual until her body has almost been stripped to the bone, until she feels vulnerable enough to join with others. Then she is able to dream of ancestors and be healed. As Antoinette Holm suggests, Kerewin "expands beyond the confines of a romanticised heroine to occupy a new space" (84). She is able to welcome Joe, who dropped out of Catholic seminary in his youth but has now been "ordained" (*The Bone People* 378) by the Maori elder, back into her life. Finally, Kerewin, who shrinks from touch, can embrace her formerly estranged family and Simon. As Le Cam argues: "Hulme is not interested in . . . reinstating the standard Maori divide between the *tapu* (sacredness) of the insider and the *noa* (ordinariness) of the outsider. Her prophetic bias is no longer exclusive and tribal as in the past, but indeed inclusive" (77). Commensalism involves a spirituality that creates a new kind of intimacy and a joy in relationship that spirals back to the beginning of the novel and brings healing to the postcolonial condition.

Both Burford and Hulme tell positive stories about women who find intimacy with a group of others and connect with their racial and ethnic identities. They must work to maintain this intimacy, but that work enables them to be artists and to share their visions of new relationships and of the hybrid cultures in which they live. These stories demonstrate the costs of racism and colonialism, but they are also stories of hope that break down traditional boundaries and forms. They are stories that write beyond the ending of the heterosexual romance plot to describe different kinds of opportunities for human connection.

Chapter 3

National Identities:
The Search for Place in Buchi
Emecheta's *Kehinde* and Anita
Desai's *Clear Light of Day*

"Place is security, space is freedom," proclaims geographer Yi-Fu Tuan. "[W]e are attached to the one and long for the other. There is no place like home. What is home?" (3). Biddy Martin and Chandra Mohanty answer Tuan's meditative question with a dose of contemporary reality: "'Being home' refers to the place where one lives within familiar, safe, protected boundaries; 'not being home' is a matter of realizing that home was an illusion of coherence and safety based on the exclusion of specific histories of oppression and resistance" (196).[1] Particularly if "home" is conceptualized as "nation," there are many histories of oppression and violence that belie the illusion of security. Benedict Anderson defines "nation" as an "imagined political community," a "fraternity that makes it possible . . . for so many millions of people, not so much to kill, as willingly to die" (6–7). For Anderson the symbol of nation is a tomb of the Unknown Soldier. Where is the security and where is a woman's place in this "fraternity?" Ania Loomba comments: "If the nation is an imagined community, that imagining is profoundly gendered" (215). The "'fraternity' which represents the nation does not explicitly include them [women] as equals, however, it always implicitly claims to represent them" (198).[2] It is no wonder that Virginia Woolf in her 1938 polemic against fascism said, "[A]s a woman I have no country" (*Three Guineas* 109). And yet there still remains for women as well as men a longing for a place of familiarity, a location of safety and an experience of freedom.

This longing for a sense of place is explored in two contemporary women's novels of adulthood, Buchi Emecheta's *Kehinde* and Anita Desai's *Clear Light of Day*. *Kehinde* investigates the meaning of transnational and diasporic identities in the story of a Nigerian woman living in Britain who searches for "home" both in Nigeria and in the diaspora. Anita Desai's heroine remains in the same country, even the same city, but her search for a place takes her through the estrangement and dangers of colonialism and the partition of India. As Anindyo Roy explains, in the postcolonial world "vulnerable, historical and cultural boundaries . . . continually refract the shapes in which 'homes' are imagined" (114).[3] As the novels open, both protagonists are adult women, probably in their late thirties or early forties, who have already established many aspects of their identities and made many decisions about their lives. Emecheta's protagonist, Kehinde Okolo, is married, has two children, and is working in a bank and living in London. Desai's protagonist, Bim Das, is a teacher at a women's college who has turned down marriage but taken on the responsibility of keeping up their family home and looking after her retarded younger brother.

In terms of their careers and their caring for others, both these women have reached the stage of maturity where, Erik Erikson says, the primary task is that of "generativity," the use of one's "productivity and creativity" in "guiding the next generation" (*Childhood and Society* 267). In *Binding Cultures: Black Women Writers in Africa and the Diaspora*, Gay Wilentz uses a similar term to describe the way African women throughout a wide diaspora have passed on cultural values to their communities: "generational continuity" (xviii). Sudhir Kakar, who has shown the parallels between Erikson's adult stages of development and Hindu concepts of dharma (which Kakar translates as "moral duty" or "right action"), links Erikson's adult task of generativity to the "teaching of *dharma*" and the extending of "care" to a younger generation (*The Inner World* 37, 43). Both Kehinde and Bim are already involved in care, but before they can truly pass on values and create that generational continuity, they must find their own places and sort out the meaning of "home" and "national identity" for themselves.

Both novels illustrate Homi Bhabha's questioning of Benedict Anderson's "homogeneous and horizontal view associated with the nation's imagined community" (*The Location of Culture* 144). Both women reside in what Bhabha calls a "liminal" or "borderline" area—Kehinde in the space of the diaspora, Bim in a historical space of changing nationhood. Bhabha says it is these stories to which we must pay particular attention:

> It is precisely in reading between these borderlines of the nation-space that we can see how the concept of the "people" emerges . . . as a double narrative movement. . . . We then have a contested conceptual territory where the nation's people must be thought in double-time. (*The Location of Culture* 145)

Both Kehinde and Bim must locate themselves within their "contested cultural territories."[4] Kehinde has lived in London for eighteen years, but she has stayed within the Nigerian emigrant community there and always thought that she and her husband would eventually return to Nigeria and build a house in Ibusa, "their *home* village [my emphasis]" (Emecheta, *Kehinde* 41). In *The Clear Light of Day* Bim has always been in the same place, but the meaning of that place has changed radically after the partition of India and her older brother's desertion of their home and marriage to a Muslim girl. Furthermore, because of her British colonial education, Bim is caught in two worlds, the world of her British education and her duty as a Hindu daughter. Rajeswari Mohan comments on the effects of that education and the place of the Indian middle-class woman at this point in history:

> [G]ender ideologies are obviously an important area undergoing reconfiguration under colonialism. Under the pressure of territorial displacement, class formation and religious identification during the independence movement, these ideologies assume complicated and indeed hardened forms that, despite their apparently liberatory potential, more often than not circumscribe options available to women. . . . *Clear Light of Day* . . . figures the contradictions at the centre of emerging ideals of nation and femininity. (50)[5]

As the narrative shifts back and forth from Bim's adulthood to the time of partition to childhood, Bim thinks about the changes in nation, family, and house that have created her adult female identity.

Like Tambu Sigauke in *Nervous Conditions* and Elaine Risley in *Cat's Eye*, Kehinde and Bim must confront the "multiple, fluid structures of domination which intersect to locate women differently at particular historical conjunctures" (Mohanty, "Introduction: Cartographies of Struggle" 13) and at different ages. As adults, Kehinde and Bim are not immune from these oppressions, and each must sort through her own multiple structures of dominations. As a member of the diaspora, Kehinde must find a way between national identities, between "a national British identity . . . built upon a notion of a racial belonging, upon a hegemonic white ethnicity that never speaks its presence" (Mirza 3), which has no place for her as black, and a Nigerian national identity that has too small a space for her as female. Chikwenye Ogunyemi says that in *Kehinde* "Emecheta locates woman's anguish in the insecurities, from womb to the grave, of not being assured a home or a place she can call her own" (*Africa Wo/man Palava* 279). Bim must redefine for herself the idea of "home" and find a place for herself within family and nation, institutions that at varying times restricted and idealized women's lives and were sometimes complicit with colonialism in erasing women's lives.

Buchi Emecheta herself has lived in the double-voiced liminal space she writes about for the past thirty-seven years. She went to England in 1962 to join her husband who was a graduate student there. As she explains in her autobiography *Head Above Water*, they, like many Africans in Britain, thought of themselves as "emigrants" who would "work their way through college [and] . . . go home after their studies" (140). Emecheta says that she goes to Nigeria "at least twice a year" (Ogundele 448) and remains close to her relatives and agemates, "the Saltless Women" as they are known because they grew up during World War II when Nigeria did not have salt ("Feminism with a Small 'f'!" 177), but she lives in England. She describes her struggles with English racism and the difficulty of raising five children alone after leaving her husband in her two early autobiographical novels, *In the Ditch* (1972) and *Second Class Citizen* (1974).[6] It is not surprising that many critics refer to the many voices[7] echoing through her novels. John Hawley says that most of Emecheta's female protagonists "are doubly rooted. They do not live *between* countries, but instead attempt to form a psychic bridge across the metaphysical space separating them" (339).

One of the most contested "metaphysical spaces" for Emecheta is that of feminism. The distrust that some African women feel for feminism is revealed in some of Ogunyemi's early comments on Emecheta's novels. In a 1985 article in *Signs*, Ogunyemi says that Emecheta's first two novels are "deeply grounded in the British and Irish feminism in which she was nurtured" ("Womanism" 66). Ogunyemi castigates Emecheta for feminizing African males, for turning away from her African identity, and for being narcissistic (67). It is not surprising that in spite of her focus on female characters Emecheta, too, is wary of the term *feminist*. In a 1984 interview Emecheta says emphatically: "My novels are not feminist; they are part of the corpus of African literature" (Ravell-Pinto 50). Cynthia Ward summarizes Emecheta's dilemma: "Success in speaking unequivocally in the service of feminism produces a voice that serves neocolonialism; speaking for anticolonialism produces a voice that serves patriarchy" (86). Emecheta relents somewhat and acknowledges her ambivalence when at a 1986 conference she described herself as "a feminist with a small 'f'!" ("Feminism with a small 'f'" 175). In her 1986 speech Emecheta shows much greater comfort with the term when she characterizes "feminism" as not just being against marriage (her 1980 comment to the Umehs, "Interview" 23) but as embracing a particular literary perspective:

> I write about the little happenings of everyday life. . . . I see things through an African woman's eyes.[8] I chronicle the little happenings in the lives of the African women I know. I did not know that by doing so I was going to be called a feminist. But if I am now a feminist then I am an African feminist with a small "f." (175)

The focus on "the little happenings of everyday life" is not only feminist but also, according to Bhabha, a characteristic of writing from a liminal perspective: "The scraps, patches and rags of daily life must be repeatedly turned into the signs of a coherent national culture" (*The Location of Culture* 145). When these "scraps, patches and rags of daily life" are those of an emigrant African woman, a feminist with a small "f," the national culture can be remade to provide places for a variety of its peoples.

An important part of Emecheta's portrayal in *Kehinde* of daily life in the borderline nation–space of the Nigerian emigrant community in London are the "scraps" of different languages throughout the novel. Although Kehinde and Albert Okolo have lived in London for eighteen years, they speak Igbo to each other at home. When their son hears them talking in Igbo, he interprets their use of Igbo as an attempt to exclude their children. His mother scolds him gently, "'Whose fault is it that you don't speak your mother tongue when you refuse to learn?'" He responds, "'You mean *your* mother tongue. Mine is English'" (3). Kehinde indulgently dismisses his comments as typical of the rebellious nature of a fourteen-year-old boy, but it shows the language gaps in the children's national identity. There are language varieties within the emigrant Nigerian community as well. Kehinde's best friend at the bank is Moriammo, a Muslim Nigerian woman. When they go out to lunch, they speak pidgin English to each other. "We use pidgin in a relaxed situation,"[9] Emecheta says, but pidgin also avoids the choice between Kehinde's Igbo and Moriammo's native tongue. It is, Bhabha argues, "postcolonials, migrants, minorities . . . who by speaking the foreignness of language split the patriotic voice of unisonance" (*The Location of Culture* 164) and create difference within culture.

At the opening of the novel, Kehinde ignores these linguistic signs of cultural difference and thinks of herself as a traditional Nigerian wife. She knows she can "talk to her husband less formally than women like her sister, Ifeyinwa, who were in more traditional [polygamous] marriages" (6), but the "Igbo woman in her knew how far to go. She could tell Albert what she liked, but would not malign his relatives. Not to his face, at any rate" (22). Kehinde is contemptuous of a fellow Nigerian woman, Mary Elikwu, who left her husband because he beat her. Kehinde thinks of her as a "fallen woman" (38) who allowed her marriage to fail. Kehinde is happy in her marriage and happy in London. She has a seemingly secure place in her joint ownership of the house, her well-paying job at the bank, and her status of being a married woman.

Albert, however, is anxious to return to Nigeria. His job as a storekeeper is less prestigious and well paid than Kehinde's, and his sisters urge him to return to Nigeria and take his place as head of the family. In London, Albert plays the role of a contented Igbo family man, but he is still dissatisfied. Kehinde senses that "behind the veneer of westernisation, the traditional Igbo man was alive and strong, awaiting an opportunity to reclaim his birthright" (35). Albert reveals the selfishness in his desire to return home when he forces Kehinde to have an abortion so that she will not miss her promotion at the bank and thus be able to pay for their passage home. Both as a Roman Catholic and as a Nigerian, Albert knows abortion is wrong, but he rationalizes that they are "in a strange land, where you do things contrary to your culture" (15). Albert does not fully realize, however, exactly how contrary to his culture the abortion is. After the abortion, Kehinde has a dream in which Taiwo, her *chi*, her personal spirit who is also the spirit of her twin who died in the womb,[10] comes to tell her that the baby that she aborted was the spirit of their father who was returning to protect Kehinde. Kehinde is devastated and feels estranged from Albert. Unaware of her feelings, Albert returns to Nigeria, and before long, the children follow him to go to boarding school. Kehinde stays behind to sell their house.

Although Kehinde still has her job and the house and a new friendly Caribbean tenant named Michael Gibson, she feels estranged from the London Nigerian community. She thinks that without a husband she is viewed as only "a half-person" (59). Her *chi* urges her to go to Albert, lest he get a girlfriend. Even Moriammo urges her to go to Nigeria and enjoy her status as a "rich, been-to madam" (47). Kehinde quits her job and leaves her house in the care of her tenants, but she does not realize that her place in Nigeria has been usurped by Albert's older sisters and his second wife.

In interviews Emecheta is sanguine about polygamy. In 1984 she explained: "In a polygamous society every woman has a husband whom she shares with a number of other women. This gives her more freedom in some respects: she has the opportunity of pursuing a career as well as having children. . . . The children belong to an extended family with a number of mothers, and the women, after the initial jealousy, share a kind of sisterhood" (Ravell-Pinto 51). In 1986 she continues the defense, saying: "People think that polygamy is oppression, and it is in certain cases. But I realize, now that I have visited Nigeria often, that some women now make polygamy work for them" ("Feminism with a small 'f'!" 176). In her novels, however, Emecheta concentrates on the jealousy and not on the sisterhood of polygamy. This is true to a certain extent in *Joys of Motherhood* and even more so in *Kehinde*. Kehinde has always been aware of the sufferings of her older sister Ifeyinwa in a polygamous marriage, and she had thought that Albert agreed with her because he had seen the sufferings of his own father's two wives. When she arrives in Nigeria, however, Kehinde finds that the place allotted to a senior wife, even a "been-to madam,"[11] is a lot different than she had imagined. She is ushered into a small bedroom with a single bed, not the double bed that she had helped pay for and had had sent to Nigeria. When Kehinde calls to Albert to ask about her room, Ifeyinwa reminds her that it rude to call a husband by his given name. Kehinde must now call him "Joshua's father" or "our husband" to acknowledge the role of his new wife Rike. When Kehinde gets in the front seat of the car beside Albert to go visit her children at school, she is reprimanded by Albert's older sister:

> "What is wrong with you? . . . [W]ho do you think you are? Don't you see your mate, Rike . . . sitting at the back with her maid and baby. When we, the relatives of the head of the family are here, we take the place of honour by our Albert. . . ."
> Kehinde almost died of shame. (88)

Kehinde cannot get a job in Nigeria because she has no degree, and she is no match for the sophisticated Rike, who has a doctorate and teaches at a university, or for her husband's powerful sisters. Even her children are happy at boarding school and no longer need her. In the land of her birth Kehinde is forced because of gender to inhabit a smaller and more constricted space than she had in London. She had dreamed that her return to Africa would be a time of celebration in which she was honored as a "been-to" madam: "Instead, she found herself once more relegated to the margins" (97). Even Rike is not protected from marginal status. Ifeyinwa gets revenge upon Rike for her treatment of Kehinde by being the one to tell Rike that Albert has taken a third wife, an even younger Fulani woman from the north.

Kehinde is nostalgic for the space and freedom and even the weather of London: "[T]his was October, autumn in England. The wind would be blowing, leaves. . . falling" (96). Kehinde thinks of the small cherry tree in the garden behind the house that she still owns and envisions its bare branches against the sky while she sits inside by the gas fire watching her favorite TV serials: "Her eyes misted" (96). She feels "nostalgia" for all of her past life in England, even "for the wet stinking body-smell of the underground" (96). Kehinde writes to Moriammo of her predicament. It is Moriammo, her British-Nigerian friend and age-mate, who, although she shares neither a religion nor a native language with Kehinde, offers Kehinde an alternative place by sending her a plane ticket back to London. At this point even the damp cold autumn weather of London seems inviting to Kehinde. Bhabha comments on the relationship of English weather to its multicultural inhabitants:

> [T]he English weather . . . invoke[s], at once, the most changeable and immanent signs of national difference. It encourages memories of the

"deep" nation crafted in chalk and limestone; the quilted downs; the moors menaced by the wind; . . . [It] also revives memories of its daemonic double: the heat and dust of India; the dark emptiness of Africa; the tropical chaos that was deemed despotic and ungovernable and therefore worthy of the civilizing mission. These imaginative geographies that spanned countries and empires are changing, those imagined communities that played on the unisonant boundaries of the nation are singing with different voices. If I began with the scattering of the people across countries, I want to end with their gathering in the city. The return of the diasporic; the postcolonial. (*The Location of Culture* 169)

Kehinde represents the return of the diasporic, the postcolonial. Fortunately, Kehinde still has a place in London since she never sold her house. When she returns to London, she pulls up the "For Sale" sign in front of her house and claims her place: "'This house is mine'" (108). Hawley comments: "Tearing down the For Sale sign, therefore, ends the tentative emigrant status that would not let Kehinde—or Emecheta—settle. Her liberating act as a woman is also her liberating act as a Nigerian—one who chooses to redefine the possibilities of nationality for women such as herself" (344). Emecheta comments in several interviews about the freedom of European women in comparison to African women. She said to the Umehs in 1985: "The comparative ease with which the women in Europe move around became clear. One can live alone; one can have children. The women in Britain have much more freedom than Nigerian women. It is when you're out of your country that you can see the faults in your society" ("Interview" 22). Later Emecheta admits that her years in England have changed her: "In Nigeria women are riddled with hypocrisy, you learn to say what you don't feel. . . . I find I don't fit in there any more" (James 38).

Returning to London only resolves one of Kehinde's multiple oppressions, however. She still has to face economic hardship and racial prejudice in Britain.[12] Although Kehinde returns to school to get a university degree in social work, she is unable to return to her job at the bank and is forced to support herself by working as a maid at a fancy hotel. There she experiences problems of economic class that cross cultural and religious lines as well as racial lines. When Kehinde is sent to clean the hotel's most expensive suite for an Arab sheik, her fellow black maid comments that at least she is making up the room "for a non-white person." Kehinde expects no such solidarity based on color. Kehinde senses that economic class is a greater force when she responds "'Ah, but the oil money makes people colour-blind, my sister'" (126). When she goes to the Arab's suite, he surprises her by acknowledging ties based on religion and education. After hearing her speak, he asks her if she will tutor his wives in English. He presumes that because Kehinde is a Nigerian that she is also Muslim. Kehinde, however, is wary because she senses that economic difference is more powerful than religious understanding. She thinks of her Muslim neighbors in Lagos, where she grew up:

> They had sold meat and hides, prayed several times a day and given alms to beggars. The Ebute Metta Muslims carried water in kettles with them, so they could wash and pray wherever they were, and they chewed kolanuts. They had not prepared her for this man in his silk robe, speaking in a low voice she found hard to understand. (128)

Later her suppositions are proven correct. After Kehinde gives an English lesson to his fifteen-year-old wife, the Arab asks Kehinde to remove her clothes because he wants "to see what a naked black woman looks like" (131). Unfortunately, in the hybrid culture of wealth neither classism nor racism is restricted to the English alone. Kehinde runs from the room and loses both her job as English teacher and her job as maid.

Eventually, however, Kehinde finishes her degree and gets a professional job. Emecheta is interested in how women cope "with the changes from one culture to the other and survive" (Ogundele 455). Kehinde is the most successful of all of Emecheta's London heroines. In London, Kehinde finds a home, an education, a career, and a lover in her Caribbean tenant, Michael Gibson. Even her son Joshua has to learn that his mother owns the house and that being male gives him no rights over it in England. Kehinde has found in London a place from which to speak, and she can join her new Caribbean friend in what Paul Gilroy calls the culture of the "Black Atlantic," a culture of the African diaspora that creates a space for black men and women not just in Africa, or even America, but all around the Atlantic. In *Kehinde*, an African woman can negotiate nationalities and create a new sense of place. The "scraps, patches and rags of daily life" (Bhabha, *The Location of Culture* 145) can be collected into a new story about a hybrid, borderline national culture that has a place for different voices.

Anita Desai, who has been called "the foremost contemporary Indian woman novelist in English" (Dharwadker and Dharwadker 103), is like Buchi Emecheta in that she, too, occupies a multilingual, hybrid space, although she spent her childhood and young adulthood in Delhi and after her marriage lived in Calcutta and other Indian cities. Since Desai's mother was German and her father Bengali, she grew up speaking German at home, Hindi to her friends, and English at school.[13] She writes in English not only because it was the language in which she learned to read and write but also because for her it is "the most flexible, the most elastic, the most capable of taking on foreign tones and accents, the most rich in nuances and subtleties" (Desai, "Against the Current" 533). Although these various languages do not appear in *The Clear Light of Day* as much as they do in Emecheta's novel, their myths and histories and poetry do. The lyrical tones of Desai's novel are partially a result of these many multilingual allusions. During Desai's childhood, old Delhi was a multicultural city; she describes it as "a curious world . . . made up of all these different fragments. There was the British element, there was the Islamic element . . . and there was the ordinary basic and enduring Indian element—the Hindu element I suppose—although I don't like to call it that" ("Interview" 171).[14] All these traditions echo through the novel. Desai acknowledges the influence of Virginia Woolf on her work[15] ("Interview" 173), and snatches of T.S. Eliot's poetry occur throughout the novel. These allusions are blended with quotes from the Urdu poet Iqbal and Hindu songs about "Radha's pining for Krishna" (*Clear Light of Day* 30). It is precisely this nation of many, often conflicting traditions that Desai portrays in *The Clear Light of Day*.

Desai's novel is characterized not only by the blending of various voices and intertextualities; it also explores the complex relationship between female identity in Hinduism and female identity as it evolved in terms of Indian national identity. Indian psychologists Ashis Nandy and Sudhir Kakar and historian Partha Chatterjee explain this complex intertwining of ideas of "femininity" and "nation" in India. Nandy says that the concept of femininity is different in India than in the West: In India "the concept of *naritva*, so repeatedly stressed by Gandhi . . . included some traditional meanings of womanhood in India, such as the belief in a close . . . conjunction between power, activism and femininity" (*The Intimate Enemy* 53). In his article "Woman versus Womanliness in India" Nandy traces the association of women and power back to pre-Aryan times and explains how the "dominance of woman [in this matrifocal agrarian culture] was retained . . . in the symbolic system" of the Brahmanic tradition" (305). Thus, "the ultimate authority in the Indian mind has always been feminine" (305); in particular, this authority is associated with motherhood. Interwoven with this religious tradition is the literary feminine ideal, Sita, the heroine of the epic *Ramayana*, parts of whose story are similar to Chaucer's Griselda. Sita personifies chastity, purity, and self-sacrifice (Kakar, *The Inner World* 63-67). Wives, Kakar explains, are expected to be subservient; it is only when a woman becomes a mother that her status in her husband's family begins to rise (76).

These understandings of womanhood and the idealization of motherhood were associated with the idea of nation in the writings of early Indian nationalists: "Bakim Chandra Chatterji and Vivekananda linked this traditional image of sacred motherhood to the modern concept of motherland, hoping thereby to give a new sanctity to the concept of nation in an essentially apolitical society" (Nandy, "Woman versus Womanliness" 311). Gandhi, Nandy argues in *The Intimate Enemy*, used both the sense of activism and power associated with femininity and the ideal of self-sacrifice to undermine some of the hypermasculine ideals of British colonialism (48–55). Nandy sees many of these nationalist strategies as effective in combating colonialism, but he also notes the cost to Indian women: Although many cultures idealize the mother, "only in a few cultures have the loneliness and self-abnegation of woman as a social being found such elaborate justification in her symbolic status as a mother" ("Woman versus Womanliness" 307).

Partha Chatterjee further explains how nationalists used these associations politically against colonialism. The nationalist movement emphasized that India and the East were superior to the West in the spiritual domain. Social space was then divided into inner and outer realms: "the home and the world. . . . The home . . . must remain unaffected by the profane activities of the material world—and woman is its representation" (238–39). A "respectable woman" could "acquire the cultural refinements afforded by modern education without jeopardizing her place at home" (246); the "'new' woman defined in this way was subjected to a *new* patriarchy" (244).

Ania Loomba sums up Indian nationalism's relationship to women by saying: "Indian nationalism takes up and discards the woman question, depending on the exigencies of the moment" (195). It is precisely this complex history of woman's relation to nation that Bim must confront. She sees the restrictions placed on women by the history of "mother India." She also knows from her own experience of the vacuous life of her well-colonized birth mother and the injustices suffered by the "aunt" who brings her up the damage that both colonial and indigenous patriarchy have inflicted on women.

At the opening of the novel, Bim is caught between these conflicting definitions of "home" and "womanhood" in her old house in Delhi whose atmosphere is that of decay and stasis. She seemingly has all the trappings of a Westernized, independent existence. She is a teacher at a girls' college and has turned down an offer of marriage. She has stayed on in the home of her birth to look after her retarded younger brother, Baba. As Vrinda Nabar argues, Bim is "comfortably off, anglicized, even neocolonial. However . . . Bim is also conditioned by her Indian environment. It is *this* environment which positions her as the moral and physical caretaker of the Das household after her parents die" (229). This acceptance of duty fits what physician Kushalata Jayakar argues is one's dharma: "the duty bestowed on an individual by virtue of his or her being in a given place or space at a given time. . . . In Indian culture, the individual's role is to follow the expected path" (170–71). Even though her older brother Raja feels free to leave his home and family business in 1947 and join their former neighbor in the Muslim community in Hyderabad in southern India, Bim feels obligated by her position as the eldest daughter to stay in Delhi and become the caretaker. Joanna Liddle and Rama Joshi argue that in India

> the class structure, rather than destroying the gender divisions within the caste system, may be building upon them, whilst changing their form. . . . [Women's movement into the professions of] medicine and teaching. . . happened partly in response to demands for education and health care amongst female relatives of middle-class men, and partly because the maintenance of sex segregation and female seclusion demanded that these services be provided by other women. (73)

Bim, seemingly comfortable in her profession and the choices she has made, nonetheless feels caught between the contradicting gender codes of her British education and her Hindu sense of duty. In order to find a place between these conflicting traditions, Bim must go back in time to 1947 to sort out her feelings about that violent summer and the birth of her modern nation as well as to her earlier childhood and the mother figures that dominated it.

The two mother figures of the Das household represent the conflicting traditions in which Bim is caught. As mother figures they participate in what Sangeeta Ray calls the "ubiquitous trope of nation-as-woman in all nationalist discourses" (100). Their illnesses represent the damages done to women by these interlocking forces. Mrs. Das, Bim's birth mother, is a wealthy and highly colonized upper-middle-class woman whose husband has a successful insurance business. She represents a class so assimilated into the colonial regime that she literally vanishes from her children's lives and can offer them no model of how to live in the modern nation. The other maternal figure is a poor relative, Mira-*masi*, or Aunt Mira, who comes to care for the Das children after Baba, the youngest child, is born. She represents a woman whose space has been so constricted by traditional Hindu patriarchal practices that the only way out she finds is alcoholism.

Neither Bim nor her younger sister Tara have much access to their birth mother who spends her time playing bridge at the "Roshonara Club" (*Clear Light of Day* 50). When Tara plaintively asks why her parents spend all their time playing cards, Aunt Mira tells them for the first time about their mother's diabetes: "It helps your mother to forget her pain" (*Clear Light of Day* 115). The explanation that their mother's withdrawal from her children was caused by diabetes is actually a relief to the children, but the diabetes also causes what seems at first to Tara a sinister act of her father's. When Tara first witnesses her father give her mother a shot of insulin, she thinks he is murdering her:

> As the needle went in, the mother's head tilted back and sank deeper and deeper into the pillow, the trembling chin rose into the air and a little sigh issued through her dry lips as if the needle had punctured an air-bag and it was the very life of her that was being released. (114)

Tara's fear that her father is implicated in her mother's suffering is brought out by the narrator's diction and echoes several times throughout the novel. Although technically Mr. Das is giving her a life-prolonging shot of insulin, Tara's impression that the shot is a death-dealing drug implies that patriarchy is colluding with colonialism in destroying Mrs. Das. In fact, that might well be so since diabetes was very rare among lower socioeconomic groups in India who had less access to food and a more physically rigorous lifestyle (Babu). Mr. Das's financial success in the insurance business and the leisure of his wife might well have contributed indirectly to her diabetes. Mrs. Das is so distanced from her daughters, however, that by the time of her death they feel only a vague loss, no real grief. The colonized mother has provided an English education for her daughters but little else. She is not a role model for them; they remember primarily her illness.

Bim and Tara are actually raised by Aunt Mira, but the portrait of the traditional poor Indian woman is even grimmer than that of their birth mother. As Pushpa Parekh says, "Bim and Tara inhabit a space where privilege and agency for educated, upper-middle-class women is mounted on the silence and erasure of poorer and often socially ostracized women, such as the widowed Aunt Mira" (276). Her erasure began even before she came to the Das household. Aunt Mira was widowed at age twelve when her student husband caught cold and died in England. The family blamed her horoscope for his death, and she became a servant in her husband's household to expiate her guilt. Only her rapid aging saved her from a worse fate: "being used by her brothers-in-law who would have put the widow to a different use had she been more appetising" (*Clear Light of Day* 108). In spite of her low social position, she is able to provide crucial nurturing for the Das sisters. When she first arrives, Tara asks whether she is going to look after them as well as Baba. Aunt Mira replies, "I am to look after Baba . . . but I would like to play with *you*" (105). For Tara, Aunt Mira "was solid as a bed, she smelt of cooking and was made of knitting. Tara could wrap herself up in her as in an old soft shawl" (109). Aunt Mira is a good mother for Bim and Tara, and she nurses their older brother, Raja, through tuberculosis, but she cannot heal herself. When Raja travels to Hyderabad in 1947 to marry their former Muslim neighbor's daughter and Tara escapes into marriage at eighteen, Aunt Mira slowly sinks into alcoholism. As she is dying in the grip of delirium, she tears at her clothes as if they represented the constraints of tradition, poverty, and class that have always surrounded her. As Mohan says, Mira-*masi* "plays out in her symptoms her anxiety, confusion, and above all, anger at her situation. In so doing, she becomes the riveting point where the obscene violence of the postcolonial conjunction of indigenous and colonial patriarchy stands exposed" (60). That this combination of indigenous and colonial patriarchy can continue to control women's lives into the postcolonial generation is vividly illustrated by Bim's next-door neighbors, the Misra sisters. The two sisters have been abandoned by their husbands who were "too modern and too smart" (*Clear Light of Day* 151) for them and sent home where, grey-haired, thin, and fatigued, they support their father and brothers by teaching Hindu songs and dancing.

In turning down an offer of marriage from the doctor who comes to treat her brother's tuberculosis and Aunt Mira's dementia, Bim rejects both the experience of her mother and that of Aunt Mira and the Misra sisters. Like Bim's mother, Dr. Biswas is completely Westernized. He says, "[W]hen I first heard Mozart, Miss Das, I closed my eyes, and it was as if my whole past vanished, just rolled away from me—the country of my birth, my ancestors, my family, everything—and I arrived in a new world" (83). Bim does not want to live the life of her mother as the wife of a colonized Indian. Dr. Biswas misreads her rejection and romanticizes her into a stereotype of the self-sacrificing Indian woman: "Now I understand why you do not wish to marry. You have dedicated your lives to others—to your sick brother and your aged aunt. . . . You have sacrificed your own life for them" (97). Liddle and Joshi explain that sacrifice "is a powerful concept for women in orthodox Hinduism. It embodies the ideal of what women should be in a male-dominated society—silent, subservient, self-effacing" (200). Neither Aunt Mira nor the Misra sisters had any choice but to act out this role. Bim, however, is not making that choice. She and Raja later laugh at Dr. Biswas's interpretation. Arun Mukerjee points out Desai's use of irony here because Bim is also clearly rejecting

> the sacrificial, sentimental heroine popularized by the stalwarts of Bengali fiction and cinema. By creating a heroine who wants autonomy rather than domestic bliss, and having her turn down the Bengali doctor, Desai creates a new script for Indian women at the same time as she mocks the earlier ones. ("Other Worlds, Other Texts" 354–55).

Bim's mockery of Dr. Biswas and his sentimentalized concept of Indian women starts Bim on her search for her own sense of place.

In commenting on the concept of place in her novels, Desai says that a "writer cannot write of a place with no other tool than observation. He must also employ memory, dream and reverie" ("'Feng Sui'" 106). Before Bim can fully reconcile the conflicting traditions that have molded her, she must go back in memory and reverie to confront the past history of her nation and her family. Although a historian by profession, Bim is still mired in the events of the summer of 1947. The second section of the novel includes Bim's memories of national events, the assassination of Gandhi, the rioting in the streets, and the mass migration of Muslims from Delhi, interwoven with her memories of family illnesses and departures. The split in the country is reflected in microcosm in the split in the Das family. Raja, inspired by British romantic poetry and Urdu poetry, has said that he wants to be a hero when he grows up. When the fighting occurs, however, Raja is bedridden with tuberculosis, a real illness but also a temporary solution to his unwillingness to join the Hindu cause. When he gets better, he decides to go live in southern India with their wealthy Muslim neighbor and landlord, Hyder Ali, and eventually marries his daughter. Mohan argues that like "Raja, Bim is caught within the ideological binds of her colonial education, but without his male prerogatives and with a strongly inculcated sense of her responsibility for the family, she ends up being the one to pay the price for his freedom" (57). Bim's anger at Raja's desertion and refusal to acknowledge her contribution is concentrated by a letter he sends her after Hyder Ali's death, saying she can pay the same rent to him as she had previously to Hyder Ali. Raja has become her expatriate landlord, not her idolized brother. The intertwining of national and family history has left Bim in a state of bitterness.

As in *Kehinde*, it is another woman, in this case Bim's sister Tara rather than an age-mate, who helps Bim find a way out of the constricted space of her resentment. As Parekh explains: "Throughout their childhood and adulthood, men—their father, Raja, Bakul [Tara's husband]—had occupied the central stage, minimizing the potentiality of one woman's importance for the other. But with the passage of time the two women, apparently dissimilar, become each other's healers" (280). Although Desai said in a 1988 interview that she wasn't a feminist in writing this novel because she "wasn't even aware of such a concept as feminism" ("Against the Current" 524) at that time, nonetheless it is the women who help each other retrieve the past and discover how to relate to it. It is in community with each other that they are each able to resolve their memories and accept the choices that they made. Tara is able to let go of her guilt at deserting Bim as they recall an episode where Bim ran into a bee's nest and Tara ran away to get help. In finally apologizing for leaving her sister with the bees, Tara is able to express her regret and guilt at leaving Bim with the responsibilities of Baba, Aunt Mira's illness, and the house.

Likewise, Tara helps Bim to let go of her anger at Raja and consider reconciling with him. Tara urges Bim to tear up Raja's letter and to visit him: "You live in the same country and never visit each other" (143). Tara urges Bim to acknowledge the family ties and shared history that are more important than regional and religious loyalties.

Initially, Bim's anger simmers, and she even lashes out at Baba, threatening to sell the shares of her father's insurance business and send him to Raja. In the face of Baba's uncomprehending silence,[16] Bim realizes that "she loved him, loved Raja and Tara and all of them who had lived in this house with her. . . . Although it was shadowy and dark, Bim could see as well as by the clear light of day that she felt only love and yearning for them all" (165). In accepting "all of them who had lived in this house with her," Bim is accepting both her own and her nation's past. She can mourn the losses, the division, and the violence and come to a new understanding of place and nation. Afzal-Khan argues that it is "this acceptance of the past and all its myths that leads to a wholeness for Bim" (84).

In accepting the past but changing some of its definitions of "home" and "house," Bim does create a new script for the Indian woman in which she maintains tradition but creates greater freedom for herself.[17] Bipin Panigrahi argues that Bim achieves a "spiritual wholeness" based not in sacrifice but in the choice "to bridge the rift with others . . . [and] find her own social relevance" (78). Panigrahi links this emotional decision to Bim's house: "The historicity of her house provides Bim with a perspective to approach reality, to perceive life as a continuum [which Panigrahi connects to Indian concepts of flux] in which the contradictions . . . are reconciled into the attainment of an authentic self-hood" (79). In her essay on "the spirit of place," Desai explains that she has borrowed the Chinese term "Feng Sui," which refers to "the spiritual atmosphere" of a house. She explains that the Chinese believe that a house with a negative atmosphere can be changed by the virtuous living of its inhabitants ("'Feng Sui'" 101). In changing her attitude toward her house and its past, Bim can change its atmosphere and remove the sense of constriction in which she has been caught.

Ashis Nandy finds in a "fluid self-definition" a sense of liminality that offers a new kind of nationality. He says that the "alternative to Hindu nationalism is the peculiar mix of classical and folk Hinduism and the unselfconscious Hinduism by which most Indians, Hindus as well as non-Hindus, live. . . . It is that liminality on which the greatest of Indian social and political leaders built their self-definition as Indians" (*The Intimate Enemy* 104). For Nandy the "uniqueness of Indian culture lies . . . in the society's traditional ability to live with cultural ambiguities. . . . [T]he culture itself demands that a certain permeability of boundaries be maintained in one's self-image. . . . This is . . . the clue to India's post-colonial world view" (107). Bim, who has previously restricted herself too tightly, remaining at home but constricted by the definitions of womanhood that she had inherited, can now open herself up to a new liminality that combines her Indian heritage with her education and allows new permeable boundaries both for self and for a sense of place. This is a different kind of nationalism that allows more flexibility for women as well as men, a chance to break out of the "false [binary] essentialisms of home/world . . . feminine/masculine" (Chatterjee 252) that Partha Chatterjee felt dominated earlier stages of modern nationhood in India. Bim can find a new place for women in the liminality of a postcolonial nation.

Desai herself describes Bim as one of the rare Indian "women who triumph" ("Against the Current" 524). Desai acknowledges the suffering of Indian women and agrees that in many ways her books are a "lament" ("Against the Current" 524, 532) for that suffering and the violence of history and yet at the same time they are celebrations of place: "[F]or every writer there is a starting point, and for me it very often is place" (533). The elegiac tone that ends *Clear Light of Day* makes it clear that for Bim there must be an acceptance of sadness and loss as well as love in her reconciliation to family and homeland. That acceptance of both anger and loss undoes the former sense of constriction and allows Bim to reenvision her place in the family and in Delhi. As Nabar comments, "[T]he kind of reconciliation with the self that Bim achieves, inseparable as it is from her family set up, emphasizes that *Clear Light of Day* cannot be anything other than an 'Indian' novel. . . . [I]ts central conflicts can only be satisfactorily explained in an Indian context" (229).

Kehinde Okolo and Bim Das have imagined themselves new places, new homes. Kehinde enters a new diaspora within the heterogeneous city of London. Bim has gone back into memory and the past to redefine for herself the traditions that have held her fast. She finds a new liminality in which she can reconcile both past traditions and her education without being confined by either one. The freedom that a newly imagined place provides allows both women to participate in "generational continuity" without sacrificing their own space. They both have not just rooms of their own but their own houses. Kehinde explains to her son that she owns her house; he is welcome to live there, but she is not going to give it to him. Bim has turned her "home," with its past association of restrictions, into a house to which she can invite both her students and her estranged family. Although Bim does not go to Raja's daughter's wedding with Tara, she urges Tara to invite Raja and all his family to visit her, to return to the family house that Bim has preserved and made into a place where she can live freely as an Indian woman and make others welcome. Kehinde and Bim, in novels about postcolonial women's triumphs as well as their sufferings, achieve new places for themselves.

Chapter 4

Social and Political Identities: The Search for Space in Margaret Drabble's *The Radiant Way* and Nadine Gordimer's *None to Accompany Me*

If geographical space is associated by Tuan with freedom and the openness of the ocean (3–4), political and social space is much more complex. It is crisscrossed with rules and conventions and restrictions. It is much more like a complex and intricate dance, the metaphor that is used by both Margaret Drabble and Nadine Gordimer to describe the complex sets of political and social roles that women in their late forties and fifties often face. Drabble's *The Radiant Way* and Gordimer's *None to Accompany Me* are novels about women in late middle age who are coping with political change. In novels of political change, whether the controversial dismantling of Britain's welfare state in the 1980s in *The Radiant Way* or the long-hoped-for end of apartheid in South Africa in *None to Accompany Me*, the politically committed female characters are relegated to the sidelines like the chaperons sitting "at the edge of the dance" in Victorian novels (Drabble, *The Radiant Way* 13). It is not coincidental that these political novels by Drabble and Gordimer portray women in middle adulthood. It is particularly after decades of political commitment and sacrifice that the force of political change, for good or ill, and the consequent shift in social roles, is felt most strongly.

From very different geographical and national points of view these novels chronicle the end of a commitment to liberal politics. In England, liberalism ends with the election of Margaret Thatcher as prime minister in 1979. In South Africa the end of apartheid in the early 1990s also dismantles the liberal white opposition. Margaret Drabble, who was raised a Quaker, belongs to "the tradition of radical dissent, religious and political" (Myer 17). Her three female characters in *The Radiant Way* benefit themselves from the welfare state and are deeply critical of its dismantling. Gayle Greene says: "*The Radiant Way* is a political novel . . . [whose] characters think politically, see all issues politically, fall in and out of love on account of politics. And its politics are bleak: it documents the end of 'the great social dream,' of hopes for progress or unity" ("Bleak Houses" 317).

Nadine Gordimer actually reacted against liberalism long before the end of apartheid. In 1974 she said, "'I am a white South African radical. Please don't call me a liberal.' Liberal is a dirty word. Liberals are people who make promises they have no power to keep" (Smith, Introduction 15). Although in the 1980s Gordimer wrote novels about revolution, such as *July's People* and *A Sport of Nature*,[1] in *None to Accompany Me* she tells the story of two women, a liberal white woman lawyer, Vera Stark, who has committed her career during apartheid to "challenging the law by means of its interstices and the great principles of justice beyond it" (164), and a black African woman, Sibongile Maqoma, who has lived in exile as a traditional wife supporting her husband's politics but who now must learn to become a politician herself. In her 1982 essay "Living in the Interregnum," Gordimer quotes Bishop Desmond Tutu, who says he welcomes

> "the participation of all, both black and white, in the struggle for the new South Africa . . . [but] the leadership of the struggle must be firmly in black hands. . . . Whites unfortunately have the habit of taking over and usurping the leadership and taking the crucial decisions. . . . Whites must be willing to follow." (266–67)

Twelve years later, Nadine Gordimer writes the story of this change in power and the radical adjustments that such political changes require. *None to Accompany Me* explores the new roles white and black women take in postapartheid South Africa. Margaret Drabble's *The Radiant Way* asks what roles liberals should play in the new conservative politics of Thatcher's England.

In "The Third Space" Homi Bhabha heralds the end of the politics of liberalism with its benign tolerance for "cultural diversity" so long as it is carefully contained. He argues that the "whole nature of the public sphere is changing so that we really do need the notion of a politics which is based on unequal, uneven, multiple and *potentially antagonistic*, political identities" (208). He says that "all forms of culture are continually in a process of hybridity. . . . [And] the importance of hybridity . . . is the 'third space' which enables other positions to emerge. This third space displaces the histories that constitute it, and sets up new structures of authority, new political initiatives" (211). An era of political change is a "third space," a space for growth and the recognition of difference. "It is only," he continues, "by losing the sovereignty of the self that you can gain the freedom of a politics that is open to the non-assimilationist claims of cultural difference" (213). It is difficult to give up the master narratives of liberalism that have often given women a valuable sense of sovereignty of self. But it is only through giving them up that, Bhabha argues, one can achieve a real freedom in politics. Furthermore, political change, like aging, is unavoidable. The question for Drabble's and Gordimer's characters is how to redefine themselves and adapt to their new social and political roles.

Drabble and Gordimer both turn to a metafictional narrative structure in order to undo these master narratives of self and explore political change.[2] Pamela Bromberg suggests that Drabble moves even "further in the direction of feminist metafiction" (8) in *The Radiant Way* than in her previous novels by adopting an allusive style and "an alternative narrative structure, a contemporary variation of the 'narrative of community'" (11) in which "the communal protagonist replaces the individual, and the plot of connections—the perception of a linking pattern—replaces the teleological plot" (12). *The Radiant Way* combines the stories of three Cambridge friends, Liz Headland, a psychiatrist, Alix Bowen, a social researcher and teacher, and Esther Breuer, an art historian. Likewise, Dominic Head argues that a "very significant characteristic of Gordimer's fiction is its metafictional quality" (*The Radiant Way* 11). Gordimer, who was influenced by and corresponded with Georg Lukács,[3] the Marxist proponent of realism, moved beyond traditional realism as her politics became more radical. Head links her metafictional style directly to her politics:

The extension of narrative possibilities in Gordimer's work . . . is a crucial aspect of her quest for a literary form appropriate to her situation, because the cultivation of narrative relativity, of a plurality of voices, is a way of conveying the complexity of the historical situation. It is also a way of deconstructing the authoritative monologic perspective sometimes associated with colonial literature. (*The Radiant Way* 16–17)

Like Drabble, Gordimer uses a communal protagonist, combining the stories of Vera Stark and Sibongile Maqoma[4] to develop a new "third space" in which white and black characters' stories can both be told.

The communal protagonists of each novel reinforce what Mikhail Bakhtin calls the "heteroglossia" or "multi-voicedness" of the novel form: "Authorial speech, the speeches of narrators, inserted genres, the speech of characters are merely those fundamental compositional unities with whose help heteroglossia . . . can enter the novel; each of them permits a multiplicity of social voices and a wide variety of their links and interrelationships" (Bakhtin 263). Both novels also include contemporary historical and political references, what Bakhtin calls "extra-artistic" genres, "everyday, rhetorical" insertions (320).[5] Drabble, for instance, refers to the "small war in the Falklands (rather a lot of people dead), and of the Falklands Factor in politics" (*The Radiant Way* 215). Drabble's narrator flattens political and social events by conflating politics and consumerism: "An ageing film star became President of the United States of America and his wife bought a lot of new clothes. The heir to the throne of England married a kindergarten assistant and she bought a lot of new clothes" (216). With equal irony Gordimer's narrator combines fictional and real characters, describing the groups that rush to Mandela's side as soon as he is let out of prison: "Vera and Bennet Stark gave a party . . . the year the prisons opened. . . . [S]ports club delegations, mothers' unions and herded schoolchildren stood around Nelson Mandela's old Soweto cottage queueing to embrace him, while foreign diplomats presented themselves to be filmed clasping his hand" (*None to Accompany Me* 5).

Robert Young analyzes Bakhtin's theories of hybridity in language and Bhabha's use of Bakhtin and his theory of third space. Young explains that there are two kinds of hybridity in Bakhtin's theory, the one intended by their authors (as in those examples quoted above), which "has been politicized and made contestatory," and an unconscious, organic hybridity that Young describes as a creolization or *métissage* or merging of cultures (*Colonial Desire* 21). Young finds both kinds of hybridity in discussions of contemporary culture. The unconscious kind is contained in the idea of "a transmutation of British culture into a compounded, composite mode" (23). The other kind, "Bakhtin's intentional hybrid[,] has been transformed by Bhabha into an active moment of challenge and resistance against a dominant cultural power. . . . [A] counter-authority, a 'Third Space'" (23). In Drabble's novel, filled with ironic references to aging film stars as presidents, the political space is the contestatory one. Can the three Cambridge friends give up their old securities and their former "sovereignties of self" and find a space in which to contest the power of conservatism?

Gordimer has been searching for the other kind of hybridity, the merging of cultures, throughout her career. Head argues that Gordimer's call for a "genuine cultural identity and national literature" for South Africa involves "a fusion of a European literary heritage with elements drawn from an African tradition" (*Nadine Gordimer* 8–9). Head calls this fusion: "Cross-fertilization . . . a hybrid between the rich pre-colonial oral tradition of South Africa, and the imported European tradition, [which would produce, in Gordimer's words,] a 'truly new indigenous culture'" (10). In *None to Accompany Me* Gordimer blends the stories of black and white women. Both Vera and Sibongile need to adapt to a new postcolonial, hybrid space in which Vera must learn to give up some of her previous political power, and Sibongile must learn to exercise hers. In *Writing and Being* Gordimer says that when South Africa left the British Commonwealth in the 1960s, she could

> speak of "my country" and mean South Africa.
> But it was not possible for me to say "my people." That I began to understand.
> The whites were not my people because everything they lived by . . . was the stuff of my refusal. . . .
> The blacks were not "my people" because all through my childhood and adolescence they had scarcely entered my consciousness. *I had been absent.* (128)

Finally, however, the politics changed. Gordimer explains:

> In April 1994 all South Africans of all colours went to the polls and voted into power their own government, for the first time. There are now no overlords and underlings in the eyes of the law. . . .

> My country is . . . whole, a synthesis. I am no longer a colonial. I
> may now speak of "my people." (*Writing and Being* 134)

A significant metaphor for these social and political changes in
both novels is that of a dance and women's varying roles within the
complex interactions of a formal dance. Drabble introduces the image in the opening pages of her novel as Liz Headleand awaits her
guests for a New Year's Eve party to herald the beginning of the
1980s:

> As a child, reading her mother's collection of Victorian novels,
> Edwardian novels, she had wondered how women could bear to re-
> nounce their position in the centre of the matrimonial stage, the sexual
> arena, how they could bring themselves to consent to adopt the role
> of chaperone, to sit at the edge of the dance. . . . How could one bear
> to be on the sidelines? Not to be invited to the waltz? Not ever again
> to be invited to the waltz? (13)

Liz Headleand, from her vantage point as a successful psychotherapist, wife of the wealthy television producer Charles Headleand,
and mother of five grown children and stepchildren, can "see the
charm . . . of the observer's role. . . . [T]he observer was filled and in-
formed with a quick and lively and long-established interest in all
those that passed before, in all those that moved and circled . . . was
filled with intimate connections" (13–14). Liz's friends Alix Bowen
and Esther Breuer join in the pleasure of observing and analyzing
society, but the politics they have observed so long are about to
change, and the "intimate connections" are reconfigured in the new
political space.

Learning how to sit at the edge of a dance, learning to step aside
out of the sexual arena, is harder for Gordimer's characters because,
as Head explains, one of the consistent themes throughout Gordimer's
novels has been a politics of the body:

> The key issue for Vera Stark, as for Gordimer's previous heroines, is
> how a public role can be allied to personal need and expression: spe-
> cifically, how the expression of her sexuality "fits" her political com-
> mitment. This kind of politics of the body has always been important
> for Gordimer, and it has, of course, a special relevance in South Afri-
> can fiction. The outlawing of transracial relationships, a cornerstone
> of apartheid in the 1950s, makes the exploration of personal and
> sexual relationships . . . an implicitly politicized activity in South
> Africa. ("Gordimer's *None to Accompany Me*" 49–50)

Not only does Vera need to reposition her political role, she also needs to reevaluate her personal life and sexual role. By the end of the novel "Vera, too old to find a partner, danced alone, no one to witness" (*None to Accompany Me* 305). Can Vera learn to live without a partner, be content to dance alone, or even sit at the edge of the dance? The question must be asked in reverse for Sibongile Maqoma, who must learn to use power, who must learn how to lead without losing her partner. Both *The Radiant Way* and *None to Accompany Me* analyze how these various women negotiate the new spaces of changing politics in late middle age.

Although in 1980 at the beginning of *The Radiant Way* all three of Drabble's protagonists, Liz Headleand, Alix Bowen, and Esther Breuer, seem to inhabit a comfortable middle-class space, they did not always feel that they were at the center of society. In fact, what first brought them together as fellow students at Cambridge was a sense of being different from the other students in both politics and religion:

> [What] held them together [was] . . . a sense of being on the margins of English life, perhaps, a sense of being outsiders, looking in from a cold street through a lit window into a warm lit room. . . . Removed from the mainstream by a mad mother [Liz], by a deviant ideology [Alix's parents' leftist politics], by refugee status and the war-sickness of Middle Europe [Esther, who is Jewish, had to flee the Nazis as a child]. (85)

Although outsiders, liberal politics and scholarships allowed them to attend Cambridge: "[A]t eighteen the world opened for them and displayed its riches, the brave new world of Welfare State and County Scholarships, of equality for women; they were . . . the chosen, the garlanded of the great social dream" (83).

Each of the three friends attains her goal. Liz, who said she wanted "to make sense of things. . . [to] understand" (81), has become a psychiatrist. Alix, who said she wanted "to change things" (81), has become a social researcher and teacher. Esther, who said she only wanted "to acquire interesting information" (81), has become an art historian and scholar. In a 1975 commentary Drabble notes that she had just read "an account of Erikson's theory of the eight stages of man. It seems to me that to stop short at self-realization, and the achieving of one's own identity, is to refuse to move into the . . . stage, in which . . . one assumes responsibility for one's community and one's succeeding generations" ("The Author Comments" 38). In their careers and in their respective families—Liz's taking on three stepsons as well as her own two daughters, Alix's raising of her two sons, and Esther's inviting her niece to live with her—all three women do take responsibility for children and for communities. They have achieved Erikson's seventh stage of generativity.

All three women are also comfortable in their physical bodies. Middle age itself with its physical changes is not a threat or a catalyst for redefinition. Liz Headleand "greets with curiosity" the "signs of age, of the ageing process":

> the amusing little sag of her incipient double chin, the veining on her cheeks . . . the slight plump soft dimpling of her upper arm, the raised veins in the back of her hands, the broadening of her hips, the decreasing flexibility of her joints. . . . One might as well welcome them, after all: there is not much point in rejecting them. It is all intended, it is all part of the plan. (14)

Alix "laughs to see her face wrinkle, she prides herself on being without vanity" (157). Esther "had not changed much over the years. There she still was, small, neat, olive-skinned . . . with perhaps just the slightest hint of a wizening, of a wrinkling, of a preservation to come" (206). Esther is aware that she has become more careful with age, however. Her niece "sits drinking cans of beer with impossible people in condemned and boarded cottages in the middle of rubble wastes. . . . Esther, who once like the *louche* herself, feels a little old for that kind of thing" (182). All three women are proud of their achievements and comfortable with their age, but then, politics change. It is the new political space that forces their reassessments.

The great social dream ends with the Thatcher government, and all three women find themselves in the midst of change. Their ties to the wider community must be redesigned, their identities rethought. Liz, who struggled to escape poverty and her mother's strange behavior, merged her identity with the wealthy, and initially liberal, widower Charles Headleand. When after their New Year's party he tells her he wants a divorce, she becomes a "wounded healer" (130) who must go back to her own childhood and social origins to reestablish her identity. Alix, who is committed to socialism and happily married to her working-class husband, Brian Bowen, "undergoes a crisis of confidence in the political assumptions that have been her guiding lights" (Greene, "Bleak Houses" 317) when both she and her husband lose their jobs. Esther Breuer, who has committed her life to the rational analysis of art and careful control of her social and economic life, must come to terms with the uncanny in her relationship with her dying friend Claudio Volpe.

The narrator, who is clearly critical of Thatcher's policies, describes this new political space. After introducing in detail many of the people at Liz and Charles's New Year's party, the narrator assumes a wide-angle lens to describe the new political climate:

> Old opinions were shed, stuffy woolly shabby old liberal vests and comforters were left piled on the shore. Some shivered in the cold breeze of change; others struck out boldly, with a sense of freedom, glad to be unencumbered by out-of-date gear and padding. . . . Cutting, paring, slimming, reducing, rationalizing: out swam the slim hard new streamlined man, in the emperor's new clothes, out of the gritty carapace. . . . The conventions were changing, assumptions were changing, though not everybody was to enjoy or to survive the metamorphosis, the plunge. . . . [C]hange is painful, transition is painful. (31)

In 1980, one year after Thatcher's becoming prime minister, liberalism has become a shabby wool vest, a carapace, to be discarded. Politicians are unconcerned that some people will not survive the change. Later in the novel the narrator drops the imagery to turn to a reporting style and direct, confrontational irony:

> 1980 continues. The steel strike continues, a bitter prelude to the miners' strike that will follow. Class rhetoric flourishes. . . . Unemployment rises steadily, but the Tory party is not yet often reminded of its election poster which portrayed a long dole queue with the slogan "Labour isn't working." (163)

Clearly for this narrator, and Drabble's three protagonists, Tory politics are not working. The narrator summarizes the comments of Alan, Liz's stepson, who points out to his younger stepsister the "oddity of a woman Prime Minister who was in fact a mother but was not nevertheless thereby motherly" (16). In a 14–15 October 1989 interview in *The Guardian*, however, Drabble says that she's "not as anti-Thatcher as I may seem. . . . Something undoubtedly had to be done about the unions, about the welfare dependency culture. . . . But the wrong things were done. The problem was addressed with a kind of savagery and a misunderstanding of how people got into the muddle in the first place" (Myer 162).

As in Gordimer's novels, marriage and sexuality are intertwined with politics. Liz, who grew up in poverty with a "mad" agoraphobic mother and a missing father, concentrates all her energies as a young woman on escaping Northam (Drabble's fictional northern city modeled on Sheffield) and getting to Cambridge. At Cambridge, Liz met Edgar Lintot, to whom she was briefly and "superficially" married (*The Radiant Way* 133). Shortly afterward, she marries Charles Headleand, a thirty-year-old widower and filmmaker whose "mixture of brutality and desire had matched something in herself" (134). Liz, as a psychotherapist, "had long recognized that Charles had replaced the fantastic, punishing father of her childhood" (136). She and Charles are sexually, socially, and politically compatible. As a young man Charles was interested in left-wing politics and later became famous for "his punchy social-conscience documentaries" (111–12). Although both Charles and Liz possessed a social conscience, they also enjoyed their rising affluence and were proud of the large house on Harley Street that they renovated. As the debris from the old house is cleared away, the "Hogarthian, Dickensian relics of an oppressed and squalid past" (18), Liz feels that she has left "solitude and insignificance and social fear" (18) behind; her own labyrinthine past and lonely childhood are buried beneath the white and gold of the renovated house and the power of the Harley Street name.

Charles, however, changes his politics. He has "in recent years been wooed by, and had, it seemed, espoused, the radical right. The unions had driven him to infidelity" (15). The narrator's use of marital imagery to describe Charles's political shift foreshadows his decision to divorce Liz and marry an aristocrat who would match his new views. Although Charles's 1965 documentary, ironically titled "The Radiant Way," attacked the class system and educational privilege, Charles has now embraced a Tory sense of class as well as politics and business practices: "Charles had always enjoyed dismissing people. . . . He had cleared the stables not of filth and corruption but of nice woolly ageing men in their fifties, polite, gentlemanly, incompetent men" (135). After the New Year's Eve party, when Charles announces his intention to marry Henrietta Latchett, Liz is shocked and devastated. Although they had had separate bedrooms for two years, Liz thought that their twenty-one-year marriage was solid, founded on loyalty and shared experiences. She feels the divorce "a negation, a denial, an undoing of past self, of past knowledge, of past joys, of past certainties, a complete and utter unmaking of the fabric of one's true self" (135).

The impact of the divorce is psychological for Liz rather than economic. In spite of the dismantling of the welfare state, Liz is financially secure as a psychotherapist:

She is not threatened by cuts in public spending, by the decline of the National Health Service. . . . [H]er income is derived from a judicious blend of public and private practice. She believes in the National Health Service, in public welfare, of course (is she not a close friend of Alix Bowen's?), but she also recognizes, as Alix does not, that the private sector must encourage experiment, excellence, variation of treatment. (171)

Regardless of her economic security, however, Liz feels her identity and her social standing are threatened. She realizes that she must give up their house on Harley Street, that it is "ridiculous, neurotic, to cling so to bricks and mortar" (114), but she feels that she no longer has a space. She feels that in spite of all her success she is "only a fake princess, a scullery maid dressed up by a Cambridge scholarship" (174).

Liz's identity as a comfortable liberal professional woman dispensing healing to a variety of patients in her secure space on Harley Street has come to an end. She must make a journey both literally and psychically back to Northam to confront her lower-class origins, her dying mother, and long-dead father before she can establish herself in a new space. Liz finally travels up to Northam to see her mother, whom she had avoided for years. After her mother's death, Liz and her sister Shirley find a newspaper clipping recounting their father's arrest for exposing himself to schoolchildren, his acquittal, and his subsequent suicide. Liz suddenly remembers her childhood complicity, reading from her childhood primer *The Radiant Way* and rubbing "herself like a kitten up and down, sitting astride her child-molester father's knee" (366). Liz analyzes herself: "A classic case. A banal case. . . . The anti-climactic nature of knowledge. So this was it. . . . Already she was losing interest in the riddle that had teased her for decades" (368–69). Liz can now clean out her mother's house, burn all the old trash and clippings, and move to a new house herself, a house with a garden in St. John's Wood. Liz, having threaded the labyrinth of her own past, can return to London and take up her life in the new political climate of the 1980s. She no longer needs Charles to protect her from her past. Supported by her two female friends and still connected to her grown children and stepchildren, Liz can let go both of the romance plot and of the liberalism of her young adulthood. She is a survivor who can create her own space.

The political climate is much harder for Alix Bowen. Alix was the one who was always committed to politics, who wanted to change things. She was brought up in Yorkshire by "Labour-voting . . . Fabian-pamphlet-reading intellectuals" (75), and she remains true to their vision. After graduating from Cambridge, she marries Sebastian Manning, a wealthy, artistic socialist, who drowns shortly after their son is born. Alix, in dismay at her lack of grief for the careless Sebastian, lives with her son in poverty in Islington,[6] eking out a living by part-time teaching. When Alix remarries, she chooses a working-class man, Brian Bowen, who had received an education in the army and now writes novels and teaches at an Institute for Adult Education. The narrator explains: "Alix herself would be the first to admit . . . that Brian's attraction for her was massively, deeply connected with his class origins. . . . Lying in your arms, Alix said once, not very seriously to Brian, I am in the process of healing the wounds in my own body and in the body politic" (159–60).

Alix's career is motivated by her political idealism. She works three days a week as a social researcher on women offenders at Whitehall and teaches English literature part-time to young female inmates at Garfield Centre. She sometimes questions the usefulness of her occupation: "[W]hat on earth was she herself playing at, crossing the urban wastes so regularly to teach a bunch of delinquent girls, a bunch of criminals, for £15.60 a night? It hardly covered the petrol" (67). It is on her way to Garfield, however, that Alix has a vision of the interconnectedness of all people:

> She aspired to a more comprehensive vision. She aspired to make connections. . . . [She sensed] a pattern that linked those semi-detached houses of Wanley with those in Leeds and Northam, a pattern that linked Liz's vast house in Harley Street with Garfield Centre. . . . The social structure greatly interested Alix. She had once thought of herself as unique. . . . [B]ut as she grew older she [saw] . . . people perhaps more as flickering, impermanent points of light irradiating stretches, intersections, threads, of a vast web, a vast network, which was humanity itself; a web of which much remained dark . . . peopled by the dark, the unlit, the dim spirits, as yet unknown, the past and the future, the dead, the unborn. (68–69)

Before Alix can come into the light, however, these connections take her through the dark places. One of the young offenders Alix teaches is Jilly Fox, a deeply disturbed, middle-class girl jailed for drug use. When she is let out of prison, she begs Alix to see her. Although against prison policy, Alix finally agrees to see her and goes to a derelict squat whose interior walls are painted with severed heads and cockatrices. Alix finds Jilly high on drugs and fantasizing about death. Alix's car is vandalized during her visit, and she walks to Esther's apartment to call Brian. The next day Alix finds Jilly's severed head in her abandoned car. Jilly has become the next victim of a serial murderer, the "Horror of Harrow Road." Alix is aghast: "I see horrors. I imagine horrors. I have courted horrors, and they have come to greet me. Whereas I had wished not to court them, but to exorcise them. . . . I am defeated. . . . Is it the wrong battle I have been fighting, all these years?" (320). Because of this murder and Alix's visit, she loses her job at Garfield Centre, and then her Whitehall office closes. Brian cannot help Alix. He, too, has lost his job, been made "redundant," and has thrown himself into radical politics, going on protest marches to support the striking miners. His friend Stephen Cox remarks: "Brian's tragedy is that he lives now, in this time, in these times. These times are not good for men like Brian, who mean well" (250).

Like Liz, Alix must journey to Northam. Brian finds a job teaching at a community program in Northam, which had a "freak by-election . . . which had reversed the national trend to the right" (45). Thus Brian will have "good public money, [a] left-wing Council, a lot of support" (340). In a 1985 article on the city of Sheffield, Drabble notes how different the politics of her own native city are from the rest of the nation: "Despite the large Tory majority . . . the manufacturing cities remain solidly Labour" ("A Novelist in a Derelict City" 78). These northerners, she explains, "accuse Mrs. Thatcher's government of knowing nothing of their situation, of caring nothing for them and of never traveling north of Waterford—a commuter town just outside Greater London" (77). Despite the national trend, the left-leaning City Council of Sheffield maintains "a high expenditure on social services, education, subsidized transport" (79). The contestatory spirit, a requirement of the new politics for Bhabha, is alive in Sheffield.

Drabble's fictional counterpart, Northam, provides jobs for Brian and even Alix, who is hired by a well-known elderly modernist poet to sort through his papers. Alix is still not comfortable in her new space. She mourns the defeat of the miners and the division of the nation. She thinks ironically that her job and Brian's have been reversed: "I sit in an ivory attic, while Brian toils . . . with the disadvantaged, the illiterate. . . . I have been driven into paradox. . . . It is not satisfactory. But what else can I do?" (373). Alix is still discouraged about contemporary politics, but Drabble has left her in a new geographical space for a reason. Drabble has faith in the North. In a 1989 article she writes: "The North is a state of mind: It is a mixture of harshness and good humor, of grit and greenery. . . . There is life in the North yet, a peculiar, resistant, stubborn life" ("The North beyond the Grit" 15).

Esther Breuer has a different kind of confrontation to face from Liz and Alix. Esther, whose aim in life has merely been "information," has in response to the terror of fleeing the Nazis in her childhood confined herself to the world of scholarship and the rational. Rubenstein notes that ironically Esther Breuer's "name glosses Freud's first mentor, Josef Breuer" and that like Freud, Esther is "a Jewish Viennese refugee; additionally, her flat (Liz eventually realizes) resembles Freud's Viennese consulting room, with red walls and Persian carpets of geometric design" ("Sexuality and Intertextuality" 99). Esther, however, does not want to analyze or involve her emotions. She wants to remain in the two-dimensional world of paintings and live on a rational level. She lives "in a small flat just off the bad end of Ladbroke Grove, earning a pittance from odd lectures, odd articles, a little teaching" (*The Radiant Way* 22). She says to Charles Headleand: "You don't seem to realize, Charles, that I live below the reach of the economy, as an economic unit I simply don't exist" (22). Almost in spite of herself, Esther becomes well known, lecturing at the National and Tate Galleries. When the funding for her evening class on the Italian Renaissance is cut, Esther complains that she "cannot see why harmless leisure activities, in a society of increasingly high levels of unemployment, should not be more encouraged. But she does not worry about it very much" (177). She thinks she can leave emotional analysis to Liz and political concerns to Alix. She believes that she is safe in the realm of the rational, but even words have changed by the 1980s. Drabble notes that "rationalization" is now British Steel's "euphemism for cutting the labor force" and increasing unemployment ("A Novelist in a Derelict City" 77). Just as Esther's old defenses are beginning to break down, the uncanny enters her life.

Bhabha comments on Freud's essay "The Uncanny": Freud associated the uncanny "with the repressions of a 'cultural' unconscious; a liminal, uncertain state of cultural belief when the archaic emerges in the midst of margins of modernity" (143). The emergence of the uncanny can lead to the questioning of "homogeneous and horizontal" views of society. It can function as a "transgressive, invasive structure" (144). It is the emergence of the "uncanny" in the story of Claudio Volpe, Esther's "lover," that finally breaks through her carefully defended surface. Esther analyzes the uncanny in Renaissance paintings, the images of speaking wounds and severed heads and cockatrices, without becoming emotionally involved and even laughs at Alix's horrified reactions to the images at Jilly Fox's squat: "'You would have expected us to have marched forward into the new light by now? The rational, radiant light?' asked Esther" (*The Radiant Way* 314). Esther can control the pictorial images of the uncanny and accept the medieval and Renaissance images that contradict her rationality, but when it enters her narrative, Esther feels it in a different way. Claudio Volpe, "the married satanic anthropologist" (100), had long courted her, but Esther realized that "her emotional relationships throughout her life had been based partly on her desire to avoid normal sexual intercourse. She did not need someone like Liz Headleand to tell her this" (328). Esther is thus shocked to hear of Claudio's lecture at the Institute in Rome on his encounter with a werewolf.[7] Claudio's longtime "interest in witchcraft was said to be more than scholarly" (95), but his lecture is a personal narrative, not a scholarly analysis at all. Although his audience rationalizes that perhaps this is a new form of structuralism or even postmodern criticism, Esther tells Liz that she thinks it is Claudio's "power of . . . self-hallucination" that produced this story, but she adds, "[W]hen I'm with Claudio, I find myself believing these things" (241).[8]

Esther is forced to analyze Claudio and her relationship to him when she is called to his deathbed soon after the lecture. She is shaken by her own emotions: Had she "wasted her entire adult emotional life on a fantasy. On a werewolf" (328)? When Esther arrives at his deathbed, "she was relieved to sense that he was not yet harmless. . . . Relieved to find him as mad as ever . . . [speaking of] hidden power and forbidden knowledge . . . Medusa . . . and Salome" (329). When Esther recounts her story of the murder and severed head of Jilly Fox, he replies that it is "not a mortal murderer . . . it is a spirit . . . a mass hallucination, unleashed from the fear of the people. By disbelief you can disarm it" (329). Before her disbelief can function, however, Esther must be able to acknowledge, to imagine, the "uncanny," the "werewolf," the "horrors." Rationalization, liberalism, and self-control have not erased Esther's childhood experience of Nazism nor the "savagery" of contemporary politics. Esther must acknowledge evil, must, like Alix, admit that she too "can imagine horrors" (320), acknowledge darkness. Then disbelief can function, can refuse to let evil dominate.

Although Esther does not believe Claudio's conviction that she can "disarm" the murderer by the force of her will, in fact there are no more murders. One evening while the three friends are eating dinner at Esther's flat, the police arrest Esther's upstairs neighbor, a quiet young man named Paul Whitmore with whom Esther has exchanged occasional words about her potted plants. He is the "Horror of Harrow Road." Later Esther's flat is scheduled to be torn down, cut "out of the city, like a cancer" (356), but Esther now knows that evil cannot just be cut out; it must be faced. Esther decides to move to Bologna and live with Elena, Claudio's Marxist lesbian sister, and write a book with her friend and fellow art historian Robert Oxenholme. Esther accepts now that any city can have its "horrors," any politics its "savagery." She also knows, however, that she need not fear emotions, that politics can be contested, murderers caught.

Although the politics of this novel remain "bleak" and "the great social dream" is over (Greene, "Bleak Houses" 317), the ending of the novel is more ambiguous[9] as the three friends go on a hike in the country together to celebrate Esther's fiftieth birthday. Bromberg argues that against the "apocalypse of social and individual evil, the novel positions the counter movement of a narrative of community" (21). A new kind of narrative space offsets and balances the new politics. Alix's vision holds. In spite of the darkness, there are "flickering impermanent points of light irradiating stretches, intersections, threads, of a vast web" (*The Radiant Way* 69). The new political space in which these women find themselves has darkness, but it also has points of light and connections.

Nadine Gordimer's *None to Accompany Me* also opens with a party that welcomes a new decade, this time 1990. This anniversary party of Vera and Ben Stark celebrates the opening of the prisons and a new political climate. For the Starks, for Vera's Legal Foundation colleagues, for black community leaders, and for returning exiles and Communist Party members, this is the beginning of a period of light after the long darkness and oppression of apartheid. Although this new space is still threatened by old kinds of violence and some new kinds, there is a new sense of freedom for all the characters. They still carry with them, individually and in their relationships, the marks of the apartheid regime. The novel goes back and forth in time to trace these marks.

For all the characters apartheid was a time of danger, secrecy, and lies: Before 1990, South Africa "had been a place and time when integrity in many matters could be maintained only by dishonesty, when truth had to survive by lies" (*None to Accompany Me* 27). This atmosphere molded the marriages of both Vera and Ben Stark and of Sibongile and Didymus Maqoma. Each marriage is grounded in a compact necessitated by the politics of apartheid. Vera, trained as a lawyer, goes to work for the Legal Foundation, "not out of the white guilt people talked about, but out of a need to take up, to balance on her own two feet the time and place to which, by birth, she understood she had no choice but to belong" (20). In order for her to pursue this work, Ben has to give up sculpture and take a job at Promotional Luggage. The narrator comments that in other countries, in other times, such "an obvious moral contradiction in the activities of a man and woman might destroy the respect that goes with love. But here, for these two, while the great lie prevailed, it was part of a shackle of common experience of what was wrong but aleatory" (29). The very nature of Vera and Ben's intimacy in marriage was embedded in politics.

In exile Sibongile and Didymus also have a compact underlying their marriage. As a freedom fighter Didymus was always at risk and forced to keep secrets from his wife:

> She and Didymus were the best of comrades. . . . [S]he had gone about her work in London . . . without knowing or asking where he was, the letters . . . came to her unsigned through some country other than the one he was in. . . . [W]hat other relationship between a man and a woman could prove such trust? . . . [T]his was a grand compact beyond the capacity of those who live only for themselves. (75)

Sibongile and Didymus's marriage is also grounded in their work for their people and freedom. Sibongile is Didymus's closest comrade, but there is much she does not know about his life. She accepts the secrecy as the cost of their political commitment.

When Sibongile and Didymus greet Vera and Ben after twenty years of exile, their reunion is also built around a secret. Neither Didymus nor Vera reveal that they had seen each other five years ago when Didymus was working undercover in South Africa and needed to have someone reliable send letters out of the country. In Vera's mind this secret is linked to a sexual secret in her own past. Her eldest son, Ivan, just might be the son of her first husband rather than of Ben, the result of one last lovemaking when her first husband came home from the war to get his things before their final parting and divorce: Meeting Didymus "was not the first time Vera had experienced something she never revealed. . . . [T]he precedent of lying by omission becomes a facility that serves a political purpose just as well" (42–43). Gordimer intertwines the pervasive atmosphere of lies and secrecy in which these characters worked and lived during much of their lives with the new political space created by the end of apartheid. What changes will now have to be made in these marriages so grounded in secrecy and the compacts demanded by political complicity? How will Vera and Sibongile learn to negotiate this new space?

The old politics and relationships are symbolized by the photographic[10] postcards and posters that are interspersed throughout the novel. In her 1982 James Lecture in New York, "Living in the Interregnum," Gordimer said that white South Africans will have to find their way "home . . . out of the perceptual clutter of curled photographs of master and servant relationships, the 78 *rpms* of history repeating the conditioning of the past" (270). The opening lines of the novel describe a slightly different photograph of the past, a postcard of a group photo of Vera and her friends at a mountain resort that she sent to her first husband in Egypt during the war. She had circled Ben's image to communicate her rejection of the husband of her adolescence and her taking of a new lover. Vera finds the postcard "lying on a shelf under some old record sleeves" (5) in 1990. What is the significance of this snippet of the past to Vera now? "There's always someone nobody remembers" (3), the narrator comments. The question that echoes through the passage is: Which records of the past must be destroyed to prevent the conditioning for old ways and which kept?

Likewise, a poster of Didymus and other famous men sits fading in a window: "Who are the faces arranged in a collage round the great man himself? The posters are curling at the corners and some have faded strips where sunlight from a window has barred them day after day, month after month" (92). Now in the bright light of a new space, Didymus's old image is faded. He is "unrecognized; disguised, now, as himself" (92). What will his authority be now in the Movement, which must balance positions between those who fought in exile and those who were imprisoned at home? What kinds of loyalty does Sibongile, whose political position is now as a representative for new women's groups, owe to her marriage partner and comrade? "You don't know who this is?" This is the unspoken phrase that arises when looking at old photos, undecipherable postcards, faded posters. It's also the phrase Didymus says to Vera when he comes to her in disguise, and it's the phrase a cleaner in overalls uses to Sibongile while she is out shopping: "You don't know who this is?" The woman explains, "I'm Sela's child, your mother's cousin" (52).

Exile has hidden both authority and acts of bravery. It has separated people from their family and culture. If Vera and Ben must find a "home," a place for whites within the new politics in the country they've never left, Sibongile and Didymus must struggle with the gaps in their experience at home and reconcile the new experiences they've absorbed from abroad; they must create a hybrid space for themselves within their own homeland. Curling photographs are reminders of the past but no guide to the future.

During apartheid both Vera Stark's legal career and her sexuality were immersed in secrecy and contested the law of the land. During those times the Legal Foundation worked against the removal of black Africans to "homelands," and Vera used her "strategical experience" to oppose "the law through its interstices" (102). Vera realizes that although the Foundation could not undo the political power that was destroying people's lives, it could at least look "for the legal loopholes that will delay or frustrate" the "logic" of apartheid (13). Dominic Head argues that Vera's "sexuality 'fits' her public commitment" ("Gordimer's *None to Accompany Me*" 49) at this stage in her life because it, too, is expressed in the loopholes of the law. She was attracted to her present husband Ben when she was married to her first husband, who was away at war. Then after twenty years of marriage to Ben, she has an affair with a German filmmaker, Otto Abarbanel. Vera thinks to herself that it was Ben who actually "made another man possible, wanted, because he it was who had shown her, up in the mountains with those friends of a group photograph, what love-making could be" (*None to Accompany Me* 61). For Vera her sexuality "was something that concerned her alone . . . a private constant in her being, a characteristic like the colour of eyes, the shape of a nose, the nature of a personal spirit that never could belong to anyone other than the self" (62–63).

This affair is not a cross-race affair like that in several of Gordimer's other novels, but it, too, is linked to racial politics, that of the Nazis to whom Gordimer compares the apartheid regime. Because of his Sephardic name, Vera assumes and is "gratified by the idea that her lover was a Jew, orphaned by racism" (67). When Otto reacts to the savagery of the white policemen he has been filming, Vera explains: "You haven't lived here long enough to know. The Nazis didn't end in the war where your parents died, they were re-born here" (68). The irony of Vera's comment is that "Abarbanel" is only the name of Otto's adoptive parents. He explains that his genes are pure Nazi: "You know what a Hitler Baby is? . . . I'm one. My mother was mated like a cow to produce a good German child for Hitler. I don't know who the Aryan stud was. She didn't know" (69). Racial politics are always more convoluted than one expects. Head links Vera's sexual affair directly to former South African laws:

> It is Vera's acceptance of Otto—a kindling of (more intense) desire despite his past—that humanizes him, and which facilitates a personal exorcism. Yet given the magnitude of the historical associations—and the manifest parallel with the genetic engineering built into the apart-heid project—this exorcism does carry a great deal of symbolic weight. . . . [In] Gordimer's politics of the body . . . sexual expression and transgression flout the biological policing intended in the racist social structure of South Africa; and the biological hybridity implied in free sexuality indicates, by extension, a cultural hybridity. . . . But the . . . connection . . . is double-edged. ("Gordimer's *None to Accompany Me*" 50)

There is a cost to Vera's affair. Vera herself falsely connects her af-fair with Otto to her daughter Annick's lesbianism, but the real cost is to Ben. Vera recognizes Ben sitting in a restaurant as she and Otto drive by:

> He was alone. By the sight of him she was overcome with desolation, premonition like the nausea of one about to faint. How could he look so solitary? Did all the years together mean nothing? A childish fear of abandon drained her. His lowered head and bowed shoulders knew without knowing that he was no longer her lover. His aloneness was hers; not here, not now, but somewhere waiting. (*None to Accompany Me* 71)

In an interview with Nancy Topping Bazin, Gordimer confirms her "radical" view of sexuality, saying: "It is for you to dispose of and use according to your own needs" ("Interview" 574), but she acknowledges that in the novel that view "doesn't always work for" Vera; "she gets . . . a premonition of perhaps herself being discarded or set aside" (575). Vera is taken back to the place of her affair when her assistant Oupa Sejake rents the same apartment that Otto had had. The photographic like revisiting of a place, however, undermines the significance of the affair for Vera. Head concludes that with "hindsight, the affair now appears self-indulgent" to Vera ("Gordimer's *None to Accompany Me*" 51). Head explains that the "biological and cultural hybridity which defeats racism empirically— is a gesture . . . presented as belonging to the past" (52). Now that the politics have changed, the significance of the affair lies in her premonition of loneliness rather than the transgression it once symbolized. Neither the curled photographs nor the memory of physical places is a guide to the future.

Twenty years later Vera Stark finds herself in a new space. Neither the legal tactics nor the sexual affairs designed to flout the law of the land are valid any more. In "Living in the Interregnum," Gordimer comments on the strange space the white radical finds herself in:

> [H]owever hated and shameful the collective life of apartheid and its structures has been to us, there is, now, the unadmitted fear of being without structure. The interregnum is not only between two social orders but also between two identities, one known and discarded, the other unknown and undetermined. (269–70)

Politically, Vera still has work to do. The "Foundation has not, as might be expected, become redundant" (*None to Accompany Me* 13); there is still plenty of legal work to do for people whose land was stolen from them during apartheid. Vera works with Zeph Rapulana, a schoolmaster and leader of a squatters' camp, to reclaim land for his people from an Afrikaaner farmer. The new political system has not removed the threat of violence. The Afrikaaner farmer and his commandos attack the squatter camp and kill some of Zeph's people and wound him. Because of this violence, Vera and Zeph are able to force the administration to buy the land for his people, and Zeph rises politically and economically as one of the new leaders. Vera herself encounters a different kind of violence after a Foundation trip when she and her colleague Oupa stop by a township so he can visit his wife and children. On the way back their car is hijacked by criminals. Vera is shot in the leg, and Oupa eventually dies of his wounds. Oupa had admired the courage and bravado of the criminals he had been incarcerated with when he was a political prisoner. Ironically, he dies at the hands of black criminals, not Afrikaaner commandos. Zeph's and Vera's wounds heal, but work remains to be done to alleviate both poverty and old and new kinds of violence and desperation.[11]

Vera does not give up in the face of violence, however. She is learning to live in a new space and to find a new identity within it. She discusses with Zeph, whose judgment and position she respects, her nomination to the "Technical Committee on Constitutional Issues." Vera is reluctant to accept the job because, she explains, power scares her: "I've belonged so long to a people who used it horribly." Zeph responds, "[I]f this Committee does the job, it'll mean real empowerment for our people. . . . [W]hen he spoke of 'our' people it was as a black speaking for blacks, subtly different from when he used 'we' or 'us' and this meant an empathy between him and her" (282). In her relationship with Zeph and her new work, Vera is finding her way in a new political space, one that she must continue to negotiate. It requires her sensitivity to past abuse of power by whites and her willingness to donate her legal and political skills while letting blacks lead. She has to give up some of her former ideals and commitments: "Empowerment, Zeph. What is this new thing? What happened to what we used to call justice?" (285). In the new politics Vera has to work with compromise rather than to contest evil, as she did before. She has to learn to follow, to find her way in the political space that lies between "our" and "us."

Vera finds a new role politically, but emotionally she begins to be more and more alone. Now in her early sixties, she is aware of her aging. Her haircut is that "of a woman who has set aside her femininity" (39–40). When she greets Sibongile upon her return, "Vera had the generosity, toward women who still make their appearance seductive, of a woman confident that she was once successfully seductive herself and now knows she may . . . herself be merely pleasing" (46–47). Vera thinks of old age as loss of sensuality. When Ben's dying father comes to live with them, Vera says to Sibongile, "[I]t's going to be awful to be really old, no one wants to touch you any more" (131). Although Vera dresses her age and seems to accept it, she is reluctant to give up her ability to attract men. When Zeph grasps her arm as they are planning depositions, Vera's mind flashes back to a similar gesture made years ago by Otto Abarbanel that was "the compact to begin a love affair" (120), but she soon realizes that

Zeph's gesture was not sexual. She becomes aware that the relation-ship between herself and Zeph is only a political one: "a level of knowledge of one another, tranquil, not very deep . . . a level that was neither sexually intuitive nor that of friendship" (122).

Although Vera forges a new political compact with Zeph, her old one with Ben cannot withstand the pressures of the new social roles. Ben's business venture fails, and he realizes that Vera has been "his vocation" (292). He took the job at Promotional Luggage only to provide for her. Vera, however, rejects Ben's sacrifices. She says to her son Ivan: "Ben made a great mistake. . . . He gave up everything he needed, in exchange for what he wanted. The sculpture. Even an academic career. . . . He put it all on me" (223). Ben eventually goes to London to visit Ivan and begins to think that "Vera never ever really wanted a husband" (298). She only wanted for a while a do-mesticated lover who shared her political beliefs. Ben is lonely and angry, but Vera does not want his emotional dependence on her.

The narrator describes her at home alone: "Vera, too old to find a partner, danced alone, no one to witness, in the living-room of her house" (305). For Vera, marriage was "a stage on the way, along with others, many and different. Everyone ends up moving alone toward the self" (306). The compact she and Ben had forged long ago no longer works for her in this new political space. All alone now, Vera sells her house and moves into a small cottage behind Zeph's house. As she clears out her house, she sees the photographic postcard of the group in the mountains one last time. She realizes, "I'm the one in the photograph whom no one remembers" (294). Vera now must dance alone and no one remembers her from the photographs of the past.

Vera's solitary state is underlined by the last scene in the novel in which one night a pipe bursts at her annex, and she goes into Zeph's house to get a wrench. In the dark Vera runs into Zeph's mistress with her warm body and the scent of recent sex. Vera walks back outside alone, her "breath scrolling out, a signature" (324) in the cold night air. Head argues that this passage evokes the novel's epigraph, the Japanese haiku "No one to accompany me on this path/ Nightfall in autumn." Head says that "the evocation of an ageing woman, sexu-ally inactive, superseded, now living the autumn of her life, suggests a straightforwardly elegiac close, which articulates both the loss and the courage of old age" ("Gordimer's *None to Accompany Me*" 53). Vera has found her space politically and learned to negotiate, but she has cut herself off from her intimate contacts with family, and although she faces age with courage, she has not done anything to prepare for it.

In contrast, Sibongile Maqoma, younger than Vera, continues in her marriage. She does not have to dance alone; she has to learn a new dance. After her many years of being the faithful comrade, the traditional wife, coping with exile and supporting her husband's dangerous political commitments, she experiences political power and activity, but she, too, must pay a cost in terms of her personal life. For over half their married life, Didymus was the dominant and risk-taking partner. When they were first married, they lived in Soweto, and Didymus carried a pass and worked against the system from within the country, but they had had to leave over twenty years ago. Living in exile, Didymus worked on international missions. He was a "veteran of prisons and interrogation. That fox at infiltration, raiding under the eyes of the police and army" (*None to Accompany Me* 47). Like other returning exiles, the Maqomas are thrilled to be returning home: "Home: that quiet word: a spectacle, a theatre, a pyrotechnic display of emotion for those who come from wars, banishment, exile" (44). The cost of return for Didymus, however, is the loss of status and authority. Didymus firmly believes that in "a democratic movement the personality cult must be kept to a minimum" (92) and that "all that mattered was . . . political legitimacy for the long-outlawed Movement. You had your role, your missions, you took the risks of your life . . . and there was no presenting of the bill for those years to anyone, the benefit did not belong to you and your achievement was that you wanted it that way" (97).

In spite of their idealism and commitment to the new politics, however, both Sibongile and Didymus are disappointed when he is not elected to the National Executive Committee of the Movement. Sibongile is angry for him: "Those sly bastards! They planned it! They wanted you out" (97). The new politics and compromises have made Didymus invisible. Sibongile, however, is elected to the National Executive Committee by the women's branch. Didymus tries to focus on her achievements and urges compromise: "[Y]ou have to work with everyone on the Executive, don't make enemies for private reasons" (99). In spite of Didymus's conviction, emotionally he feels left out. He runs errands and takes their daughter to school. Sibongile, "graceful with her well-dressed big hips" (75) and "her obvious undocile femininity" (78), rises in power and travels all over the world in the service of her new politics. Sibongile's experiences in exile have made her an effective ambassador for the new regime: "How confidently and attractively Sibongile, in African robes and turban she wore for such occasions, picked up whatever conventions of ceremony and protocol came from different cultures" (238). Sibongile worries, however, whether some of Didymus's activities when he had infiltrated a prison camp as an interrogator would be held against her in her new political position. When she learns that his code name was not released, she feels safe. Their roles have been reversed. Didymus realizes that she is simultaneously "a stranger and . . . as familiar as his own body; that must have been how he was for her, those years when he came and went" (125).

Sibongile is impatient with Didymus's inability to adjust. She complains to Vera: "He's got to stop wallowing in this self-pity. . . . He's become history rather than a living man. How can anyone be expected to accept that about himself" (132). When Sibongile returns from an assignment in another African country, she brings Didymus an ebony walking stick, which Didymus, hurt, thinks of as a "present for a retired man" (130). Then suddenly the threat of violence[12] that has accompanied the political change involves them personally, and Didymus has a new role. Sibongile is now powerful enough to become the object of an assassination threat. Didymus becomes her bodyguard: "[H]e is no white suburban husband, needing to be instructed how to 'handle' a gun. . . . Didymus has long been accustomed to heavy odds in his way of life and all he can do is lead Sibongile through them" (286–87). Didymus and Sibongile form a new partnership: "When every old distinction of privilege is defeated and abolished, there comes an aristocracy of those in danger. All feel diminished, outclassed, in their company" (291). Sibongile will not be able to spend much time with Vera in the future; she does not want to put any of her friends at risk. She belongs to a new political aristocracy, a place of great influence but also one of danger.

The other family member to feel the effect of exile and return is Sibongile and Didymus's sixteen-year-old daughter Mpho, their "late-born" child (48), who has lived in London all her life: "This schoolgirl combined the style of *Vogue* with the assertion of Africa. . . . Out of her mouth came a perky London English. She could not speak an African language, neither the Zulu of her mother nor the Xhosa of her father" (49). Sibongile recognizes that they all have been alienated from their heritage as well as their country,[13] but her feelings are complex. Sibongile wants her child to learn African languages and African culture, but she doesn't want Mpho to live in a space of deprivation. Sibongile is surprised when Mpho bonds with her paternal grandmother and visits her in a nearby township. Sibongile thinks to herself:

> How could a child brought up with her own bedroom, fresh milk delivered at the front door in Notting Hill Gate every morning . . . be expected to stand more than one night in such a place, *gogo* or no *gogo*? Going out across a yard to a toilet used by everyone round about! Heaven knows what she might pick up there! A return to a level of life to which Sibongile, Didymus, had been condemned when they were their child's age—what did a sixteen-year-old born in exile know of what it was like when there was no choice? (50–51)

Sibongile does not want Mpho to stay in the township. They find a house in a white suburb and enroll Mpho in a predominantly white school so she can complete the A-levels she began in England. Mpho, however, has few black friends, and yearning for that contact with her own people, she begins an affair with Vera's legal assistant, Oupa Sejake, who is ten years older than she and has a wife and children in an outlying area. Distressed at having introduced them, Vera says to Didymus: "[T]hey've both been displaced, their relative ages don't tally naturally with their actual experiences, there's a dislocation that couldn't be corrected. He missed out her teenage stage, in jail; she has a worldly sophistication beyond her years, because of European exile" (177–78).

When Mpho gets pregnant, Sibongile is furious. She says to Didymus: "We should never have brought her from London. She should have been left at school there. You wanted her home; 'home' here, to get pregnant at school like every girl from a location" (173). "Home" has suddenly lost its hallowed meaning for Sibongile. She bitterly feels the cost of alienation and exile in her daughter's experience. Although Mpho's grandmother, who disapproves of abortion, offers to look after the baby, Didymus and Sibongile are firm about the need for an abortion, and Mpho complies. When Vera later asks Didymus about Mpho, he replies: "The whole thing's never mentioned at home. She laughs a lot, girl-friends in and out, very busy. It's what we wanted, I suppose" (201).

Although in this novel, Gordimer celebrates the end of apartheid, she does not underestimate the costs of moving into a new political space. Vera pays both a bullet wound and the dissolution of her marriage as the cost of her new commitments. Sibongile pays with the threat of assassination and their daughter's abortion. There is still the threat of violence in public space and the threat to intimacy in the private space. But in spite of the costs, the greater violence and lies of the apartheid regime are now gone. The photographs with Gordimer's captions in *Lifetimes under Apartheid* (Gordimer and Goldblatt) have now passed into history. After Vera agrees to accept a position on the Technical Committee on Constitutional Issues, she and Zeph stroll toward his gate. Zeph reaches out and plucks a yellow rose from a bush. As he hands it to her he says: "Mind the thorns" (285). Both Vera and Sibongile know there will be thorns, but the yellow rose represents a new hybrid, a third space, for a new politics. Temple-Thurston says: "The novel implies that cultural and racial interfusion will increasingly take place. Hybridity is an organic process and cannot be stopped" (143).

Both Drabble and Gordimer have written narratives of community, of women who have immersed themselves in the politics of their communities only to find that politics can change, for good or ill. The dances that they've learned must be rechoreographed; they sometimes must learn to dance alone or to sit at the edge of the dance. In these social novels that spread over many years and many characters, identities that have been carefully honed throughout adulthood suddenly change. Yet neither Drabble nor Gordimer gives up in the face of change. Their characters pay the price of change and work to find new roles within their new spaces. In Drabble's novel it is a new space of "contestation" and multiple political identities; in Gordimer's novel, a blending together of formerly unassimilable forces in a new hybrid political space.

Chapter 5

Cultural Identities:
The Search for Integrity in Paule Marshall's *Praisesong for the Widow* and Jessica Anderson's *Tirra Lirra by the River*

If the story of a young person growing into adulthood is called a *bildungsroman*, it is fitting that stories about facing old age are called *reifungsromane*, or novels of ripening.[1] Typical of this stage of life that novelists describe as "ripening" is the construction of a personal narrative, what gerontologist Robert Butler calls a "life review, [which he describes] as a naturally occurring ... mental process characterized by the progressive return to consciousness of past experiences, and, particularly, the resurgence of unresolved conflicts" (66).[2] It is often triggered by dreams or the reflection of an aging body in a mirror (68). Two postcolonial *reifungsromane*, Paule Marshall's *Praisesong for the Widow* (1983) and Jessica Anderson's *Tirra Lirra by the River* (1978), use this same construction, but the life review in each novel consists not just of an analysis of the memories of an individual life but also of a journey in search of cultural wholeness.

Both protagonists not only must recover a lost cultural identity but also must divest themselves of false layers of culture that prevent integration and wholeness. In Paule Marshall's *Praisesong for the Widow*, an African American protagonist, Avey Johnson, travels to the Caribbean where she undergoes both the divestment of some of her Euro-American culture and the recovery of some of the African values that had been suppressed by the external forces of American culture and repressed within herself. Jessica Anderson's white Australian protagonist, Nora Porteous, must remove the layers of nostalgic distortion that are embedded in the English culture that she has inherited and confront the white settler Australian culture underneath it. Both novels use memory to access repressed history and have a recursive structure[3] that alternates past and present. This structure allows both the recovery of cultural codes and the transformation of them as they are moved into the present. In allowing for the transformation and evolution of cultural identity, both novels share Stuart Hall's understanding of culture as containing "the ruptures and discontinuities" of history as well as its continuing narratives. In his essay "Cultural Identity and Diaspora," Hall says that cultural identity

> is a matter of "becoming" as well as "being." It belongs to the future as much as to the past. It is not something which already exists, transcending place, time, history and culture. Cultural identities come from somewhere, have histories. But, like everything which is historical, they undergo constant transformation . . . are subject to the continuous "play" of history, culture and power.[4] (394)

In engaging the theme of a need for cultural wholeness, these two novels go beyond the busyness of middle adulthood's involvement in social roles, politics, and generativity to a solitary search for integrity in one's later years. These novels begin where Gordimer's *None to Accompany Me* ended, although her title is prophetic of the need to review and evaluate life at the onset of old age. Gordimer's novel ends with Vera in her sixties still involved in her life's work. In contrast, Marshall's protagonist is sixty-four,[5] and Anderson's is in her late seventies. They both confront the task that Vera is still ignoring. In order to achieve Erikson's final stage of integrity[6] or "wisdom," it is not enough to be involved in the community and influence another generation; one must also evaluate one's life and the traditions one has embraced. Picking up the same image that novelists have used, Erikson says that it is at this point that "the fruit of the seven [earlier] stages gradually ripens. . . . [One must achieve] an emotional integration faithful to the image-bearers of the past." Strength in this stage, according to Erikson, results from "*wisdom* in its many connotations from ripened 'wits' to accumulated knowledge, mature judgment, and inclusive understanding" (*Identity, Youth and Crisis* 139, 140). It is the integration of past with the judgment of the present that allows the achievement of wisdom based in cultural identity.

The juxtaposition of these two novels creates an intriguing contrast since one protagonist is black, one white, yet each has experienced a cultural loss and must use a journey to recover it. In Marshall's novel the protagonist's African culture has been lost in the oppression of slavery and her assimilation into a middle-class, Western way of life. Avey Johnson must give up her American vacation, the Caribbean cruise on *Bianca Pride*, and journey instead to Carriacou, a small island near Grenada, to experience African cultural forms and recognize the echoes of that recovered culture in childhood memories. In Anderson's novel the journey is reversed. Nora Porteous has been living in London for thirty years and journeys back to Australia to come to terms with the land of her birth. In order to confront cultural identity in a white settler community in Australia, Nora must peel away the layers of falsehood and nostalgia[7] that have obscured her understanding of her cultural inheritance and of her homeland. For the white settler in Australia, the past is not so much lost as distorted. One of Nora's earliest memories is of looking through a window at the Australian landscape, made green by January rains: The "distortions in the cheap thick glass gave me my first intimation of a country as beautiful as those in my childhood books. . . . [M]y Camelot" (Anderson, *Tirra Lirra by the River* 8–9). Nora must work through two layers of nostalgia—first, the white settler's idealized image of England and, second, her own imaginings of Australia as Camelot. For both women the physical journey brings about a journey of memory in which they reevaluate their childhoods, their marriages, their values, and their adult life structures.

The disjunctures and ruptures in both characters' pasts are conveyed in each novel by a trope of physical illness, a temporary nausea for Avey and a more serious pneumonia for Nora. Illness forces both characters to acknowledge their bodies from which they have been alienated. As the two characters are forced to come to terms with their bodies, they open up a space for memories and lost traditions of the past that they had repressed. In her commentary on one of her husband's last books, Joan Erikson emphasizes that wisdom is not a purely cerebral concept but is rooted in the body: "[W]isdom belongs to the world of actuality to which our senses give us access" (7). To

achieve wisdom, both characters must battle illness and ground themselves in their physical bodies as well as use their memories in order
to recover and restore physical, psychic, and cultural wholeness.

At the opening of Paule Marshall's *Praisesong for the Widow*, Avey
Johnson, with her elegant tasteful clothes and secure middle-class niche
in the New York suburb of North White Plains, seems impervious to
change. She dismisses the suggestions of her youngest daughter Marion
that she accompany her to Africa for her vacation. Rather, Avey joins
two women friends for a cruise to the Caribbean, as she has in previous years. Avey's six suitcases of clothing and her fleeting thoughts of
her silver and china in her sideboard at home attest to her middle-class
American lifestyle. Nonetheless, at the opening of the novel, Avey
Johnson is packing her clothes, ready to leave her friends and aban-
don the rest of the cruise. Three seemingly unrelated events have combined to make Avey Johnson break out of the glittering confines of the
cruise ship. G. Thomas Courser suggests that the "initial reactivator
of Avey's ethnic consciousness is, significantly, an *aural* memory. The
patois spoken by natives on Martinique [which] faintly echoes the
Gullah spoken by the older blacks in Tatem, South Carolina[,] . . .
reawakens her condensed cultural memory, which was transmitted
orally" (108) by her great-aunt whom Avey used to visit in Tatem as
a child. This aural memory opens up Avey's repressed childhood memories, and she dreams of Aunt Cuney beckoning her to come to Ibo
Landing. At this point, however, Avey resists her.

The second event is similar to the life-review triggers that Robert
Butler describes; she sees a reflection of herself in a mirror. In Avey's
case, it is not that she sees a reflection of physical aging in the mirror but that she does not recognize herself at all.[8] She recognizes the
reflection of her friends Thomasina and Clarice, but "for a long con-
fused moment Avey Johnson could not place the woman in beige
crepe de Chine and pearls seated with them" (*Praisesong for the
Widow* 48). Avey realizes suddenly that this has happened before; she
had seen herself in department store mirrors but not recognized the
image of a well-dressed black woman with "carefully co-ordinated
accessories . . . muted colors. Everything in good taste" (48). Avey's
problem is not so much old age but the loss of identity. She has become her clothing; her body is encased in a suit with all its accessories. Even in her dreams she is wearing high heels and is wrapped in
a fur stole.

The third event is a vague feeling of indigestion when she is served dessert at dinner. Like Nyasha Sigauke in *Nervous Conditions*, Avey's cultural conflicts are experienced in her body. Nyasha's rejection of assimilation and colonialism is experienced as bulimia; Avey's surfeit of Euro-American culture is experienced as indigestion.[9] Although Avey at this early stage in her journey does not recognize the cause of her discomfort, she decides to leave the ship and go "home." By the time she disembarks in Grenada, she sees the cruise ship as "huge, sleek, imperial, a glacial presence in the warm waters of the Caribbean" (16–17). Although she does not yet consciously define it as such, it has become a symbol of dominating Western culture, the antithesis of the home she will find in Carriacou. This initial section of the novel in which Avey recovers only fragments of memory is entitled "Runagate." Barbara Christian points out that this title "is taken from Robert Hayden's famous poem of that name, a poem that stresses the slave past of New World blacks and their fugitive escape from bondage" (151). Like her New World ancestors, Avey is on a journey to escape bondage, but this time it is a journey to escape the bondage of materialism and cultural repression.

The second section of the novel is entitled "Sleeper's Wake." It is, as Christian notes, both "a wake for the past, as well as an awakening from the past" (152). After leaving the ship, Avey goes to a fancy hotel to await a flight back to New York. As she sits in her hotel room, still dressed in her hat and gloves, her linen dress and girdle, she has a vision of her husband, Jerome, and remembers their life together in Halsey Street in Brooklyn in the late 1940s and early 1950s, which is grounded in the blues, the dance halls, and the poetry of the Harlem Renaissance. Before Avey can recover the past of her ancestors, she needs to understand her own personal past and her marriage. As Jerome appears to her in his Masonic burial clothes, she hears him berating her for wasting the $1,500 she had spent on the cruise.[10] She thinks first of the economic hardships of their twenty years on Halsey Street and of Jerome's sacrifice of his own private life to make money for her and their three girls.

Gradually Avey allows herself to go further back in memory to the good times she had with Jerome, when he was only "Jay" in the early years of their marriage. She found herself thinking "of the small rituals and private pleasures" of Halsey Street (*Praisesong for the Widow* 122). She now remembers Jay, her young husband, who would come home from work, put on the old 78 recordings, and dance with Avey in their living room. On Sundays she remembers his quoting Langston Hughes, Paul Laurence Dunbar, and James Weldon Johnson to their young girls and singing along with the Fisk Jubilee Choir. She remembers the joyful sexuality she and Jay shared and his comparing her to African goddesses.[11]

When she suddenly awakens, Avey mourns Jay's death for the first time. Denniston suggests that "Avey mourns not the death of the rigid and compulsive Jerome but the more sensitive and culturally attuned Jay. She also mourns her own cultural loss" (136). Avey asks herself whether they could have achieved financial security "while preserving, safeguarding, treasuring those things that had come down to them over the generations. . . . They could have done both, it suddenly seemed to her, bowed over in tears there on the hotel balcony" (*Praisesong for the Widow* 139). Avey realizes that both she and Jay had lost their cultural roots in their drive for material success. Her task now is to mourn that loss and to try to recover cultural wholeness. Angelita Reyes argues that this realization is not a rejection of "economic progress. The problem is to reach and maintain a compromise between material excess and spiritual propriety . . . [and to assume] a balance between Euro-American culture and African-American heritage" (181). To achieve that balance Avey must divest herself of some of the trappings of Euro-American culture and open herself up further to the African values that she has repressed. She starts subconsciously to follow the suggestions of her dream in which Aunt Cuney pulls off her mink stole. She removes the layers of clothing that represent her middle-class American existence and puts on a light, unironed dress to walk out to the beach.

Avey has begun her task of recuperating the past, but to go from the recovering of her personal past to the recovering of a communal past, she needs a guide. In the third section of the novel, "Lavé Tête," a title that interweaves personal memory with Christian and African rituals of water and bathing, Avey finds this guide in the ninety-year-old Lebert Joseph, owner of a rum shop into which she steps to get away from the intense Caribbean sun. Lebert Joseph, whom Joyce Pettis calls "Aunt Cuney's live counterpart" (121), is closely in touch with his African cultural inheritance. Abena Busia argues that he is

an iconographic figure [who] . . . performs the role of the deity Legba. The name given in Ewe religious practice to the god of households and thresholds, and to the Yoruba god of crossroads who is the messenger of the gods, is, in Afro-Caribbean practice also, the lame god of the crossroads. It is he who acts as the widow's guide, leading her back, at this crossroads in her life, to those ancestors whose spirits she has neglected or sacrificed. (204)

When Lebert asks Avey, "What's your nation?" (167), she responds, "I'm a visitor, a tourist" (167). She does not yet have an understanding of her cultural identity, but she does begin to tell him the story of her dream of Great-Aunt Cuney and reveals her longing for knowledge. When Lebert invites her to accompany him on the excursion to Carriacou, Avey surprises herself by finally agreeing to go.

Before she arrives in Carriacou with Lebert to learn the dances of her ancestors, Avey must take the boat ride from Grenada to the island. This boat ride recalls two other voyages, one personal and one historical. The first memory is a pleasurable one from her childhood of a family boat ride on the Hudson River. Avey remembers the colorful clothes of her mother and father and remembers feeling the connection to all her people, both her great-aunt down in Tatem and the throng of people standing beside the Hudson pier. She imagines

> hundreds of slender threads streaming out from her navel and from the place where her heart was to enter those around her.... She visualized the threads as being silken ... and of a hundred different colors. And although they were thin to the point of invisibility, they felt as strong entering her as the lifelines of woven hemp that trailed out into the water. (190–91)

Helen Lock says that "these 'slender threads,' that have been reaching out of the past to tug at her visceral memory, [are] prompted by her subconscious need to remember both her individual and her communal identity" (206). In a 1995 interview Marshall confirms the significance of communal identity, saying that in most of her fiction she is "concerned on the one hand about the individual, realizing self; there's always that sort of quest for an identity... [but] the individual struggle had to be matched with the struggle of communities to realize themselves, as well, to achieve empowerment" ("To Be in the World" 103).

The second memory, even more visceral, reinforces the site of Avey's body as the place of cultural conflict. The seasickness she feels in the cramped quarters of the boat to Carriacou both recalls a childhood nausea at an Easter service and reenacts the misery of her African ancestors' Middle Passage on slave ships: "[S]he had the impression as her mind flickered on briefly of other bodies lying crowded in with her in the hot, airless dark. A multitude it felt like lay packed around her in the filth and stench of themselves. . . . Their moans, rising and falling" (*Praisesong for the Widow* 209). Avey's vomiting is both a reenactment of her own and her ancestors' past and a rejection of the Western patterns of consumption that have kept her from that past. She is finally purged of the rich cruise food and ready for cleansing. Avey accepts the consolation of the women around her and is humiliated but grateful to Lebert's daughter, Rosalie Parvey, for helping her to bed and bathing her the next morning. Rosalie's touch reminds Avey of the Christian ritual of "laying on of hands" (217) and of Aunt Cuney's bathing her as a child in a wash-tub in Tatem, South Carolina. In submitting her body to the touch of another, she connects both to memory and to community.

The last section of the novel is called "The Beg Pardon," which is the song that Lebert Joseph sings to honor the ancestors and to pe-tition them on behalf of all their descendants. Although Avey feels weak after her illness, she goes to the celebration to listen to the Beg Pardon and watch the nation dances. Suddenly after the creole dances begin, for those "who can't call their nation" (175), as Lebert has explained earlier, Avey finds herself thinking of the Ring Shout and "the flatfooted glide and stamp. . . . the dance that wasn't supposed to be dancing" (248) that she remembered from her visits to Tatem. Avey rises and joins the dancers and eventually starts moving her hips and torso as she had done long ago with Jay in their living room dances. As her body moves, she gathers together the threads of her cultural inheritance, "that myriad of shining, silken, brightly colored threads" (249) that she remembers imagining as a child. Joan Erikson notes that "the word for 'ear' and for 'wisdom' in the Sumerian lan-guage" were the same. For Erikson this connection illustrates an important aspect of the concept of wisdom: "If wisdom is conveyed through sound as well as sight, then singing, rhythmic gesture, and dance are included as its conveyors and amplifiers" (7). In joining the dance Avey pulls the threads of her past back into her own body and achieves cultural integrity.

The next day as Avey returns to Grenada and makes plans to go back to New York, she has made up her mind to sell her house in North White Plains and to rebuild the house in Tatem that her Great-Aunt Cuney had left her. She will invite her grandchildren to visit and become a modern griot, telling them the stories that Great-Aunt Cuney's grandmother had told her, such as the story of the vision of those "pure-born Africans" in "Ibo Landing":

[T]hey seen everything that was to happen . . . slavery time . . . the hard times today. . . . They just turned, my gran' said, all of 'em . . . and walked on back . . . over the river. . . . [T]hey just kept on walking like the water was solid ground. (38–39)

Avey can now accept the African name, Avatara, she inherited from Great-Aunt Cuney's grandmother, and like her ancestor, her "body . . . might be in Tatem but her mind . . . was long gone with the Ibos" (255). Courser argues that Avey's separation of mind and body here is "a healthy condition: she is *in* America but not entirely *of* it, engaged in American life but mindful of a valuable African legacy" (111). The story of Ibo Landing and of her stay in Carriacou will be Avey's version of "The Beg Pardon," an affirmation of an ongoing cultural tradition that accepts the suffering and strength of past ancestors and the threads that link past and future generations.

In her decision to renovate her great-aunt's house and connect with her grandchildren, Avey has a plan for her old age that will allow her to pass on the cultural traditions and wisdom she has learned. Busia comments that because of Avey's journey and change "Africa is once more reinvested with worth, the continent is no longer fractured from human history but restored to consciousness with valid meaning. Through the healing of one of Africa's lost daughters, a scattered people are made whole again" (199). It is both this individual and communal healing that the title "praisesong" celebrates. Busia explains that for

Africans, a praisesong is a particular kind of traditional heroic poem. . . . [P]raisesongs . . . are always specifically ceremonial social poems . . . and can be used to celebrate communal triumph. . . . [T]hey can also be sung to mark social transition . . . as a part of rites of passage. (198)

Avey has not just taken a journey; she has undergone a rite of passage, a transition, in which she now becomes a respected elder. Wilentz comments that in *Praisesong for the Widow* "the search for one's heritage—in this case, to remember one's tribe and legend—is seen as a woman's search. In the novel, telling the tales which must be passed on from generation to generation to maintain cultural continuity and wholeness is the function of women" (100). Women, however, can only perform this function when they have made the difficult journey that uncovers cultural identity and produces wisdom.

Tirra Lirra by the River, Jessica Anderson's fourth novel[12] and winner of the prestigious Miles Franklin award (Gilbert 129), reverses the journey that Avey Johnson has taken. Anderson's protagonist, Nora Porteous, left Australia at age thirty-five for England to escape a stifling marriage and lack of job opportunities. Now in her late seventies, Nora has returned to her childhood home in Queensland. Pam Gilbert says that one of the dominant themes in all of Anderson's novels, and one that resonates in many contemporary Australian women writers, is an interest in "'impersonation,' in the various faces that women must wear" (131).[13] The feeling of "impersonation," of wearing masks or false faces, reveals an insecure cultural identity. It is precisely the closeness between the English heritage and white settler culture in Australia that makes it seem like a false mask or face. Helen Tiffin notes that for the "non-indigenous peoples of Canada, Australia and New Zealand, there are no . . . formulated [metaphysical] systems which may be recuperated to challenge the imported or imposed European one" ("Post-Colonialism, Post-Modernism" 173). Furthermore, the imposed culture is often distorted and layered with nostalgia. Forced to return to Australia in her late seventies, Nora must finally come to terms with her various selves and faces. When she and her two women friends lose their London flat because of rising rents, Nora must journey home alone. She must finally give up the joking persona she has used to entertain her friends and find her true self between the masks imposed by her assimilation of Englishness and by Australian white settler culture. Anderson admits to being strongly influenced by English traditions:

> I feel I belong to the English and American traditions. . . . I did read Australian novels, but they didn't supply much for me. They were mostly blokey and outback. They didn't supply much for a girl or a woman. Women were either mates or martyrs in the kitchen, or chopping wood, or killing snakes. (Willbanks 63)

Anderson's identification with the English literary tradition, however, does not prevent her from seeing the falseness with which it is sometimes applied to Australian culture. Her use of Arthurian myth, such as the novel's title from Tennyson's poem "The Lady of Shallot," illustrates the false romanticism, distortion, and nostalgia within Nora's search for Camelot.

Like Avey Johnson, Nora Porteous's life review and recovery of repressed memories are triggered both by her reflection in a mirror and by illness. Nora's reflection, however, is not that of nonrecognition but of a sudden awareness of old age.[14] The novel opens with Nora's entry into the childhood home she has not seen for over thirty years:

> I enter the hall, finding the echoes immediately familiar. . . . Through the long mirror of the big black hall stand I see a shape pass. It is the shape of an old woman who began to call herself old before she really was, partly to get in first and partly out of a fastidiousness about the word "elderly," but who is now really old. She has allowed her shoulders to slump. (2)

Nora's shift into the third person illustrates her alienation from her body and her multiple sense of self. She is exhausted after her journey, and her exhaustion soon turns into pneumonia. She is forced to acknowledge the limitations of her body and feels her age.[15] As she drifts in and out of consciousness, she finally allows herself to face memories long repressed.

The seven recursive sections of the novel that alternate present and past take her back to evaluate the events of her life. Like Avey Johnson's aural memory and physical discomfort, Nora's process begins with fragmentary memories, what Dominique Hecq calls "the involuntary memories which assault [Nora's] . . . well-protected consciousness during sickness and confinement . . . [and reveal] the fear of impending death" (172). Nora still maintains her joking persona when she tells her neighbor, Betty Cust, that the one question she forgot to ask the doctor was whether she was dying. Betty reassures her, but the fear jolts Nora's memory. She assesses her life and examines the journeys she has made first to England and now back to her homeland. Nora needs to find out whether she, like her counterpart in "The Lady of Shallot," made the wrong decision in leaving Queensland initially. Did her journey "crack the mirror" of her life as the mirror was cracked for the Lady of Shallot when she looked out toward Camelot and heard Lancelot singing, "Tirra lirra by the river"? As a child Nora had looked through a "cheap thick [window] glass" whose distortions created an image of Camelot for her: "miniature landscapes, green, wet, romantic, with silver serpentine rivulets, and flashing lakes, and castles moulded out of any old stick or stone" (8–9). Throughout her life Nora has been journeying to find a "Camelot," first to Sydney, then London. Now she must scrape away the layers of myth and try to find the reality of her experiences.

As Nora lies in bed, she begins to see her life in a pattern; it is not a linear pattern, like that of her London friends, but rather a circular globe:

> Liz used to say that she saw her past life as a string of roughly-graded beads, and so did Hilda have a linear conception of hers, thinking of it as a track with detours. But for some years now I have likened mine to a globe suspended in my head, and . . . I have been careful not to let this globe spin to expose the nether side on which my marriage has left its multitude of images. (25)

Nora likes to be in control of the spinning of that globe, and for many years she has repressed the anger and resentment she felt for the controlling husband of her youth, Colin Porteous. Nora realizes that she has been defensive about her past. She has turned distressing events into humorous stories for her housemates. She asks herself as she begins to remember: "Have I given an accurate account of Colin Porteous. . . . Perhaps the real man has been so overscored by laughter that he will never be retrieved" (73). Previously, as Donat Gallagher suggests, Nora has been guilty of "selectivity, suppression and distortion" (102). Finally now in her seventies, faced with illness, Nora begins to let the globe of her past spin to its dark side. She is finally willing to confront her memories and separate myth from personal history.

Like the Lady of Shallot, Nora is a weaver and an artist. As Nora begins to turn the globe of her memory, she wonders whether she squandered her artistic gift, choosing a "Prince Charming" as her mother and sister call Colin Porteous, and later using her embroidery skills for dressmaking to support herself. Betty Cust has gathered three tapestries that Nora had made as a young woman before she left Brisbane. The first is a stylized orange tree made for Betty's mother. The second belongs to the doctor who is treating Nora, Dr. Rainbow, whose mother, Dorothy Irey Rainbow, was a childhood acquaintance of Nora's. It is a realistic portrayal of a "swag of jacaranda leaves with the head and breast of a big magpie" (101). The third is owned by the elderly mother of another of Nora's friends, Olive Partridge, and is an abstract motif of "swirling suns, moons and stars" (128), which Nora thinks is the best of the three. Elaine Barry says that these are all "Australian motifs" (9), but Roslynn Haynes argues that the first and third are too abstract to be identified clearly as Australian and that the third can in fact be linked to a line from "The Lady of Shallot": "Below the starry clusters bright/ Some bearded meteor, trailing light,/ Moves over still Shallot" (317). Nora also compares the last embroidery to the paintings of a French artist. At this point Nora is still judging her work, as well as her life, by European and English standards. Although Betty Cust admires the realistic Australian tree and magpie, Nora thinks that that embroidery is "muddled in execution. I suspect it was something I actually saw, and tried, with mistaken fidelity, to reproduce" (101–2). In rejecting the second piece, Nora denigrates Australian culture and idealizes the Western standard of abstraction.[16]

The two owners of the embroidery make Nora think of her two childhood friends. Olive Partridge, whose mother owns the abstract piece, left Brisbane at age twenty-five, moved to England, and became a novelist. This is the artistic model Nora understands. The realistic Australian scene was won in a raffle by Dorothy Irey Rainbow, who married young and never left Australia. Lying in bed and thinking of the past, Nora begins to question her idealizing of English culture. Nora acknowledges that she made all these embroideries while living at home in Brisbane. She begins to wonder if she would have been truer to her art if she, like Dorothy Rainbow, had stayed at home in Brisbane, devoted to her art like Lady Shallot in her tower.[17] Nora looks at the embroidery of the swirling stars and says to Betty Cust: "I wonder what would have happened if I had never left this place. . . . I have never done anything of this quality since" (128).

As the seven sections of reminiscences that alternate with scenes of her house in Brisbane progress and Nora lets her globe of memory spin, she comes to realize that her absence from Australia has distorted its spaces just as the cheap window glass distorted her view as a child. She did escape to Sydney, which in her mind "had stood proxy for Camelot" (18), but Sydney was no Camelot. Her husband Colin is rigid and contemptuous of her, and his mother, with whom they live, is unbearable and berates Nora for being barren. Nora's only friends are a dressmaker who teaches her to make clothing and a gentle homosexual artist named Lewie Johns, who becomes her confidant. These years coincide with the depression, and Nora is forced to steal coins from her husband's trouser pocket since he refuses her an allowance. Lewie eventually vanishes as creditors begin to chase him. When Colin finds another woman and initiates a divorce, Nora is thrilled and uses her divorce settlement to go to London in search of another Camelot. She even has a shipboard romance, only to arrive in London pregnant. With the help of her seemingly liberated but still judgmental friend Olive Partridge, Nora finds an abortionist, but the experience is so traumatic that Nora decides not to have any more sexual relationships. Helen Tiffin argues that the

> internalization of these dreams/ideals, i.e., the Anglo-written world of patriarchy and imperialism, have emotionally and imaginatively severed Nora from her childhood place in the Australian city of Brisbane, and from her own body. This dissociation from her body through the colonial idealization of . . . her quest for "romance" in the "motherland" culminate[s] ironically in the abortion. (221)

Nora's decision to turn away from sexuality is at this point her only way to protect herself from the Lancelots and Prince Charmings who have imposed their patriarchal control over her. Nora manages to support herself in London by dressmaking, waiting out the years of World War II and suffering bouts of pleurisy. After the war she finally books a passage to return home.

Nora is still concerned about her image and the "face" she must wear, so she decides that before she returns to Australia, she will have a facelift. Still alienated from her body, Nora thinks she is losing her beauty in her midforties and does not want to go home without the proper mask: "Overnight, it seemed to me, the homage of glances was withdrawn, and I became an invisible woman. The comeliness of my face had depended on moulding rather than sculpture" (104). Nora arranges for both a facelift and her passage home. Kathleen Woodward notes that cosmetic surgery is rooted in the false illusion that one can reclaim one's lost youth. "What is further lost in the process of surgery . . . are the traces of one's history. Thus cosmetic surgery serves to silence subjectivity. It is a form of self-repression" (*Aging and Its Discontents* 163). It illustrates Nora's continuing separation from her self and her body. Even worse for Nora, the facelift goes wrong. She does not just have a false face without history but a distorted one. Nora, as an artist herself, understands how this can happen: "Even the most skilled and conscientious craftsman—like him [the surgeon], like me—is fallible, and has, every now and again, a moment of irretrievable error. I knew that well" (107). Unwilling to admit a mistake, the doctor casually remarks that the "benefit" of a facelift "lasts for about five years" (107). Nora thinks to herself that "the operation had been my last throw of the dice" (107), and she returns to her flat and attempts suicide. The dice are thrown again for her, however, when some workmen, who have come by to fix the water pipes, take her to the hospital. Nora lives but loses her desire to return to Sydney.

When Nora returns from the hospital, she is visited by a new friend, Hilda, who suggests that Nora take a job making theatrical costumes. Nora decides to try it. "Before a week was out it was clear that I had fallen among people who would accept me for what I was, whatever I was, and in that same week the work itself began to engross me. . . . I found it an illumination and a synthesis" (110). Not only is Nora accepted regardless of her "face," but she has a new relationship to the English culture she had idealized. It is only costumes and masks. It has always been costumes and masks, however artistic or romantic. Furthermore, she now controls the design.

Nora also realizes that she will always be an outsider in England. At best she can become what one of her friends calls "a pommiefied Aussie" (84). A "whinging pommy" was Australian slang for a weak English immigrant, not a match for the tougher Australians.[18] When Nora first went into the dressmaking business for herself after World War II, Nora confided to a homosexual friend who reminded her of Lewie: "'I have come a long roundabout way . . . to find out who I am'" (87). Her friend, David, responds: "'Some people are homeless wherever they live . . . You are, and so am I'" (87). At first Nora can't understand and argues, "'But you are an Englishman in your own country.'" David says again, "'I am homeless on this earth. . . And so are you. Once you admit it, you know, you'll find it has advantages'" (87). Slowly, Nora begins to understand the effects of patriarchal and imperial English culture that has alienated her from her own body and also outlaws homosexuals like Lewie and David. Finally Nora begins to reframe that cultural inheritance as a theatrical costume that she can put on and take off. She can use it, but it is not her identity. Art and myth, Camelot itself, are only part of a cultural tradition that she can redesign. They are masks that she can take off and put on. Unlike cosmetic surgery, Woodward explains, "masking can sometimes both display symptoms *and* work as a cure"(*Aging and Its Discontents* 163). One can still hide behind a mask and use it for protection, but there is always the awareness that the mask can be removed and that it is only a mask.

Although Nora has now framed English culture as theater, as costume, she still remains in England another eighteen years. The mask provides some comfort even if it is recognized as an illusion. Back home in Australia, Nora describes this comfort as nostalgia: "I grew to love those big cluttered low-ceilinged rooms, and the memory of winter afternoons there—the light, the smell, the visitors and the voices—can still fill me with nostalgia" (112). Nora recognizes her feelings for what they are, a nostalgia for an illusory beam of sunlight, a costume, a myth, a story. When her hands develop arthritis, Nora lives in retirement with Hilda and another female friend in a flat in an old Victorian house. They tell stories of their pasts, design masks, to entertain each other. This quiet period, however, does not last. When Fred, the owner of the house, becomes paranoid and is hospitalized, his sister increases the rent, and the three women must leave. Nora learns that Grace, her older sister, has died and has left their childhood home in Brisbane to Nora to live in for the duration of her life. Reluctantly, driven by economic necessity, Nora returns to Australia to face that part of her past.

Now Nora must give up her English mask and come to terms with her image of Australia. Was it, once all her distortions of memory are removed and her globe is allowed to spin, the real Camelot? It might still seem as if she would have been better off to stay in Brisbane, waiting forever in her tower and never journeying down the river to the sea. Then finally Nora learns the story of her friend Dorothy Irey Rainbow who did stay at home and married a banker after World War I. Dorothy Irey was six years older than Nora, and Nora often admired her from afar. She "was said to have Polynesian blood. . . . The effect she gave, of darkness, freshness, and white lace, left me incredulous. She was rare and beautiful" (13–14). The doctor who has been attending Nora is Dorothy Rainbow's youngest son, but he is very taciturn whenever Nora mentions his mother. Finally, Betty Cust tells Nora that Dorothy Rainbow murdered her husband and all her children with an axe, except for the youngest, who managed to hide. Then she committed suicide. As Nora thinks about Dorothy's grisly acts and death, she recognizes the stresses that the colonial culture of early-twentieth-century Australia placed on women. The mirror did crack "from side to side" for Dorothy Rainbow, and nobody anticipated it. Everyone thought she had been completely assimilated into white settler culture, but she had not. Tiffin comments that

> Dorothy Rainbow is the figure who erupts into the text, threatening the symmetry of the Australia/Britain, settler-invader colony/imperial

power relations that the rest of the text explores. . . . [Her] Polynesian blood . . . invokes the brutal history of "blackbirding," the kidnapping and enslavement during the nineteenth and early twentieth century of Pacific Island peoples to provide labour for Queensland sugar plantations. . . .

But although Dorothy Rainbow is thus a marker of radical "difference" in *Tirra Lirra by the River*, she is also persistently *associated* with Nora. ("The Body in the Library" 222)

Nora, in her identification with Dorothy, realizes that her journey was necessary. The white settler culture could have destroyed her, too. Nora had experienced the gender oppression. Now she realizes that although she could create beautiful tapestries in Australia, difference and rare exotic beauty were threatened there. Although journeys are always dangerous, Brisbane, with its narrow conception of identity, was no safe haven. As Nora's globe of memory goes into "free spin, with no obscure side" (140), Nora can face the dark side of both her personal experience and Australian white settler culture.

The mirror image returns as Nora begins to get well and sees her reflection as an old woman. She now does not idealize either English traditions or female beauty, but she does not regret her years in exile. As she looks into the mirror, Nora acknowledges and accepts her wrinkled face and looks down at her arthritic hands without resentment. In old age Nora for the first time accepts her body.[19] At the end of *Writing a Woman's Life* Carolyn Heilbrun muses that "the old woman must be glimpsed through all her disguises which seem to preclude her right to be called woman. She may well for the first time be woman herself" (131).

Nora still has one more memory to recover, however. The Lancelot images of "the step of a horse, the nod of a plume" (141) still keep coming back to her, and they are accompanied by grief. Finally Nora recognizes them as images from the funeral cortege of her father who died when she was six. Woodward notes that there is a strong fear and denial of death built into Western culture. She quotes Ernest Becker's argument "that a culture is built primarily, not on the repression of sexuality, as Freud believes, but on the repression of death, whose symbol is the human body" (Woodward, *Aging and Its Discontents* 70). Having accepted her own aging body, Nora now can face death and loss. Tiffin says that the "plumes of Lancelot are remembered as those on the curbed horses at her father's funeral, and the ideal male promise, and the colonial's ideal world of England, the motherland, are associatively remembered now as death" ("The Body in the Library" 221). This memory, Tiffin argues, leads "to reconciliation, not just with the lost body of her father and her own, but with the Australian landscape and culture" (221). For many years, Nora has buried her loss in nostalgia, which Roberta Rubenstein describes as "the imagination's attempt to override, neutralize, or cancel loss" ("Fixing the Past" 33). Now finally, facing loss directly, Nora can grieve[20] for her father, for the distortions caused by false adherence to English culture, and for the damages that her homeland has done to women like Dorothy Rainbow. In accepting the pain of loss and oppression, Nora can also accept her homeland and her identity as both an Australian and an artist. Nora has finally removed the mask of English myths and romances and is content to search for integrity in a transformed Australian identity.

Retrieving and coming to understand cultural identity, as both novels show, can be a lonely and painful process. Only the brave can construct an ongoing cultural identity because it involves an assessment of personal history as well as a recovery and assessment of communal history. Avey Johnson must face her complicity in idealizing materialism and in the loss of both memories and joy in her marriage. Nora must recognize her own willingness to embrace distortion, her distancing herself from her body and relationships, and her inability to see beyond her own oppressions to those of others like Dorothy Rainbow. With this honest assessment of history, however, and the purging or grieving that the assessment brings about can come new transformation—an understanding, a ripening into wisdom and a new ongoing cultural identity rooted in, but not controlled by, history.

Chapter 6

Facing Death:
The Search for a Legacy in Joan
Riley's *Waiting in the Twilight*
and Doris Lessing's *The Diary*
of a Good Neighbour

From the vantage point of age ninety-three, Joan Erikson has suggested that there is a ninth stage of life that needs to be added to the eight stages that she had often worked on with her husband, Erik Erikson. She says that although

> at age eighty we began to acknowledge our elderly status, I believe
> we never faced its challenges realistically until we were close to ninety.
> Our lives had not been beset with unresolvable difficulties. At ninety
> we woke up in foreign territory.[1] . . . At ninety the vistas changed; the
> view ahead became limited and unclear. Death's door, which we al-
> ways knew was expectable but had taken in stride, now seemed just
> down the block. (4)

Two novels that portray both the bodily limitations and emotional yearnings of this last stage of life are Joan Riley's *Waiting in the Twilight* (1987) about a disabled Jamaican immigrant, Adella Johnson, who has lived much of her adult life in England and is now dying from complications of an earlier stroke, and Doris Lessing's *The Diary of a Good Neighbour* (1983), the story of a ninety-two-year-old "crone," Maudie Fowler, who is dying of stomach cancer. Both novels use social realism and vivid physical description to remove both the "foreignness" and the "invisibility"[2] associated with old age.

In her writings about a ninth stage of life, Joan Erikson points out that in extreme old age and in severe illness all the achievements a person may have accumulated over a life course can begin to be lost. Even basic achievements, such as control over elimination, are no longer taken for granted. Autonomy is now threatened: "When you were young, all the elders were stronger and more powerful; now the powerful are younger than you" (*The Life Cycle Completed* 108). The urgency of industry and the drive for competence are gone. Identities shift; loved ones die. Generativity is no longer expected. One may no longer even have the energy for a life review, characteristic of the search for integrity in the eighth stage of life:

> Loss of capacities and disintegration may demand almost all of one's attention. One's focus may become thoroughly circumscribed by concerns of daily functioning so that it is enough just to get through a day intact, however satisfied or dissatisfied one feels about one's previous life history. (113)

E. Ann Kaplan adds additional emotional losses to Erikson's description to define aging as trauma: "It is especially the increasing series of losses—of bodily function and appearance, of mental agility, of ideologies and values one grew up with, of friends and family—that may be traumatic for everyone in western culture. . . . [There is also loss] of a community of shared beliefs and world views" (173). These physical and emotional losses and limitations are exacerbated by cultural ones. Joan Erikson quotes her husband's comment that Western civilization lacks "'a culturally viable ideal of old age'" and adds herself that "elders are seen no longer as bearers of wisdom but as embodiments of shame" (*The Life Cycle Completed* 114).

In spite of these limitations and losses, Joan Erikson suggests that some can achieve a transcendence in old age that she separates from a purely religious experience by calling it a "transcen*dance*," a coinage that echoes her own career as a dancer. She explains:

> [T]ranscen*dance* . . . speaks to soul and body and challenges it to rise above the dystonic, clinging aspects of our worldly existence that burden and distract us from true growth and aspiration. . . . Transcen*dance* may be a regaining of lost skills, including play, activity, joy, and song, and above all, a major leap above and beyond the fear of death. (127)

Joan Erikson's optimism is shared by psychologist David Gutmann, who argues:

> The phasing out of sexual and aggressive instincts in the later years [allows] . . . the aged person . . . [to be] set free to search for those objects that finally will be sustaining and security giving. The aged have learned that all things of seeming substance pass and fade: their parents and the leaders of their youth are gone, peers are dying, the social mores change, and their bodies fail them. . . . Since substance has failed, they seek the sustaining object in the insubstantial abstractions that cannot be lost. (Gutman 492)

As Joan Erikson herself acknowledges, however, this search for "transcendence" is dependent in Western society upon having enough money for basic care: "[Good] homes for the elderly are planned to serve their needs in every way . . . except that the cost is high, much too high for most" (*The Life Cycle Completed* 117). For those who cannot reach "transcendence," Woodward suggests that there is another mitigating factor seen in Erik Erikson's approach to aging and death. Woodward says that in facing the disintegration of the aging body Erikson did not turn "the mirror to the wall" in despair. Rather, he "consistently looked into a mirror populated by several generations. He is not *shocked* by aging because he has been anticipating it and expecting it, not repressing it. . . . This would be to emphasize genealogical continuities" (*Aging and Its Discontents* 71). Although Woodward is speaking primarily of Erikson's ability to look back in time at previous generations and their aging process, the term "genealogical continuity" can also express the legacy that is left for following generations, examples of courage and self-respect in the facing of aging and death.

In Joan Riley's and Doris Lessing's novels about disability, aging, and facing death, there is less opportunity for "transcendence" because their novels are about lower-class women in England who are coping not only with illness and age but also with poverty. Both Riley's character, Adella Johnson, and Lessing's character, Maudie Fowler, are struggling for a much more basic value, respect. The memories that they retrieve are not so much part of the life review process as an attempt to create a sense of respect for themselves. Adella, in reaching out to one of her daughters, and Maudie, in making a new friend, Jane Somers, are both attempting to create a legacy to leave behind them. They want someone to tell the stories of their lives. In the dedication to *Waiting in the Twilight*, Riley says that she is writing the novel not only to record what life was like for West Indian women in Britain but also to show "the great legacy and strength" that the descendants of these women inherit. What both Adella Johnson and Maudie Fowler want to achieve, even in the midst of poverty and illness, is a story, a legacy, that will provide some measure of "genealogical continuity."

Specifically, both characters are searching for a legacy of self-respect to hand down to a child or a surrogate child. In Maudie Fowler's case, the memories serve as an opportunity for reciprocity. If she can entertain Jane Somers by the stories of her youth, then Jane will continue to visit her, and Maudie can achieve both self-respect and friendship, something she has rarely had before. This search for a legacy to leave behind them in the face of death differs from the search for integrity that Avey Johnson and Nora Porteous pursue in Chapter 5. Avey and Nora, who recover from illness, can reconstruct a past and teach it to succeeding generations. In contrast, in these novels of advanced old age and frailty, all that can be left behind are bits and pieces of stories that sustain relationship and provide respect. These novels, like the middle-class novels of "dependency and death" studied by Barbara Waxman, May Sarton's *As We Are Now* and Margaret Laurence's *The Stone Angel*, "do not depict old age as a mellowing period, but as a turbulent one, filled with pathos" (Waxman 139). Riley's Adella Johnson experiences both despair at her failing health and many losses and pride in her younger daughters. Lessing's Maudie Fowler expresses rage at her disintegrating body but joy in her newfound friendship with Jane Somers. Both women struggle against death. They do not transcend it, but they leave a legacy behind them of their courage in facing the trials of their personal lives and of their deaths.

Joan Erikson's ninth stage of life is not restricted only to those in their nineties. Kathleen Woodward notes that aging, in "addition to being a state of mind, . . . is a biological phenomenon and a social construction. . . . [S]ocial age . . . is mediated by chronological age (how many years old we are) and biological age (the state of health of the body)" (*Aging and Its Discontents* 149).[3] A lack of health could put one in the ninth stage of life at any chronological age. E. Ann Kaplan adds that "the specific contexts within which one ages clearly make a huge difference outside of the possibly general existential human predicament: I have in mind not only gender and race, but also one's culture, nationality, religion and even geography" (172). Riley's Adella Johnson is only fifty-eight years old but is crippled from a stroke she had at thirty-four. She works two shifts as a cleaning woman for the city and hopes "the new people at the town hall really meant to retire everyone over fifty-eight" (*Waiting in the Twilight* 4). Although Adella's grandmother, Granny Dee, lived to be ninety-five in Jamaica, Adella herself at fifty-eight can barely cope with the demands of her job, the cold English winters, and the pain in her legs and back. As her health worsens throughout the novel, Adella becomes more and more dependent on her daughters and confined to her small "council flat." Although chronologically middle-aged, Adella fits the ninth stage of life biologically.

Joan Riley is a medical social worker as well as a novelist, and her four novels[4] portray the problems of Caribbean immigrants and working-class Jamaicans with vivid social realism. As Isabel Suárez says, "Riley's exhaustive accounts of black experience in Britain are careful not to romanticise its reality in any way" (305). Riley focuses on the problems of racism in Britain and the difficulties of immigrant life in all her novels, but in *Waiting in the Twilight* she also explicitly writes about age. She says in an interview with Donna Perry: "[W]hen I was writing *Waiting in the Twilight* . . . I went out and talked to lots and lots of older people and absolutely listened to them for the first time with a view to hearing how their minds worked— the way it skips and the way it flows and convolutes" ("Interview" 283). Riley not only captures the immigrants' Jamaican patois in her characters' speech but also the rhythms of age in Adella's thoughts. Before getting into Adella's mind, however, Riley uses vivid realistic details to describe the physical exhaustion and debilitating illness of Adella's body.[5] The novel opens with a scene of Adella at her cleaning job. She can barely cope with the physical movement her job demands:

> She was mopping again, carefully pushing the bucket along with her foot. The scraping protest it made no longer gave her the crippling ache behind her eyes that she had lived with in her first few years of cleaning. It was a slow process, good arm gripping the mop, crippled one locked round it in a steadying vice. She moved the mop head slowly across the floor. . . . Feet braced against her heavy bulk as she swung it wide before bringing it laboriously to the murky water of the bucket. (2)

Walking home is equally laborious as she drags her bad leg behind her and struggles against the icy January wind that blows through her "thin canvas coat" and the wet that seeps into her split plastic shoes. "Her crippled hand swung limp at her side, fingers clamped like a vice around her purse" since those fingers felt no pain and thus offered more protection against "bag snatchers" (5).

Adella Johnson needs all her energy to get through her workday and get home, but when she finally reaches her favorite chair and television, her thoughts provide little comfort. In addition to physical exhaustion and pain, Adella's primary burden is coping with shame. She feels a debilitating sense of shame in several areas of her life. The first is her physical body. Psychoanalyst Gregory Rochlin says, "'No experience brings out the effect in self-esteem more immediately than when it is associated with the body. The integrity of one's shape and bodily function holds the deepest and perhaps longest-standing investment in respect to self-esteem'" (Woodward, *Aging and Its Discontents* 69–70). Adella feels a tremendous sense of loss when she realizes that she no longer has the ability to sew. She had been proud of her skill at embroidery and earned good money when she first came to England. After her stroke, however, Adella is fired from her sewing job. She is even rejected for sewing machine work at a factory. "'What do you think this is?'" the foreman at the factory asks her when she goes in for an interview, "'Some kind of charity for cripples? Labour shortage ain't that bad yet'" (85). Finally Adella is forced to take a job as a "cleaner." Riley says to Donna Perry: "If you really want to talk about people suffering you can't get a more common denominator than a cleaner. And it's not only black people. Cleaner is a job you start with whenever you migrate. . . . It's a question of class" ("Interview" 272).

Adella's shame in her disabled physical body is not only caused by society's rejection of her abilities and loss of class status but also by her husband's reaction. Stanton tells her, as he plans to run off with her cousin Gladys, who came over from Jamaica to help Adella with the children: "'Fram yu have de stroke, yu change, Adella. A doan recognise yu de way yu get bitta'" (89). Walking out the door, he adds, "'Yu should look pan yuself. . . . Yu get ole and ugly. Yu let yuself go so bad a doan tink any man gwine waan look pan yu much less waan move wid yu'" (92). Adella is made to feel that she caused her own illness and disability by "letting herself go," and her body is brutally rejected by her husband, who says that no man will look upon her anymore.[6] Ironically, in spite of his cruel treatment, Adella feels a social sense of shame for losing her husband. Riley explains: "When you are a poor Jamaican there's nothing worse than to lose your man. You're good for nothing. You have no home training. You're worthless—all of the things you can think of" ("Interview" 272). Adella knows her Caribbean friends in London and all the people at the open market where she shops, as well as her relatives back home, will blame her for Stanton's leaving. She internalizes Stanton's rejection of her, thinking to herself: "That wasn't Stanton's fault though. He was still young and sharp looking; you couldn't expect him to let a crippled woman tie him down" (49).

The reason why Adella makes excuses for Stanton in spite of his cruelty and desertion is not mere nostalgia for a few good years. Stanton was the only man who treated her with respect, even if it was only briefly. Adella hangs on to her memory of him and her hopes that he may some day return not to fool herself but to remind herself that she has been loved by a man and has been a respectable married woman. All Adella's other relationships with men have caused her only shame. Her shame is so intense that she feels she can never return to Jamaica. Adella's daughters suggest that perhaps she can retire and go back to live with her sister in Kingston, but Adella won't even tell them that she feels she can never go back to Jamaica. Adella was originally sent from her village of Beaumont to Kingston to live with her cousin because Granny Dee knew that the widowed pastor of her village had an eye for the young girls,[7] but when Adella gets to Kingston, she is seduced by a Beresford, a policeman who turns out to be married. When she becomes pregnant, her cousin, who is a devout Seventh Day Adventist, throws her out. Adella is forced to live as a concubine during which time she bears two sons for Beresford. "If you get pregnant in Jamaica," Riley explains, "you are finished. You are fair game. Going to Jamaica is like going back into the nineteenth century" ("Interview" 278). Adella finally gets up the courage to leave Beresford, and it is then that she meets Stanton. Stanton loves her in spite of her illegitimate children, and when she gets pregnant by him, he marries her and they have several happy years. Then Stanton decides to go to England.

It is the combination of their individual infidelities, the alien culture and difficulties of immigrant life, and her physical illness that finally undoes Adella and Stanton's marriage. When Stanton finally sends for Adella, she has a shipboard affair that results in another daughter. Stanton accepts that daughter but berates Adella for only giving him daughters and not sons. He has always had other women, but until her stroke, he always returns to her. After her stroke, Stanton beats her and eventually takes off with her cousin, leaving Adella with five children to raise. Although Adella finally gets a job as a cleaner, she is forced to supplement her income sometimes by going with other men. Adella knows that she has been "read out in church" back in her village of Beaumont and condemned for these sexual sins, so she can never go back. She yearns for the warmth of the Jamaica sun and the love of her now-long-dead grandmother, but Adella knows that she can never return. Suárez argues that Adella "is a victim of the double standard that allows her husband to change women but condemns her for relationships that she had to maintain in order to feed her children. She alone has struggled to bring them up, but she still perceives herself as a failure" (298).

Adella suffers from the image of her disabled body and her sense of social and sexual sin, but she at least expected to receive some respect in old age. She thinks of Granny Dee and an older relative, Mada Beck:

> Mada Beck had been so wise, and Adella wondered if she had looked ahead and seen approaching death. The thought brought heaviness inside her. Would she see approaching death, would she recognise it? Die with dignity like Mada Beck? "All dat respeck," she sighed, in remembrance and regret. Everyone had looked up to that woman, loved her for her age. But then she had died in her own place and among her people. (8)

England is very different. In England not only is there no respect for age, but racism and class prejudice further denigrate poor black women. Adella can hardly believe the way the young white women in the office she is cleaning speak to her. As Adella struggles with the mop, one of the office girls turns to her, saying, "I hope you emptied the ashtrays this morning. . . . You listening to me, Johnson?" (2–3). Adella bites her tongue and reminds herself: "How different England was. She could remember being a young girl, going to Kingston. Always you had to respect the older heads. . . . Now she was here, had found out too late that it was only in the islands that respect for the old existed" (3). Adella not only suffers physically and psychically from her illness and old age; external forces like geography and culture intensify her misery. This realization, however, helps

Adella to dissolve some of the burden of shame that she has been carrying. She can mentally fight against these external forces and see the cultural sources of ill treatment.

As Adella begins to let go of shame, she lets herself think about the one financial success that she achieved before her stroke. Although she and Stanton are forced to look only at houses in black areas, Adella is finally able to buy a large, run-down house. As she tells her husband: "'Dis house is my house, Stanton. . . . Is me save de money and is me get loan fram de bank. Yu neva waan fe know nuting bout it and yu neva help wid it at all'" (63). When her husband leaves her, Adella still manages to raise her five children by working double shifts as a cleaner and by renting out rooms in her house. Eventually, however, her local council condemns the house; the money she gets in compensation barely pays off the mortgage. Adella is left in old age renting rooms. Carole Boyce Davies's comment about Riley's first novel, *Unbelonging*, is also applicable here: "Rooms . . . become metonymic references for reduced space . . . alienation and outsideness" (*Black Women, Writing and Identity* 102). Once again Adella is reminded that in spite of all her achievements she doesn't really "belong." She thinks ironically about the recruiting slogans that covered the Caribbean after World War II: "They had promised her a land where the streets were paved with gold; the Motherland where you could get everything" (2). She had joined her husband along with other Caribbean immigrants in response to these slogans, but all she ever achieved was her house. Then the council took that away: "They had pulled the heart out of her when they took her house" (13). Suárez says that all Riley's characters suffer from an "absence of place, of belonging, the absence of an authentic motherland" (299). Because of race and class prejudice, England has never been a motherland for Adella, but neither was Jamaica where she was rejected because of religious prejudice and demands for "respectability."

As Adella sits in her chair in her rented rooms, she does not foresee death, but she does recognize the "old-age signs. The need to seek out the past, look deep into the years she had lived. The present had too many aches and pains. Too many worries" (43). The memories that come to Adella's mind are stories of loss. All her life she has yearned for respect. She was denied it as an unwed mother in Jamaica; she is denied it as an old, heavy-set, disabled black woman working as a cleaner in England. She is denied it in her struggles with dismissive doctors and national health insurance procedures. She sums up her life: "All her young life spent struggling to raise her children, all her old without respect" (2). In addition to being a way of coping with shame, her memories are a process of mourning. In *Aging and Its Discontents* Woodward explains the function of mourning in the theories of French psychoanalyst Elliot Jacques:

> [R]eparation in terms of our anticipated loss of our own lives is possible. . . . [It] is accomplished, paradoxically, by mourning. . . . "Mourning for the dead self can begin, alongside with the mourning and reestablishment of the lost objects and the lost childhood and youth." (185)

Adella mourns in particular for her grandmother, Granny Dee, the only one who offered her unconditional love and acceptance. She mourns for the few good years she had with Stanton, her husband. She mourns for the house she had been so proud of. This mourning for lost objects of love, while she is sitting in the twilight, creates for Adella the self-respect that she cannot get from the society around her. When Adella suffers a second stroke, her daughters rush her to a hospital, but she dies in the hospital corridor waiting for a bed. Before she dies, she has a vision of Stanton returning to be with her. That image then blends with the faces of loved ones long gone, Granny Dee, Mada Beck, and others who seem to be welcoming her with love and respect. "'All dat respeck,'" Adella murmurs to herself as she closes her eyes for the last time (165). Adella's memories represent for her both the mourning for the many losses and hardships of her life and the respect that she has so yearned for throughout those hardships.

Riley comments on the representative nature of Adella's experience reflected in the title: Adella "dies waiting for a bed in King's College Hospital. . . . [F]or so many of these women, their whole life is waiting . . . waiting to do the cooking, shift cleaning, waiting to retire, waiting for the husband to come home, always in the twilight because they have to save electricity. But also in the twilight because they can't really live" ("Interview" 272). Adella has not "really lived" except in the mourning process of her memories and in the attention and achievement of two of her daughters, who go to the university and get good jobs. Riley says in an introductory note that she has written this novel to "celebrate the courage of one woman and a whole generation of women, who took ship and sailed into the unknown [stepping into a society of alien values] to build a better future for their children" (n.p.). Although Adella's own story, and the story of many of the black Caribbean immigrants of her generation, is bleak, there is the hint of genealogical continuity and the legacy of a better life for at least some of her children.

The Diary of a Good Neighbour, which was published under the name of Jane Somers in 1983, is the first novel in Doris Lessing's *The Diaries of Jane Somers*. It approaches old age and dying as vividly as Joan Riley's novel but more obliquely. Lessing's novel is doubly mediated. Maudie Fowler's story is narrated by Jane Somers, a middle-class, middle-aged woman who learns to "see" the poverty-stricken old women of London who before had been invisible[8] to her. The novel was also published pseudononymously. Lessing says in her preface that she wanted to be rid of "labels" and "be reviewed on merit" to show up some of the politics of publishing (vii) and that she wanted to take a break from the persona of Doris Lessing and the science fiction novels, *Canopus in Argos: Archives*, that she was writing in the 1980s: "Jane Somers knew nothing about a kind of dryness, like a conscience, that monitors Doris Lessing whatever she writes and in whatever style" (viii). Claire Sprague argues perceptively that there are other motivations at work:

> [Lessing's] altruism is suspect. Artistic deception is never that simple. The Jane Somers caper involved more profound personal and artistic needs. Through Jane/Janna Somers Lessing confronts more directly than she could in earlier novels or in the Canopus novels her own guilt [at rejecting her mother] and her own fears about aging and dying. (111)

With the protection of a pseudonym and a middle-aged narrator, Lessing is able to portray in vivid detail the physical decay of the body and the deprivations that accompany the combination of old age and poverty.

Both Sprague and Carey Kaplan see *The Diaries of Jane Somers* as intricately related to *Canopus in Argos: Archives*, especially the novel immediately preceding *The Diaries of Jane Somers*, *The Making of the Representative for Planet 8* (1982). That novel chronicles the death of planet 8; a few of its inhabitants leave their bodies to merge into a single consciousness, thereby becoming the "representative." Sprague says that "*The Making of the Representative*, fabular and haunting as *Jane Somers* is not, can nonetheless be described as a dress rehearsal for the later novel. In *Making* Lessing confronts species annihilation as a form of transcendence" (111). Carey Kaplan suggests that in her science fiction series Lessing "may very well be an ageist [i.e., prejudiced in favor of the aged]. That is, the Canopeans have all the virtues associated with age: experience, wisdom, aloofness from emotional hysteria, long-sightedness, resignation to cosmic rhythms" (155). Kaplan links this focus on age in the Canopean series to the Jane Somers novels: "Many readers wondered where Lessing's lifelong commitment to realism went when she created Canopus. Jane Somers may provide an answer: she is an underground *doppelgänger* of Doris Lessing. . . . . [B]oth series deal with decay, dissolution, and aging" (156).

If *The Making of the Representative for Planet 8* is about cerebral resignation and transcendence of the body, *The Diary of a Good Neighbour* discusses the other side of old age, the side of the body and raging emotions associated with dying and death. In an "Afterward" attached to *The Making of the Representative for Planet 8*, in which Lessing discusses the influence of Robert Falcon Scott's exploration and death in Antarctica on the theme of ice and resigned desperation in her novel, she adds:

> Or perhaps something else was going on. I finished writing it the day after the death of someone I had known a long time; though it did not occur to me to make connection until then. It took her a long cold time to die, and she was hungry too, for she was refusing to eat and drink, so as to hurry things along. She was ninety-two, and it seemed to her sensible. ("Afterward" 144)

In her next novel, Lessing describes the death of a ninety-two-year-old woman, Maudie Fowler. There is nothing sensible or resigned to death in Maudie Fowler, but she has much to teach her new middle-aged friend, Jane Somers.

In the preface to *The Diaries of Jane Somers* Lessing says that one "influence that went to make Jane Somers was reflections about what my mother would be like if she lived now: that practical, efficient, energetic woman, by temperament conservative, a little sentimental, and only with difficulty . . . able to understand weakness and failure" (viii). In *Doris Lessing: The Poetics of Change* Gayle Greene comments that the pseudonym allows "Lessing to deal with matters she could not confront as Doris Lessing, still cathected matters related to the mother" (190). Greene continues: "This new interest in and empathy for the aged has to do with the fact that Lessing herself is aging, but it also has to do with her reevaluation of her mother" (193). Jane, or Janna as she calls herself in *The Diary of a Good Neighbour*, thus functions on two levels. On the one hand, her personality type is like that of Lessing's mother, and Lessing has the opportunity, as she never did in life, to teach her, to remold her and make her more sympathetic. On another level, Jane may represent Lessing herself, someone who rejected her own mother[9] and, now protected by a pseudonym, can reach out to a surrogate figure to expiate the guilt of ignoring a mother figure who was too dangerous to engage in real life. As Sprague argues, the "specific private failures that haunt Janna may well have haunted Lessing" (116). The novel progresses on both levels. On the one hand, it is a portrayal of the emotions and body of a dying ninety-two-year-old woman; on the other, it is the story of a middle-aged woman learning about age and learning to foresee, as Woodward argues Erik Erikson did (*Aging and Its Discontents* 71), what aging and dying will be like.

Jane Somers is portrayed initially as a rather limited person. She has to learn to overcome barriers of class and age before she can befriend Maudie Fowler. In a radio talk Lessing comments that "Jane Somers is very English. I mean, she is *very, very* English. She has hardly been outside England" ("Doris Lessing Talks About Jane Somers" 5). Jane Somers is particularly English and very like Lessing's mother[10] in her class consciousness. Lessing notes in the second volume of her autobiography how shocked she was by the English class system:

> And then there was this business of Britain's class system. It shocked me—as it does all colonials. Britain is two nations, all right . . . though it is a bit better now—not much. When I first arrived, my Rhodesian accent enabled me to talk to the natives—that is, the working class— for I was seen as someone outside their taboos, but this became impossible as soon as I began talking middle-class standard English: this was not a choice; I cannot help absorbing accents wherever I am. A curtain came down—slam. (*Walking in the Shade* 2:59–60)

When Jane runs into a social worker at Maudie's home early in their acquaintance, the social worker asks if she is Maudie's "Good Neighbour," a paid helper who visits the elderly and helps them with their needs. "'No,'" Jane replies, "'I am not a Good Neighbour, I am

Mrs. Fowler's friend.'" It is only then that she realizes the class implications of what she has said: "This was quite outrageous, from about ten different viewpoints, but most of all because I was not saying it in inverted commas, and it was only then that I thought how one did not have *friends* with the working classes. I could be many things to Mrs Fowler . . . but not a friend" (38).

Jane does not intend to become Maudie's friend; she merely runs into her one day in a chemist's shop, not long after her husband and her mother have died from cancer. Jane managed to remain emotionally aloof during both these deaths; her sister and coworkers tell her she is reacting out of guilt when she befriends Maudie, but there are a number of complex motivations. Their first encounter is actually initiated by Maudie. Jane Somers relates:

> I saw an old witch. . . . A tiny bent-over woman, with a nose nearly meeting her chin, in black heavy dusty clothes, and something not far off a bonnet. She saw me looking at her and thrust at me a prescription and said, "What is this? You get it for me." (12)

Jane slowly walks out of the shop with Maudie, out of curiosity more than anything at this point, and realizes

> how I rushed along the pavements every day and had never seen Mrs. Fowler, but she lived near me,[11] and suddenly I looked up and down the streets and saw—old women. Old men too, but mostly old women. . . . I had not seen them. That was because I was afraid of being like them. I was afraid, walking along there beside her. It was the smell of her, a sweet, sour, dusty sort of smell. I saw the grime on her thin old neck, and on her hands. (13)

Suddenly, gripped by her own fear of age, Jane Somers recognizes her complicity in the invisibility of old age. She "sees" old women for the first time.

In befriending Maudie, Jane Somers also learns for the first time what poverty is. She learns physically from the smells and difficulties of Maudie's filthy living space what it is like to be old and working class. In the midst of affluence, not far from Jane Somers's fashionable flat, Maudie lives in a rent-controlled basement room, with a coal fireplace, cold water, and an outdoor privy. Maudie can barely manage to walk down the street to the Indian grocer to buy a few groceries for herself and her cat. When Jane goes to the store for

Maudie, Mr. Patel, the grocer, says to her: "'When I was in Kenya, before we had to leave, I thought everyone in this country was rich'" (106). Now as an immigrant he knows better and even admits how Western attitudes toward aging have changed his own culture: "'Once, with us, we would not let one of our old people come to such a life. But now—things are changing with us'" (107). Now both Mr. Patel and Jane Somers are appalled at the poverty of the old in the middle of a wealthy capitalistic society.

Another lesson that Jane Somers learns is a new attitude toward the physical body. Jane is a women's magazine editor and has complete control of her body and her fashion. Her hair and fingernails are perfectly colored; every button, piece of lace, and fine fabric is exactly in place. Now through Maudie, Jane faces the disintegration of her internalized image both of gender identity and of the body.[12] Although Jane writes the story of Maudie's young life as a romance and understands that "we need our history prettied up. It would be intolerable to have the . . . truth . . . all grim and painful" (141), Lessing does not spare the grim physical details of age and illness. As Maudie's stomach cancer progresses, she begins to lose control over her own body. It takes all her energy to get up and get outside to the toilet, but she refuses any pills that will "stupefy" her mind. She needs all her wits to maintain what autonomy she can: "A general planning a campaign could not use more cleverness than Maudie does, as she outwits her . . . terrible tiredness. She is already at the back door; the toilet is five steps away; if she goes now it will save a journey later" (115–16).

Eventually Maudie loses control of her bladder and bowels. Once when Jane arrives to visit, she finds not only a filthy kitchen and bedroom but a soiled Maudie as well, sitting helpless in a rage, afraid to call the social worker, lest she be put in a Home, but desperately ashamed of her physical condition. Jane, who never had children and avoided the "physical awfulness" (7) of her own mother's death, strips off Maudie's stinking clothes, boils some water, and physically washes her. Maudie's reaction to shame is not resignation, however; it is anger. Jane realizes that Maudie's anger is entwined with her survival: Maudie "was chilly, she was sick, she was weak—but I could feel the vitality beating there: life. How strong it is, life. I had never thought that before, never felt life in that way, as I did then, washing Maudie Fowler, a fierce angry old woman. Oh, how angry: it occurred to me that all her vitality is in her anger" (51–52).

Although Maudie is furious that her body is betraying her and struggles to maintain her autonomy as long as she can, she also takes great joy in Jane's visits and care for her. In spite of the loss of bodily independence and control, Maudie gains a new kind of self-respect in her relationship with Jane. She says to Jane, "'I have been thinking, this is the best time of my life. . . . I'm not talking about the short joyful days, like carrying my Johnnie, or a picnic here and a picnic there, but now, I know you will always come and we can be together'" (122). Maudie's husband deserted her and stole her only son; her sister's family used her and then ignored her; she was a talented milliner, but hats went out of fashion and she lost her job. Now in spite of the misery of poverty and illness, she is happy because Jane has befriended her. Maudie is very aware of the nature of their relationship; any time Jane can refuse to come.

What Maudie can offer is stories of her youth: "'You do so much for me, and all I can do for you is to tell you my little stories, because you like that, don't you? Yes, I know you do'" (87). Eventually Jane gives up her editorship of the magazine and cuts back on her working hours to write a romance about Maudie and her friends called *The Milliners of Marylebone*: "How I did enjoy making Maudie's relentless life something gallantly light-hearted, full of pleasant surprises" (244). These stories and memories are selective for both Maudie and Jane because they are not really a life review but rather, like Adella's selective memories of her husband and her fantasy of his return, a search for respect and pleasure, a reminder in the face of death, of the joy of life. In her interactions with Maudie and her two-week bout with lumbago, Jane has learned that "I have only to slip once on my bathroom floor. . . [and] I shall be grounded. Like Maudie" (166).

Lessing's novel, in spite of the vivid repulsive details about the body's losses, is a celebration of old age. As Jane gets to know other old women as well as Maudie, she says: "These are the old ladies I once did not see at all but, since Maudie, have watched creeping about the streets with their bags and their baskets—I could never have guessed the companionableness, the interest of their lives, the gaiety" (148).

Maudie is eventually taken to the hospital in the final stages of cancer, but as Jane realizes, no matter how good the care and the nursing, "what she wants is—not to be dying! . . . [N]inety-two years old, and Maudie seems to believe that an injustice is being done to her!" (218). In spite of her intense pain, Maudie's love of life and her appreciation of a friend who listens to her stories make Maudie unwilling to resign herself to death. Jane realizes that there is a process beyond the body that is a crucial part of dying:

> What I think now is, it is possible that what sets the pace of dying is not the body, not that great lump inside her stomach, getting bigger with every breath, but the need of the Maudie who is not dying to adjust—to what? Who can know what enormous processes are going on there, behind Maudie's hanging head, her sullen eyes? I think she will die when *those* processes are accomplished. (244–45)

Maudie dies the next day without any further words, but she has left a legacy behind for Jane Somers. It is not just the romance novel of early-twentieth-century shop women's lives and pre–World War I gaiety but, rather, a new understanding of class and age, of the physical body and the possibility of, if not transcendence, at least celebration of life even in advanced old age.

In discussing the themes of the *The Diary of a Good Neighbour* and Lessing's use of a pseudonym, Cora Agatucci says that in this novel Lessing continues to explore her lifelong concerns with identity. "Identity," Agatucci says, includes "the processes of its construction and deconstruction, the role of others in its definition, the necessity of growth through continual redefinition, its enabling and crippling properties" (47). This definition fits nicely the understanding of identity in the ninth stage of life. As the body, a powerful source of identity, begins to disintegrate, it is possible to construct a new identity out of other elements of existence. Memory of past relationships or the establishment of new relationships can provide sources of redefinition and growth even in the face of increasing disability. As the writings of Joan Erikson and these novels by Joan Riley and Doris Lessing show, identities change and grow even up to death itself. The courage and respect that these characters accord themselves provide a legacy, a model for younger generations to use in their own inevitable aging process.

Conclusion

If most late-twentieth-century cultures are hybrid and heterogeneous and if identity, particularly gender identity, is best understood as narrative, it is valuable to look closely at women's narratives that are consciously written from a place of hybridity, from the interstices of culture. Whether the author's sense of dislocation or liminality comes from a geographic experience of immigration, emigration, or exile, or whether it is an awareness of geographic invasion and the superimposing of an alien culture as in colonialism, or whether it is a consciousness of a mixed ethnic and cultural heritage or even a sense of marginality, the narratives of such women come from a different space than many narratives from the earlier twentieth century, which were often nation based. In *Writing a Woman's Life*, Carolyn Heilbrun says that "lives do not serve as models; only stories do that. . . . We live our lives through texts. . . . [S]tories have formed us all; they are what we must use to make new fictions, new narratives" (37). These late-twentieth-century novels by women consciously writing from a place of hybridity are novels that engage Western tradition and yet critique that tradition from multiple viewpoints. They are stories that open up new insights into women's desires and identities and provide models for new fictions.

"What do women want?" Freud famously asked. He actually gave a surprisingly accurate answer to that question in his definition of human normality: the ability to "love and to work" (see Erik Erikson, *Childhood and Society* 264–65). To be able both to love and to work means one must grapple with various tensions, as Erikson called them, throughout the course of one's life. From their own particular geographic and historical locations, the authors discussed in this book look at these tensions and desires in women's lives. These narratives portray women's needs at a variety of ages and from various locations.

Women need to find not just adult roles that are handed down by national or political or ethnic or gender ideologies but roles that are both discovered and defined individually yet still grounded in culture and connection. This is the search described both by Tsitsi Dangarembga in *Nervous Conditions* and by Margaret Atwood in *Cat's Eye*. Women need relationships and intimacy, what Erikson in his old age defined as "the capacity for . . . commitment to lasting friendships and companionship" (Erikson, Erikson, and Kivnick, *Vital Involvement in Old Age* 37). They need the freedom to discover their own sexuality and working relationships, as described in Barbara Burford's "The Threshing Floor," or to discover intimacy outside sexuality altogether, as Keri Hulme describes in *The Bone People*.

In order to achieve what Erikson calls "generativity" and what Gay Wilentz calls "generational continuity" (xviii), women need both the security of place and the freedom of space (Tuan 30), whether they are migrants or have always lived in the same country. Buchi Emecheta's Nigerian protagonist in *Kehinde* defines a place for herself in London as a member of the Black diaspora; Anita Desai's protagonist in *Clear Light of Day* redefines her concept of home as she sorts out the heritage of gender roles left by colonists and nationalists in India. Margaret Drabble's and Nadine Gordimer's characters must revise their social and political roles in new spaces, whether those roles are the contesting of an unwanted political shift or an adjustment to a long-sought change in political regime.

Cultural identities must be recuperated through memory, both personal and collective, in order to discover integrity. That process includes the divestment of false layers of a superimposed culture and of deceptive nostalgia and the recovery of wholeness as described in both Paule Marshall's *Praisesong for the Widow* and Jessica Anderson's *Tirra Lirra by the River*.

Finally, facing death and the bodily losses described by Joan Erikson as a ninth stage of life, women want to leave a distinctive legacy behind them, as Joan Riley portrays in *Waiting in the Twilight* and Doris Lessing in *The Diary of a Good Neighbour*.

These are all narratives with female characters who resolve some of the tensions in their lives. These novels describe the traumas of colonialism, racism, war, poverty, and prejudice, but these are not just stories of victims.[1] These are novels about women who have managed to find spaces in the interstices of cultures from which to define their own identities and tell their own stories. They all portray women who, if not living in the West, are exposed to Western ideas through education and/or family inheritance but who also stand outside the Western master narratives because of some combination of nationality, ethnicity, class, sexual orientation, and/or religion.

These are all narratives in which women demonstrate both courage to face obstacles and the agency to define themselves and critique dominant traditions. Although Tambu in *Nervous Conditions* and Elaine in *Cat's Eye* cannot undo the colonial and gender ideologies of their society, they can negotiate paths between them. As Hannah in "The Threshing Floor" and Kerewin in *The Bone People* allow themselves to be vulnerable to others and bravely do not flinch from the ordeals they must undergo, they recover their artistic abilities. Kehinde in Emecheta's novel and Bim in *Clear Light of Day* assess their locations and their relationships to establish places for themselves. Liz, Alix, and Esther in *The Radiant Way* must learn new social roles and new forms of political existence. In *None to Accompany Me* Vera and Sibongile must exchange political identities: Vera must learn how to relinquish power, and Sibongile must learn how to exercise it. Avey in *Praisesong for the Widow* and Nora in *Tirra Lirra by the River* undergo lonely and painful processes of divestment in their journeys to find wholeness. Adella in *Waiting in the Twilight* and Maudie in *The Diary of a Good Neighbour* cannot escape the poverty that is intertwined with their immigrant and/or class status nor the bodily losses that disability and old age bring, but they present models of how to face death with courage and self-respect.

It is particularly in the overlap and affiliations between these hybrid stories of different cultural combinations that the new narratives of identity emerge. As Bhabha says: "It is in . . . the overlap and displacement of domains of difference—that the intersubjective and collective experiences of *nationness*, community interest, or cultural value are negotiated" (*The Location of Culture* 2). These overlaps in the narratives give us an intersubjective understanding not only of nationality and culture but also of the adult experiences of intimacy and generativity (which could be another way of describing "community interest") and even the achievement of wisdom, that ripeness of experience, "accumulated knowledge and mature judgment" (Erik Erikson, *Identity, Youth and Crisis* 140). Because the experience, knowledge, and judgment come from stories of mixtures of a variety of cultures, albeit in the Western form of the novel, the overlaps and intersubjective understandings deepen our conception of women's identities and serve as new models for the transnational narratives of a new century.

Notes

INTRODUCTION

1. Bart Moore-Gilbert calls hybridity "perhaps the key concept through-out" Bhabha's career (129).

2. Gloria Anzaldúa, speaking from the experience of a Chicana, emphasizes the dangers of the borderland: "[T]he U.S.-Mexican border *es una herida abierta* where the Third World grates against the first and bleeds. . . . A borderland is a vague and undetermined place created by the emotional residue of an unnatural boundary. It is in a constant state of transition. The prohibited and forbidden are its inhabitants. . . . Tension grips the inhabitants of the borderlands like a virus. Ambivalence and unrest reside there and death is no stranger" (3–4). See Susan Friedman (93–101) for a detailed analysis of *Borderlands/La Frontera: The New Mestiza*.

3. In *Gender Trouble* Judith Butler asks of sexual difference: "Is it natural, anatomical, chromosomal or hormonal?" (6). Butler says: "It would be wrong to assume in advance that there is a category of 'women' that simply needs to be filled in with various components of race, class, age, ethnicity and sexuality in order to become complete" (15). For Butler gender is performative: "[G]ender is an identity tenuously constituted in time, instituted in an exterior space through a *stylized repetition of acts*" (140).

4. Key articles that critiqued the universalism of 1970s feminism from a postcolonial viewpoint include Hazel Carby, "White Woman Listen," in *The Empire Strikes Back: Race and Racism in Seventies Britain* (London: Hutchinson, 1982); 212–35, reprinted in Mirza; Chandra Talpade Mohanty, "Under Western Eyes: Feminist Scholarship and Colonial Discourse," *Boundary 2* 13.1 (1984): 333–57, reprinted in Mohanty, *Third World Women*; and Gayatri Chakravorty Spivak, "Imperialism and Sexual Difference," *Oxford Literary Review* 8.1–2 (1986): 225–40.

5. Susan Stanford Friedman's "mappings" and diagrams of hybridity theories (82–93) are very useful; Ania Loomba gives a good summary of hybridity and several of its critics (173–83). In addition to the critics described by Loomba, Feroza Jussawalla criticizes hybridity not only because she thinks it is too generalized but also because it does not address racism. For Jussawalla, it "is wishful thinking in London as it is in Los Angeles" ("South Asian Diaspora Writers" 30). Like others, she worries that it leads to erasure of difference and loss of ethnic traditions. As a Parsi herself, she links Bhabha's concept of hybridity to his own identity as a Parsi, which she describes as "a diasporic immigrant community in India that frequently adapted to its changing masters like 'sugar blending with milk'" ("South Asian Diaspora Writers" 29). Several of the novels in this study, however, highlight both racism and the dangers of assimilation.

6. Sara Suleri criticizes Mohanty's early article "Under Western Eyes" as calling too much for the "authenticity" of "lived experience" (760), which can lead to a splintering of identities, but Rita Felski argues that in her later work Mohanty "insists on the need for a broader perspective . . . emphasizing the value of cross-national and cross-cultural analyses" ("Doxa of Difference" 10). Susan Friedman analyzes the term "transnational" as used in Spivak's essay "Scattered Speculations" in *Outside the Teaching Machine* and in Inderpal Grewal and Caren Kaplan's *Scattered Hegemonies* (Friedman 111–12).

7. Mohanty herself uses the term "Third World" both in the title of her first anthology and in Alexander and Mohanty, *Feminist Genealogies, Colonial Legacies, Democratic Futures*. She explains in a note that she follows Ella Shohat and Robert Stam's usage of this term in *Unthinking Eurocentrism: Multiculturalism and the Media*, where they point out that the term was adopted at the 1955 Bandung Conference by African and Asian nations to illustrate their nonalignment (Alexander and Mohanty 357).

8. Benhabib proposes this narrative model as an alternative to Butler's performative concept of gender. See Benhabib (338–41) for a discussion of the precise differences between the two.

9. I include Paule Marshall among the authors I've chosen even though she was actually born in New York of Barbadian parents. During her child-

hood, however, her mother took her home to Barbados for two years. Joyce Pettis notes that Marshall "was enrolled in the local school, where the British system dominated" (30). Two other white African novelists I've chosen, Nadine Gordimer and Doris Lessing, dropped out of formal schooling early—Lessing completely at age fourteen in Rhodesia and Gordimer from ages eleven to sixteen in the Union of South Africa—but both read widely in English and European literature.

10. Susan Friedman describes the first meaning of hybridity as "fusion" and quotes Salman Rushdie's essay in *Imaginary Homelands* where Rushdie celebrates hybridity: *"Mélange*, hotch-potch, a bit of this and a bit of that is *how newness enters the world"* (Friedman 83–84). The second meaning involves the retention and intermingling of differences. The third meaning argues that all cultures are by nature syncretic, that is, mixed and heterogeneous (Friedman 83–85).

11. Likewise, Moore-Gilbert says that Spivak's interviews in *The Post-Colonial Critic* imply that for Spivak also "the 'white settler' histories of such countries [as Australia] make their presumption of a 'postcolonial' identity, and consequently of a role in postcolonial criticism, deeply problematic" (Moore-Gilbert 16).

12. To their survey I would add two additional strong critics of post-colonialism, Carole Boyce Davies, who writes about Caribbean women and women of the African diaspora (see *Black Women, Writing and Identity*), and Arun Mukerjee, whose field is nonwhite Canadian writing (see "Whose Post-Colonialism"). They are both concerned that the postcolonial approach erases issues of race.

Moore-Gilbert also gives a survey of the history of the term and its emergence from "Commonwealth Studies" (22–33). Ever since Anne McClintock labeled the term "Commonwealth" "fuddy-duddy" ("Angel of Progress" 299), it is not used much except in a few journal titles.

13. As Erikson describes them, these are the oral stage with the task of trust, the anal stage with the task of autonomy, the genital stage with the task of initiative, and the latency stage with the task of industry. For each stage, Erikson also describes the feelings that ensue if the conflict is not resolved or the task not completed: trust versus mistrust, autonomy versus shame, initiative versus guilt, industry versus inferiority (*Childhood and Society* 273).

14. The results of Erikson's observations of school-age boys and girls' play constructions were first published in *Daedalus* 42.2 (Spring 1964): 582–607 and later incorporated into *Identity, Youth and Crisis* (1968). Lawrence Friedman summarizes the feminist criticisms of Erikson's ideas in the late 1960s and mid 1970s (423–26).

15. Papalia and Olds summarize the revised understanding of Erikson that is now the focus of developmental psychologists. They report, for

instance, that "Marcia (1993) argues that relationships and an ongoing tension between independence and connectedness are at the heart of all Erikson's psychosocial stages for *both* men and women" (373).

16. See Lillian Comas-Díaz and Beverly Greene's *Women of Color: Integrating Ethnic and Gender Identities in Psychotherapy* (1994) for an integration of cultural difference and a variety of psychotherapeutic approaches. Jean Lau Chin's essay in that volume on "Pschodynamic Approaches," for instance, refers to both Chodorow's and Gilligan's work.

17. Margaret Atwood says that her education in the 1950s in "a recently postcolonial" Canada had an advantage over a U.S. education for a young female writer: "[B]eing female was not considered the hindrance that it was in America, where Emily Dickinson fluttered halfway up the famous canon like a lone and pale flag. It was possible to be female and a writer, like Jane Austen and Emily Brontë" ("The Writer: A New Canadian Life-Form" 39).

See Mohan for a discussion of "the mixed blessings" of a British colonial education for other postcolonial women writers (48).

18. In some of her other stories in the collection called *The Threshing Floor* Burford uses seemingly "magical" events or mythic settings that she describes as science fiction.

CHAPTER 1

1. See Ruth Saxton, ed., *The Girl: Constructions of the Girl in Contemporary Fiction by Women* (1998), and Elizabeth Abel, Marianne Hirsch, and Elizabeth Langland, eds., *The Voyage In: Fictions of Female Development* (1983).

2. Lindsay Aegerter points out that in *Nervous Conditions* the "friction" between the older narrative voice and that of the naive young girl prevents the novel from falling into an "all-too-easy *bildungsroman*" pattern (236). Chinmoy Banerjee describes *Cat's Eye* as containing "a narrational braid" with three strands: the adult voice, the little girl's voice, and the story told by "dreams, fantasies, [and] paintings" (514, 518).

3. Nancy Chodorow's work in feminist psychoanalysis has been applied to both Dangarembga's novel and Atwood's. See Flockemann's essay on Dangarembga and Ingersoll's, Osborne's, and Hite's on Atwood.

4. Brown says that "Elaine's childhood illustrates with stunning clarity a transformation that I, and other feminist psychologists of late, have witnessed and documented in girls' interviews over time—a shift from a lively embodied young girl, outspoken, direct, in touch with her senses, her feelings and thoughts, to a girl at the inside edge of adolescence struggling to speak, to stay with her feelings, to know what she knows" (286).

5. In "Who Is That Masked Woman? or, The Role of Gender in Fanon's *Black Skin, White Masks*," Gwen Bergner says Fanon opens up psychoanalysis to issues of race but treats women, white and particularly black,

as abstractions and "objects of exchange in the homosocial, heterosexual colonial economy" (85). T. Denean Sharpley-Whiting criticizes Bergner's article and argues that Fanon's dismissal of Mayotte Capécia's novel is an important corrective to her "blackphobia" (157). Anne McClintock suggests that in Fanon's work "the fateful chiaroscuro of race is at almost every turn disrupted by the criss-crossings of gender" (*Imperial Leather* 361).

6. In an interview with Kirsten Holst Petersen, Dangarembga says of this opening line: "I thought I should say something stunning in the opening sentence that would focus very much on the issues I was dealing with. That sentence was really to open up people's minds. It has such an impact that nobody could ignore it." Dangarembga further explains that Tambu's treatment by her brother and her family is "not purely a patriarchal problem, it is also a result of the state of colonisation at the time" (345).

7. Tambu's aunt Lucia, her mother's sister, speaks up for herself and gets a job from Babamukuru, but she is not married and is considered by Babamukuru to be "like a man" (171) in her outspokenness.

8. Sugnet also comments on this episode: "Note Dangarembga's honesty about the limits of self-help in a colonial or neocolonial situation. Tambudzai does not succeed by selling her crop for a fair price; instead, her serious economic effort becomes an occasion of colonialist charity" (Sugnet 48, note 7).

9. See Creamer (354–58) and Thomas (32–33) for a further discussion of the role of food and food-related illness in the novel. Sugnet says motifs of eating and digestion are "metaphors for domination and resistance in the novel," and he relates them to similar images in Fanon's *Wretched of the Earth* (35).

10. Dangarembga is extremely critical of the way Christianity is implicated in colonialism in the farce of her parents' wedding, but she is equally critical of traditional African religion in her portrayal of Jeremiah's accusation of witchcraft and call for a medium to solve problems that his own laziness and lack of self-discipline have created. For an interesting discussion of how traditional African religion can revise Western psychological theory, see Spillers's discussion of two texts about mental illness among the Senegalese.

11. In reaction to her parents' disapproval, Nyasha calls herself a "hybrid." She says that she and her brother should not have been taken to England when they were young because now her parents are "stuck with hybrids for children" (78). In actuality, however, Nyasha is not a hybrid because she has no access to Shona culture; there is not a mixing of cultures in her but a gap where the culture of her birth should be.

12. Heidi Creamer notes that an article about a Black Zimbabwean woman with anorexia nervosa in a 1984 British journal emphasized that the woman's English experiences were the cause. Creamer points to a 1992 American study of multicultural patients in *Gender and Society* that is more

helpful. That article "establishes bulimia and anorexia as serious responses to injustices" (Creamer 360).

Supriya Nair suggests that "Nyasha's violent purging . . . [is] indicative of the indigestibility of patriarchal order and . . . her violent rending of colonial textbooks by tearing into them with her teeth . . . is also emblematic of the ideological diet of colonial history that literally sickens her" (136). Carl Plasa links Nyasha's anorexia to eating disorders in Charlotte Brontë's *Shirley*.

13. Nathalie Cooke and Coral Howells discuss the similarity of Elaine's early life to Atwood's own.

14. Arnold Davidson says that *Cat's Eye* "does have clear postcolonial implications. Miss Lumley advocates the conventional ordering of an imperial centre and subsidiary margins which necessarily fall short of that centre even as they are ostensibly being re-created in its image" (62).

15. Chodorow explains in a 1995 article that she was not proposing a "definition" of femininity or feminine gender identity in *Reproduction of Mothering*: "I generalized, I believe usefully, about the ways that many women and men operate psychologically and experience and define their selves. Such generalizations are useful to the extent that they speak to any particular individual's experience, to the extent that they help clinicians, or to the extent that they serve as guides for interpreting literature and biographies" ("Gender as Personal and Cultural Construction" 523).

16. See McCombs for a fascinating analysis of all the paintings of the novel, particularly those of Mrs. Smeath and of Elaine's five newer paintings described in the novel on pages 443–47.

17. Susan Strehle analyzes Cordelia in terms of Julia Kristeva's concept of abjection, or self-loathing. She finds the source of this self-contempt in Cordelia's father, a misogynistic minor character who represents the power of patriarchal control (see especially 169–75).

CHAPTER 2

1. Erikson clearly did not include either of these forms of intimacy in his early writings. He describes intimacy in his first book, *Childhood and Society*, as based in "true genitality" (294), which includes a commitment to a "loved partner of the other sex" (266). In his last book, written with his wife, Joan Erikson and Helen Kivnick, Erikson expands his definition to one that opens up a much broader understanding of intimacy:

> Intimacy . . . is the capacity for eventual commitment to lasting friendships and companionship in general. . . . [An] important (and first adult) strength is love, about which we may say the following: love is mutuality of devotion forever subduing the antagonisms inherent in divided function. It pervades the intimacy

of individuals and is thus the basis of ethical concern. (*Vital Involvement in Old Age* 37)

2. DuPlessis finds the "kunstlerromane," or artist's story, to be one of the effective ways in which early-twentieth-century women novelists wrote "beyond the ending," but many of these early kunstlerromane still pit intimacy against achievement. They have "a triangular plot of nurturance offered to an emergent daughter by a parental couple" (91) or a plot in which the protagonist liberates her artistic abilities by "reparenting" herself (DuPlessis 94).

3. One pattern that DuPlessis finds in earlier women's kunstlerromane that fits these late-century works as well is the need for breaking down isolation and experiencing vulnerability: "[A]rt work can only be made with an immersion in personal vulnerability, a breakdown, or a breakthrough . . . or as an articulation of long-repressed grief" (103).

4. Burford's own heritage reflects multiple ethnic backgrounds in that her mother was part Scot, part black, and her father was Jewish. Burford explains that she spent her very young childhood in Jamaica and then moved to England with her parents when she was ten. She attended Dalston County Grammar School for Girls, where she was the only black girl but was friends with the Jewish girls ("When Everything Else Is Done and Dusted" 24).

5. Hulme says that in spite of the similar name and heritage, the novel is "not autobiographical at all." She says that she "thought Kerewin Holmes was a really neat pun. Keri win home. I learned later on that this was not a good idea, but it was too late. That character had taken her own name over and I couldn't extricate her from that name" (Hulme and Turcotte 137).

6. Some critics initially felt that Hulme couldn't claim to be Maori if she was only one-eighth Maori, but Margery Fee answered them in her article "Why C.K. Stead didn't like Keri Hulme's *the bone people*: Who can write as Other?" She analyzes criteria often used to determine "authenticity": ancestry, socialization, indigenous language, the questions of a static or a changing indigenous culture, solidarity of feeling, and solidarity of politics. She concludes that Stead's "biological essentialism . . . blinds him to . . . Hulme's definition of Maori: 'actual' Maoriness, like an 'actual' family, has nothing to do with biology and everything to do with solidarity of feeling" (18).

7. See de Lauretis's chapter "The Seductions of Lesbianism: Feminist Psychoanalytic Theory and the Maternal Imaginary" in *The Practice of Love* for a critique of these ideas in French feminist thought, Adrienne Rich, Nancy Chodorow, and others. Judith Butler also cautions that these theories of maternal identification can reinforce "the binary, heterosexist framework" (66).

8. De Lauretis theorizes lesbian desire as constituted in maternal rejection:

> Failing the mother's narcissistic validation of the subject's body-image, which constitutes the imaginary matrix or first outline of the ego, the subject is threatened with a loss of body-ego, a lack of being. . . . [I]t is . . . the lack of a libidinally invested body-image, a feminine body that can be narcissistically loved—that threatens the subject most deeply. And it is against this threat that the mechanism of disavowal intervenes to defend the ego by producing the compromise fantasy "I don't have it but I can/will have it." (de Lauretis, The Practice of Love 262)

9. In her article on black lesbian literature, Anita Pilgrim praises Burford for addressing "some of the valid questions of Black-white dynamics" in "The Threshing Floor" (156).

10. Burford says that when she was writing "The Threshing Floor" she asked all her friends, but nobody knew any glassblowers. Then she was commissioned to write a play called *Patterns*, and she discovered that the scene designer was in the process of divorcing one of London's leading glassblowers, Peter Layton. Burford says, "[B]less her heart, she introduced me to him and the London Glassblowing Workshop ("When Everything Else Is Done and Dusted" 29). Burford spent a day at the London Glassblowing Workshop, and then when her manuscript was complete, she went back to three women glassblowers, whom she mentions in her acknowledgments at the beginning of the book, and they answered technical questions for her about glassblowing.

11. Dale analyzes the complex attitudes toward homosexuality in the novel. They range from a halfhearted pass that Kerewin receives from Joe's bisexual sister-in-law at a bar to a positive experience Joe once had with "Taki," a boy with whom he had a short affair after his wife's death, to two vivid homophobic incidents, the death of a drunken pedophile, Binny, and the insinuations of Joe's sinister homosexual brother Luce that Joe's cuddling of Simon will make Simon homosexual (see Dale 424–27). Dale suggests that homosexuality is like other "patterns, ideas and structures" in the novel "which work against each other—which 'unsettle' the stability of one another" (414). Prentice says that homosexuality in the novel "is presented neither wholly positively nor wholly negatively" (72).

12. Several critics remark on Hulme's deconstruction of the model of self-sufficiency in the Crusoe allusion. See Covi (224) and Fee (21).

13. Hulme says that

> in Maori society, certainly up until contact with Pakehas, there was no such thing as child beating. You did not hit children. It was believed that it destroyed their spirit. And there were no

orphans. . . . It seemed to me that there had been a breakdown of a strongly hierarchical, strongly spiritual system, that had dispossessed Maori men from what was seen as their main functions, basically protector and nurturer of other members of the extended family group.

So Joe has the energy and aggression which are quite characteristic, still today, of Maori people, but has nowhere to use these energies. (Hulme and Turcotte 139)

14. Young summarizes some of the virulent anti-Irish racism in England in the mid- and late nineteenth century. He comments that "racialized cultural assumptions about the Irish as simian or black lingered on" throughout the century (*Colonial Desire* 72).

15. Le Cam discusses the phoenix imagery and relates it to biblical and Maori stories (73–75).

CHAPTER 3

1. Geoffrey Kain focuses on the theme of "home" in Asian immigrant literature in the introduction to *Ideas of Home: Literature of Asian Migration*. See also George, *The Politics of Home: Postcolonial Relocations and Twentieth-Century Fiction* for a discussion of several Indian novels.

2. Sangeeta Ray notes that several feminist critics, in particular Mary Louise Pratt, have also made this point about Anderson's masculine terminology (96–97).

3. Anindyo Roy traces the difficulties of the concept of home and nation in his article on postcolonial theory. He discusses Said's concept of exile, Spivak's concept of the ignored subaltern within national boundaries, and Bhabha's concept of the "precariousness of home."

4. This is the phrase that Bhabha uses in an earlier version of this essay: "DissemiNation: Time, Narrative, and the Margins of the Modern Nation," *Nation and Narration*, ed Homi Bhabha (London: Routledge, 1990), 297. This phrase links Bhabha's idea more closely to Wilentz's concern for passing on "cultural values" (xii) and maintaining "cultural continuity" (xv) in varied historical and national spaces.

5. Similarly, Sangeeta Ray argues that *Clear Light of Day* "addresses the sociopolitical predicaments confronted by women whose position as independent, equal citizens in the nation is thwarted by the appropriation of 'woman' (and its related gendered significations) as a metonymy for 'nation'" (97).

6. See my article "The London Novels of Buchi Emecheta" for a discussion of these novels and others.

7. Carole Boyce Davies argues that this "polyvocal" quality of writing is typical not only of diasporic African women writers but of African

women writers in general because "African women's writing resides at the problematic intersection of gender and nationalism, class and culture" ("Writing Off Marginality, Minoring, and Effacement" 260).

Katherine Fishburn describes Emecheta's language as being a "dialogic heteroglossia," an English that is "'shot through' with the alien accents of [Emecheta's three Nigerian languages and] . . . her African worldview" (43–44).

8. In "To Ground the Wandering Muse," Pauline Uwakweh argues that Kehinde is not representative of "African feminism" because she is insufficiently committed to motherhood. Carole Boyce Davies, whose definition of African feminism Uwakweh is using, is actually more flexible on the subject. Davies says that "African feminism . . . respects African woman's status as mother but questions obligatory motherhood" (*Ngambika* 9). Lauretta Ngcobo, a South African novelist who wrote *And They Didn't Die*, critiques some of the ideology of motherhood in Africa in her conference paper "African Motherhood—Myth and Reality." Emecheta, who spoke at the same conference, agreed with her on several issues (Ngcobo 152).

9. Emecheta said this when she visited the National Endowment for the Humanities Institute on "Postcolonial Literature and Theory" at the University of London, 21 July 1998.

10. Brenda Berrian explores the theme of duality in *Kehinde* in her focus on this "Yoruba ibéji-orisa myth about twins" (170). She argues that Kehinde is neither "defeated by the Igbo world nor totally assimilated into the Western world" (181).

11. Chikwenye Ogunyemi's chapter on Emecheta is entitled "Buchi Emecheta: The Been-To (Bintu) Novel" in *Africa Woman Palava*.

12. Hazel Carby in "White Woman Listen!" warns against a simplistic white feminist view that presumes that "when black women enter Britain they are moving into a more liberated or enlightened or emancipated society than the one from which they have come" (48).

13. Parekh also argues that because of her parentage and education Desai occupies a "hybrid space" and brings to her fiction "the viewpoint of the insider and the outsider" (Parekh 272). Feroza Jussawalla and Reed Way Dasenbrock note that Desai speaks Urdu and Bengali as well as Hindi, German, and English (157).

14. Nandy explains Desai's reluctance in his comment that the "word 'Hindu' . . . was first used by the Muslims to describe all Indians who were not converted to Islam. Only in recent times have the Hindus begun to describe themselves as Hindus" (*The Intimate Enemy* 103).

15. Asha Kanwar writes on this influence in *Virginia Woolf and Anita Desai: A Comparative Study*. She pairs *Clear Light of Day* with Woolf's *To the Lighthouse*, paralleling Desai's theme of time and four-part structure with Woolf's similar theme and three-part structure in that novel.

16. Graham Huggan compares silence and music in *Clear Light of Day* and *The Bone People*. He sees silence as ambiguous in both novels: Baba's silence "may undergo a transformation in which the self-absorbed silence of personal withdrawal is converted into the exchanged silence(s) of . . . mutual recognition" (15). He describes Simon's muteness in *The Bone People* as either "a form of self-protection or as a gesture of resistance to prescribed social 'norms'" (16).

17. Both Ray and Mohan question whether the modern nation does not require just as much sacrifice from Bim as the earlier colonial regime required from Aunt Mira. Ray suggests that "the bourgeois moral underpinnings of an Indian nationalist ideology are so mythologized that Bimala is ultimately uncomfortable with the freedom granted women during and after independence" (112). Mohan wonders whether the "rich fecundity [of Indian soil] is nothing less than the female labour and sacrifice embodied in Mira-*masi* and Bim herself" (64).

CHAPTER 4

1. Abdul JanMohamed classifies *The Burger's Daughter* and *July's People* as revolutionary novels in *Manichaean Aesthetics*. See Louise Yelin's, "Decolonizing the Novel" for a discussion of the way *A Sport of Nature* undoes the bourgeois novel of sensibility to create a new genre of the female picaresque.

2. Both Drabble and Gordimer have been moving steadily away from traditional realism in their careers. Both started with female bildungsroman, Drabble's *A Summer Bird-Cage* (1962) and Gordimer's *The Lying Days* (1953). Jean Pickering says that a "change in narrative strategy took place between [Drabble's] . . . fifth and sixth novels [*The Needle's Eye* and *Realms of Gold*], paralleling what Drabble has acknowledged as a shift in emphasis from the private interior life to the public domain" (476). In her essay "Mimesis" Drabble says that she has "a particular affection for the realist tradition of the novel . . . [for] the humdrum, the everyday, the humble" (12) but that she uses metafictional, or what Appiah calls "postrealistic," techniques as well.

Abdul JanMohamed has classified Gordimer's first three novels written in the 1950s as her "bourgeois phase," the second three, as "postbourgeois," before her shift to a revolutionary phase in 1979. Judie Newman thinks that Gordimer's "deconstruction" of realism begins with her 1974 novel *The Conservationist* (55).

3. See Clingman (8–10) and Head (*Nadine Gordimer* 12–16) for the influence of Georg Lukács on Gordimer.

4. In her essay "*My Son's Story*: Drenching the Censors," Susan Greenstein argues that Gordimer had to "expel the internalized censors of

Black Consciousness [to]. . . create Will and Sonny" (204), the black protagonists in *My Son's Story* (1990). Head describes the Black Consciousness movement as a separatist one that rejected cooperation with whites
and "flourished in the 1970s before and after the Soweto riots of 1976–
77." Head says that this movement "provoked Gordimer into a narrowing
reformulation of her national identity: as a white South African complicit
with a repressive system" (*Nadine Gordimer* 7). By 1982, however,
Gordimer says that she disagrees with novelist Andre Brink's broad statement that whites "cannot write convincingly of the black situation" (Boyers
et al. 211).

   5. Bromberg argues that Drabble employs a "Woolfian or feminist
chronotype, the term Bakhtin uses for 'the intrinsic connectedness of temporal and spatial relationships that are artistically expressed in literature.' . . . By decentering and fragmenting her characters' life stories
Drabble resists the ideologies inscribed in what could have been constructed
as stories of falling in or out of love, or marrying and divorcing" (17).

   Bromberg's use of Bakhtin parallels Friedman's use of him to describe
how "intercultural narratives" turn away from the focus on "character as
it unfolds within a sequence of causal events" and instead "foreground
space and movement through space" (Friedman, *Mappings* 137). Friedman's
concept of a spatial narrative model that "defines the figure in terms of the
ground, describing character within and through cultural locations inscribed
in spatial configuration" (*Mappings* 137–38) can be applied to both these
novels as well, but part of the spatial configuration of these two novels is
a result of the communal protagonist structure of both since neither novel
involves an actual change of location. The intercultural narrative in these
two novels revolves around political spaces and, in Gordimer's novel, racial
spaces.

   6. See Sizemore, *A Female Vision of the City*, for an analysis of this
district of the city and the role of London in *The Radiant Way*.

   7. Kathleen Woodward explains that Freud, in his 1919 essay "The Uncanny," defines "the uncanny as something 'familiar that has been repressed'
and returns to create feelings of 'dread and horror,' such as repressed 'in-
fantile complexes' that are revived or 'primitive beliefs which have been
surmounted [but] seem once more to be confirmed'" (*Aging and Its Discontents* 63).

   8. In an interview with Olga Kenyon, Drabble says of her description
of Volpe as a Satanist anthropologist: "This was my little joke about magic
realism, a sort of response to it. I'm interested in the way the irrational fits
into the rational world. . . . There are some real Italian scholars, of whom
the most famous is Mario Praz . . . who would call down the wrath of
heaven on their enemies. I wanted a symbol of the extraordinary contrasts
in our intellectual life today" (Drabble, "Interview" 37).

9. Drabble has written two sequels to *The Radiant Way*. *A Natural Curiosity* (1989) focuses on Liz's sister, Shirley, and on Alix's prison visits to Paul Whitmore, whom she is trying to understand. The narrator admits that this is "not a political novel. More a pathological novel. A psychotic novel. Sorry about that" (194). The third novel, *The Gates of Ivory* (1991) deals with international politics as Stephen Cox journeys to Cambodia and is caught in its episodes of violence. The stories of the three friends are interwoven into these continuing narratives of community.

10. John Cooke notes that photographs are associated with "a dying order" in *The Late Bourgeois World* (126). In other Gordimer novels and short stories, Cooke says photographs "objectify a failure to connect" (128). In 1986 Gordimer collaborated on a book of photographs of people during apartheid with David Goldblatt, which juxtaposed passages from her writings with his photographs, *Lifetimes under Apartheid*.

11. In a 1999 *New York Times* article, Gordimer says she will "not duck" the recent statistics about violent crime in South Africa, but she categorically denies that the "phenomenon of crime . . . is the phenomenon of freedom." She explains the rise in violent crime as a result of the "dammed-up unemployment [that] has burst upon us from the inhuman confines of the past; it is not something *inherent in freedom*" ("My New South African Identity" 42).

12. Temple-Thurston points out that the assassination of an unnamed political leader in the novel is based on the assassination of African National Congress (ANC) leader Chris Hane in 1992 (128).

13. Temple-Thurston argues that this is the problem the whole Maqoma family must face: "The novel's concern for the Maqoma family . . . seems to come more from their alienation from African ways and their easy adoption of Western lifestyles and values due to all their years abroad" (139).

CHAPTER 5

1. In her study of women's novels of aging, *From the Hearth to the Open Road: A Feminist Study of Aging in Contemporary Literature*, Barbara Waxman attributes the term *reifungsromane* to May Sarton. Kathleen Woodward cites Meridel Le Sueur as substituting the word "ripening" for "aging" (*Aging and Its Discontents* 9).

2. Anne Wyatt-Brown applied Robert Butler's concept of the life review to novels by May Sarton, Madeleine L'Engle, and Toni Morrison in a 1993 South Atlantic Modern Language Association (SAMLA) paper. Carolyn H. Smith uses Butler's life review in an analysis of Josephine Miles's later poems in *Aging and Gender in Literature*, ed. Anne Wyatt-Brown and Janice Rossen.

3. Waxman says that *reifungsromane* often have a recursive narrative structure (16) and uses *Praisesong for the Widow* as one of her examples.

Karla Holloway considers recursiveness a technique of black women's literature that layers "ways of memory and discourse and the mythic figures within language and culture until each is folded into the other" (13).

4. Dorothy Denniston uses part of this same passage from Stuart Hall to support her argument that Marshall's "artistic vision is forward-looking, suggesting change and possibility" (xiv).

5. Denniston says Avey Johnson is sixty-two (126), and Wilentz says she is "approaching her mid-fifties" (110), but *Praisesong for the Widow* says that at "fifty-eight Clarice was six years Avey Johnson's junior" (21), which makes Avey sixty-four. Daniel Levinson, in his study of American women and men from a variety of class and ethnic backgrounds, describes ages sixty to sixty-five as a period of "Late Adult Transition," which often includes "a profound reappraisal of the past" (26).

6. Several critics have linked Erikson's stages of life to Paule Marshall's novels. Joseph Skerrett, Jr., notes that there is a progression in Marshall's novels from the bildungsroman of her first novel of girlhood, *Brown Girl, Brownstones*, to the "crisis of generativity" in *The Chosen Place, the Timeless People*, to the "crisis of integrity" in *Praisesong for the Widow* (68–69). He concentrates on the issue of generativity in *The Chosen Place, the Timeless People*, which Marshall in an interview calls her "strongly political novel" (Ogundipe-Leslie 20). See Chapter 4 for my connection of generativity with political novels.

Lucy Wilson applies Erikson's eighth stage of integrity and the journey motif to *Praisesong for the Widow* and Beryl Gilroy's *Frangipani House*. Wilson suggests that Marshall's novel evokes "the vast spiritual and historical significance of old age and ancestry" but that Gilroy's novel paints "a far bleaker portrait" of old age (192). Waxman also argues that Avey resolves a "crisis of integrity" (120).

7. Rita Felski writes on nostalgia in Modernism as a yearning for an Edenic past in history or a personal "longing for national plenitude" (*The Gender of Modernity* 59) that puts women outside of culture. In "Fixing the Past" Roberta Rubenstein discusses nostalgia in Virginia Woolf and Doris Lessing as a reaction to loss. Robert Young in *White Mythologies* points out that Gayatri Spivak also warns against a "nostalgia for lost origins" that "reproduces a Western fantasy about its own society now projected out onto the lost society of the other" (168).

8. Although she does not use Butler's ideas, Waxman comments on the mirror imagery in this novel and other *reifungsromane*. For Waxman, mirrors signal either self-scrutiny or self-alienation (122). In *Aging and Its Discontents* Woodward ties nonrecognition of a mirror image to Western culture's fear of age and death, such as the incident Freud reports of his not recognizing his own image in his essay on "The Uncanny" (65). Marshall here is connecting nonrecognition more with class status than age since Avey does not look old in the mirror.

9. Susan Willis gives a Marxist interpretation to this incident, associating the cruise ship food with "bourgeois consumption . . . decadence, overabundance, and the impossibility of ever attaining individual satisfaction" (62).

10. Eugenia DeLamotte links Jerome's concerns about wasting the money of the voyage to Aunt Cuney's story of the Ibo people walking back over the sea to Africa to escape slavery: "The Ibos' goal in walking away from their ship, back across the water, was to wind up, as Avey will in many senses, back where they started, thus squandering the money paid for the voyage that was intended to turn them into objects" (95).

11. Carole Boyce Davies interprets *Praisesong for the Widow* as a novel of multiple journeys of "reconnection. . . . [A]n understanding of her sexuality is also a significant journey in the text" (*Black Women, Writing and Identity* 119).

12. Arlene Sykes says that this novel was first begun as a short story, then adapted as a radio play that was broadcast in 1975 and finally expanded as a novel (61–62).

13. In fact, the original title of Anderson's fifth novel is *The Impersonators* (1982); its U.S. title is *The Only Daughter*. Anderson's other novels are *An Ordinary Lunacy* (1963), *The Last Man's Head* (1970), *The Commandant* (1975), and *Taking Shelter* (1989).

14. Kathleen Woodward connects Lacan's concept of the mirror stage in infancy and Freud's concept of the uncanny to Robert Butler's analysis of the elderly's reactions to a mirror image to develop her concept of the "mirror stage" of old age which involves a negative reaction to the image of the aging body, seen as foreign or uncanny to the viewer (*Aging and Its Discontents* 65–69).

15. Woodward notes that Simone de Beauvoir in *The Coming of Age* emphasized the biological dimension of old age as well as its social construction (*Aging and Its Discontents* 70).

16. Roslynn Haynes reads Nora's evaluation of her art differently. She argues that the abstract patterns are more creative and "reflective" and thus have produced better art.

17. Dominique Hecq associates the Lady of Shallot's Tower with Nora's thirty-year stay in England where she "retreats from the claims of artistic, emotional and sexual identity in an illusory tower of strength overseas" (173). If one is emphasizing the Lady of Shallot as a weaver and artist, however, Brisbane is a better analogy for the tower, since it is in Brisbane that Nora creates her tapestries.

18. Eric Partridge's *Dictionary of Slang and Unconventional English* suggests that "Pommie" is a late-nineteenth-century term that originated in dockworkers' rhyming slang, "immigrant/pomegranate."

19. At the end of her chapter on "The Mirror Stage of Old Age" Woodward theorizes that an "achieved psychic organization" is possible in

advanced old age, and "being repelled by (or even disinterested in) one's own body may be part of the process of accommodating death in the aging body" (*Aging and Its Discontents* 71). Since Nora has been alienated from her body ever since her thirties, a different process seems to be going on in this story in which full acceptance of the body is occurring for the first time.

20. Hecq's psychoanalytic reading of the role of grief in the novel produces a more pessimistic interpretation. The depression and "hollowing out of grief, this narcissistic emptiness . . . is the primary source of the protagonist's inhibition and of her failure to become a free woman and artist" (181).

CHAPTER 6

1. May Sarton says in her novel of an aging seventy-three-year-old woman, *As We Are Now*, that "old age . . . is a foreign country with an unknown language to the young and even to the middle-aged" (23).

2. Woodward describes a popular magazine article by Carolyn Heilbrun, "Coming of Age," in which Heilbrun argues that in order to get to a "new place" in old age "a woman must pass through the stage of invisibility." Woodward notes that Heilbrun is referring specifically to invisibility in terms of sexual power, but she argues that it is precisely this "notion that women as they grow older must pass through invisibility, as though we must adopt the veil" that the contributors to *Figuring Age: Women, Bodies, Generations* want to reject ("Introduction" xiv). Heilbrun does make wonderful ironic use of this idea of invisibility in a recent Amanda Cross detective novel, *The Puzzled Heart*, where an older woman is a successful detective precisely because "nobody even sees old women, let alone is able to describe them" (*The Puzzled Heart* [New York: Ballantine, 1998], 17).

3. Mary Russo's article "Aging and the Scandal of Anachronism" in *Figuring the Body: Women, Bodies, Generations*, ed. Kathleen Woodward, focuses on the difference between chronological age and biological age in her analysis of the relationship between dying middle-aged characters and vigorous elderly characters.

4. *The Unbelonging* (1985) deals with child abuse in a Jamaican immigrant family living in London. *Romance* (1988), also set in London, portrays a Guyanese woman whose rape by her sister's boyfriend in her youth causes her to immerse herself in romance novels and self-defeating affairs with white men. *A Kindness to the Children* (1992) describes the desperate situation in which mentally ill women find themselves in Jamaica. Riley says that she was shocked to discover that she "was the first black Caribbean woman writer to write about the British situation" of Caribbean immigrants in England ("Interview" 269).

5. Riley tells an anecdote that illustrates both the success of her realistic style as well as the idea that old age is so "foreign" that no middle-aged person could understand it. Once, shortly after the publication of *Waiting in the Twilight*, she had a speaking engagement in Sheffield, but no one came to meet her train. She finally phoned and realized that they had been looking for a fifty-eight-year-old, disabled woman like Adella Johnson ("Interview" 269).

6. Gabriele Griffin notes that the body functions in a similar way in Riley's novel of child abuse, *The Unbelonging*, in which the young protagonist's "body constitutes the site of oppression and becomes the source of . . . permanent anxiety" (21).

7. Riley's 1992 novel *A Kindness to the Children* portrays the disastrous effects of a fundamentalist village pastor seducing a young girl and then denouncing her as a temptress. Riley says of the incident in that novel: "You're very unsafe in church; they even have a folk song about pastor. When he offers to give you extra lessons, that's his shorthand for molesting you. And because in fundamentalism you never have to take responsibility, what happens is that you're tempting pastor and you forced him" ("Interview" 277).

8. In her novel of late middle age, *Summer before the Dark* (1974), Lessing explores taking on and putting off invisibility as her heroine tries walking down the street in an old loose dress and undyed hair and then again with makeup and carefully styled hair and dress to see men's reactions. See Waxman for a discussion of this novel in terms of aging.

9. In *Walking in the Shade* Lessing describes how she refused to have her mother come live with her and her young son Peter in London. Her mother returned to Rhodesia and died there in 1957. Lessing says,

> I was grief-struck, but this was no descent into a simple pain of loss, but rather a chilly grey semi-frozen condition—an occluded grief. As usual I pitied her for her dreadful life, but this rage of pity was blocked by the cold thought: If you had let her live with you she would not have died. . . . It was a bad slow time, as if I were miles under thick cold water. . . . There are deaths that are not blows but bruises, spreading darkly, out of sight, not ever really fading. (223–24)

10. In *African Laughter* Lessing describes her mother's and her own feelings about class when they visited Lessing's brother at his boarding school in Rhodesia: "I felt alien to the place. This was because I was alien to the English middle-class, playing out its rituals here, as if on a stage. I knew even then they were anachronistic, absurd, and, of course, admirable in their tenacity. These were the 'nice people' my mother yearned for, exiled in her red earth district surrounded by people—as she was convinced—of the wrong class" (24).

11. See Sizemore's *A Female Vision of the City* for a discussion of the greater diversity and class mix in London compared to American cities, which are more homogeneously zoned (18–25) and for a discussion of the celebration of the city in Lessing's *Four-Gated City* and *The Diaries of Jane Somers*.

12. Ruth Saxton notes that Jane has thought of her body as a "beautiful artifact to be petted and groomed and used as a high-powered tool to create an image. . . . Mounting difficulties of age and illness in Maudie bring Jane face to face with the limitations of the body and with her own mortality" ("The Female Body Veiled" 118).

CONCLUSION

1. In "Under Western Eyes" Chandra Mohanty critiqued the way Third World women were often "located as implicit *victims* of particular socio-economic systems" by Western scholars. "This mode of defining women primarily in terms of their *object status*," Mohanty continues, "(however benevolently motivated) needs to be both named and challenged" (259–60).

Bibliography

Abel, Elizabeth, Marianne Hirsch, and Elizabeth Langland, eds. *The Voyage In: Fictions of Female Development*. Hanover: University Press of New England, 1983.

Aergeter, Lindsay Pentolfe. "A Dialectic of Autonomy and Community: Tsitsi Dangarembga's *Nervous Conditions*." *Tulsa Studies in Women's Literature* 15.2 (Fall 1996): 231–40.

Afzal-Khan, Fawzia. *Cultural Imperialism and the Indo-English Novel: Genre and Ideology in R.K. Narayan, Anita Desai, Kamala Marandaya, and Salman Rushdie*. University Park: Pennsylvania State University Press, 1993.

Agatucci, Cora. "Breaking from the Cage of Identity: Doris Lessing and *The Diaries of Jane Somers*." *Gender and Genre in Literature*. Ed. Janice Morgan and Colette T. Hall. New York: Garland, 1991. 45–56.

Alexander, M. Jacqui, and Chandra Talpade Mohanty, eds. *Feminist Genealogies, Colonial Legacies, Democratic Futures*. New York: Routledge, 1997.

Allan, Tuzyline Jita. *Womanist and Feminist Aesthetics*. Athens: Ohio University Press, 1995.

Anderson, Benedict. *Imagined Communities: Reflections on the Origin and Spread of Nationalism*. Rev. ed. 1983. London: Verso, 1991.

Anderson, Jessica. *Tirra Lirra by the River*. New York: Penguin, 1978.

Anzaldúa, Gloria. *Borderlands/La Frontera: The New Mestiza.* San Francisco: Aunt Lute Books, 1987.

Appiah, Kwame Anthony. "Is the 'Post-' in 'Postcolonial' the 'Post-' in 'Postmodern?'" *Dangerous Liaisons: Gender, Nation, and Postcolonial Perspectives.* Eds. Anne McClintock, Aamir Mufti, and Ella Shohat. Minneapolis: University of Minnesota Press, 1997. 420–44.

Ash, Susan. "*The Bone People* after *Te Kaihau.*" *World Literature Written in English* 29.1 (Spring 1989): 123–35.

Ashcroft, Bill, Gareth Griffiths, and Helen Tiffin. *The Empire Writes Back: Theory and Practice in Post-Colonial Literatures.* New York: Routledge, 1989.

Atwood, Margaret. *Cat's Eye.* 1988. New York: Anchor, 1998.

———. "Waltzing Again." Interview with Earl G. Ingersoll. *Margaret Atwood: Conversations.* Ed. Earl G. Ingersoll. Princeton: Ontario Review Press, 1990. 234–38.

———. "The Writer: A New Canadian Life-Form." *New York Times Book Review* 18 May 1997: 39.

Babu, Sylvia, M.D. Conversation. 8 Aug. 1997, Atlanta, GA.

Baker, Houston, Manthia Diawara, and Ruth Lindeborg, eds. *Black British Cultural Studies: A Reader.* Chicago: University of Chicago Press, 1996.

Bakhtin, Mikhail Mikhailovich. *The Dialogic Imagination: Four Essays.* Trans. Caryl Emerson and Michael Holquist. Austin: University of Texas Press, 1981.

Banerjee, Chinmoy. "Atwood's Time: Hiding Art in *Cat's Eye.*" *Modern Fiction Studies* 86.4 (Winter 1990): 513–22.

Barry, Elaine. "The Expatriate Vision of Jessica Anderson." *Meridian: The La Trobe University English Review* 3.1 (May 1984): 3–11.

Bateson, Mary Catherine. *Composing a Life.* New York: Penguin, 1989.

Bellos, Linda. "A Vision Back and Forth." *Talking Back: Lesbians of African and Asian Descent Speak Out.* Ed. Valerie Mason-John. London: Cassell, 1995. 52–71.

Benhabib, Seyla. "Sexual Difference and Collective Identities: The New Global Constellation." *Signs: Journal of Women in Culture and Society* 24.1 (Winter 1999): 335–61.

Benjamin, Jessica. "A Desire of One's Own: Psychoanalytic Feminism and Intersubjective Space." *Feminist Studies/Critical Studies.* Ed. Teresa de Lauretis. Bloomington: Indiana University Press, 1986. 78–101.

Bergner, Gwen. "Who Is That Masked Woman? or, The Role of Gender in Fanon's *Black Skin, White Masks.*" *PMLA* 110.1 (Jan. 1995): 75–88.

Berrian, Brenda F. "Her Ancestor's Voice: The Ibéji Transcendence of Duality in Buchi Emecheta's *Kehinde.*" *Emerging Perspectives on*

Buchi Emecheta. Ed. Marie Umeh. Trenton, NJ: Africa World Press, 1996. 169–84.

Bhabha, Homi. "DissemiNation: time, narrative, and the margins of the modern nation." *Nation and Narration.* Ed. Homi Bhabha. London: Routledge, 1990. 291–322. Rpt. in rev. version in *The Location of Culture.* By Homi Bhabha. New York: Routledge, 1994. 139–70.

———. "Editor's Introduction: Minority Maneuvers and Unsettled Negotiations." *Critical Inquiry* 23.3 (Spring 1997): 431–59.

———. *The Location of Culture.* New York: Routledge, 1994.

———. "The Third Space: Interview with Homi Bhabha." *Identity: Community, Culture, Difference.* Ed. Jonathan Rutherford. London: Lawrence & Wishart, 1990. 207–21.

———. "The World and the Home." *Dangerous Liaisons: Gender, Nation and Postcolonial Perspectives.* Eds. Anne McClintock, Aamir Mufti, and Ella Shohat. Minneapolis: University of Minnesota Press, 1997. 445–55.

Boyers, Robert, et al. "A Conversation with Nadine Gordimer." *Conversations with Nadine Gordimer.* Eds. Nancy T. Bazin and Marilyn D. Seymour. Jackson: University of Mississippi Press, 1990. 185–214.

Bromberg, Pamela S. "Margaret Drabble's *The Radiant Way*: Feminist Metafiction." *The Novel* 24.1 (Fall 1990): 5–25.

Brown, Lyn Mikel. "The Dangers of Time Travel: Revisioning the Landscape of Girls' Relationships in Margaret Atwood's *Cat's Eye.*" *LIT Literature Interpretation Theory* 6.3–4 (Dec. 1995): 285–98.

Bryson, John. "Keri Hulme in Conversation with John Bryson." *Antipodes: A North American Journal of Australian Literature* 8.2 (1994): 131–35.

Burford, Barbara. *The Threshing Floor.* Ithaca, NY: Firebrand Books, 1987.

———. "'When Everything Else Is Done and Dusted': An Interview with Barbara Burford, Scientist and Writer, Bradford, England, Aug. 6, 1998." By Christine W. Sizemore. *MaComère* 2 (1999): 23–35.

Busia, Abena P.A. "What Is Your Nation? Reconnecting Africa and Her Diaspora through Paule Marshall's *Praisesong for the Widow.*" *Changing Our Own Words: Essays on Criticism, Theory and Writing by Black Women.* Ed. Cheryl A. Wall. New Brunswick: Rutgers University Press, 1989. 196–211.

Butler, Judith. *Gender Trouble: Feminism and the Subversion of Identity.* New York: Routledge, 1990.

Butler, Robert. "The Life Review: An Interpretation of Reminiscence in the Aged." *Psychiatry: Journal of the Study of Interpersonal Processes* 26 (1963): 65–76.

Carby, Hazel V. "White Woman Listen! Black Feminism and the Boundaries of Sisterhood." *Black British Feminism: A Reader.* Ed. Heidi Safia Mirza. London: Routledge, 1997. 45–53.

Chambers, Iain, and Lidia Curti, eds. *The Post-Colonial Question: Common Skies, Divided Horizons*. London: Routledge, 1996.

Chatterjee, Partha. "The Nationalist Resolution of the Women's Question." *Recasting Women: Essays in Colonial History*. Ed. Kumkum Sangari and Sudesh Vaid. New Delhi: Kali for Women, 1989. 233–53.

Chennells, Anthony, and Debrah Raschke. "Doris Lessing and the Spirit of Postcolonialism: Zimbabwe to Star Wars." *Doris Lessing Studies* 21.2 (Fall 2001): 1–3.

Chodorow, Nancy. "Gender as a Personal and Cultural Construction." *Signs: Journal of Women in Culture and Society* 20.3 (Spring 1995): 516–44.

———. "Gender, Relation, and Difference in Psychoanalytic Perspective." *Feminism and Psychoanalytic Theory*. New Haven: Yale University Press, 1989. 99–113.

———. *The Reproduction of Mothering: Psychoanalysis and the Sociology of Gender*. Berkeley: University of California Press, 1978.

Christian, Barbara. "Ritualistic Process and the Structure of Paule Marshall's *Praisesong for the Widow*." *Perspectives on Black Women Writers*. New York: Pergamon Press, 1985. 149–58.

Clingman, Stephen. *The Novels of Nadine Gordimer: History from the Inside*. 2nd ed. Amherst: University of Massachusetts Press, 1986.

Comas-Díaz, Lillian, and Beverly Greene, eds. *Women of Color: Integrating Ethnic and Gender Identities in Psychotherapy*. New York: Guilford Press, 1994.

Cooke, John. *The Novels of Nadine Gordimer: Private Lives/Public Landscapes*. Baton Rouge: Louisiana State University Press, 1985.

Cooke, Nathalie. "Reading Reflections: The Autobiographical Illusion in *Cat's Eye*." *Essays on Life Writing: From Genre to Critical Practice*. Ed. Marlene Kadar. Toronto: University of Toronto Press, 1992. 162–70.

Courser, G. Thomas. "Oppression and Repression: Personal and Collective Memory in Paule Marshall's *Praisesong for the Widow* and Leslie Marmon Silko's *Ceremony*." *Memory and Cultural Politics: New Approaches to American Ethnic Literature*. Ed. Amritjit Singh, Joseph Skerrett, Jr. and Robert E. Hogan. Boston: Northeastern University Press, 1996. 106–20.

Covi, Giovanna. "Keri Hulme's *The Bone People*: A Critique of Gender." *Imagination and the Creative Impulse in the New Literatures in English*. Ed. M.T. Bindella and G.V. Davis. Amsterdam: Rodopi Press, 1993. 219–31.

Creamer, Heidi. "An Apple for the Teacher? Femininity, Coloniality, and Food in *Nervous Conditions*." *Kunapipi: Journal of Post-Colonial Writing* 16.1 (1994): 349–60.

Dale, Judith. "*the bone people*: (Not) Having It Both Ways." *Landfall* 39.4 (1985): 413–28.

Dangarembga, Tsitsi. "Between Gender, Race and History: Kirsten Holst Petersen Interviews Tsitsi Dangarembga." *Kunapipi: Journal of Post-Colonial Writing* 16.1 (1994): 345–48.

———. "Interview with Rosemary Marangoly George and Helen Scott." *The Novel* 26.3 (Spring 1993): 309–19.

———. *Nervous Conditions*. 1988. Seattle: Seal Press, 1989.

———. "Women Write About the Things That Move Them. Interview with Tsitsi Dangarembga." By Flora Veit-Wild. *Matatu* 3.6 (1989): 101–8.

Davidson, Arnold E. *Seeing in the Dark: Margaret Atwood's Cat's Eye*. Toronto: ECW press, 1997.

Davies, Carole Boyce. *Black Women, Writing and Identity: Migrations of the Subject*. New York: Routledge, 1994.

———. "Introduction: Feminist Consciousness and African Literary Criticism." *Ngambika: Studies of Women in African Literature*. Ed. Carole Boyce Davies and Anne Adams Graves. Trenton, NJ: Africa World Press, 1986. 1–23.

———. "Writing Off Marginality, Minoring, and Effacement." *Women's Studies International Forum* 14.1 (1991): 249–63.

de Lauretis, Teresa. *The Practice of Love: Lesbian Sexuality and Perverse Desire*. Bloomington: Indiana University Press, 1994.

DeLamotte, Eugenia C. *Places of Silence, Journeys of Freedom: The Fiction of Paule Marshall*. Philadelphia: University of Pennsylvania Press, 1998.

Denniston, Dorothy Hamer. *The Fictions of Paule Marshall: Reconstructions of History, Culture and Gender*. Knoxville: University of Tennessee Press, 1995.

Desai, Anita. "Against the Current: A Conversation with Anita Desai." Ed. Corinne Demas Bliss. *Massachusetts Review* 29.3 (Fall 1988): 521–37.

———. *Clear Light of Day*. New York: Penguin, 1980.

———. "'Feng Sui' or Spirit of Place." *A Sense of Place. Essays in Post-Colonial Literatures*. Ed. Britta Olinder. Göteborg: Gothenburg University, 1984. 101–9.

———. "Interview." *Interviews with Writers of the Post-Colonial World*. Eds. Feroza Jussawalla and Reed Way Dasenbrock. Jackson: University Press of Mississippi, 1992. 157–79.

Dever, Maryanne. "Violence as *lingua franca*: Keri Hulme's *The Bone People*." *World Literature Written in English* 29.2 (Autumn 1989): 23–35.

Dharwadker, Aparna, and Vinay Dharwadker. "Language, Identity, and

Nation in Postcolonial Indian English Literature." *English Post-coloniality: Literature from Around the World*. Eds. Radhika Mohanram and Gita Rajan. Westport, CT: Greenwood Press, 1996. 89–106.

Dharwadker, Vinay. "The Internationalization of Literatures." *New National and Post-Colonial Literatures: An Introduction*. Ed. Bruce King. Oxford: Clarendon Press, 1996. 59–77.

Doan, Laura. "Jeanette Winterson's *Sexing the Cherry*." *The Lesbian Post-modern*. Ed. Laura Doan. New York: Columbia University Press, 1994. 137–55.

Drabble, Margaret. "The Author Comments." *Dutch Quarterly Review of Anglo-American Letters* 5.1 (1975): 35–38.

———. *The Gates of Ivory*. New York: Viking, 1991.

———. "Interview." *Women Writers Talk: Interviews with Ten Women Writers*. By Olga Kenyon. New York: Carroll & Graf,. 1989. 26–49.

———. "Mimesis: The Representation of Reality in the Post-War British Novel." *Mosaic* 20.1 (1987): 1–14.

———. *A Natural Curiosity*. New York: Viking, 1989.

———. "The North beyond the Grit." *New York Times* 26 July 1987, sec. 10 "Travel": 15.

———. "A Novelist in a Derelict City." *New York Times Magazine* 14 Apr. 1985: 76–81.

———. *The Radiant Way*. New York: Ballantine Books, 1987.

———. *A Summer Bird-Cage*. London: Weidenfeld and Nicolson, 1962.

DuPlessis, Rachel Blau. *Writing beyond the Ending: Narrative Strategies of Twentieth-Century Women Writers*. Bloomington: Indiana University Press, 1985.

Emecheta, Buchi. "Feminism with a Small 'f'!" *Criticism and Ideology: Second African Writers Conference, Stockholm 1986*. Ed. Kirsten Holst Petersen. Uppsala, Sweden: Scandinavian Institute of African Studies, 1988. 173–85.

———. *Head Above Water: An Autobiography*. Oxford: Heinemann, 1986.

———. "Interview with Buchi Emecheta." By Davidson Umeh and Marie Umeh. *Ba Shiru: A Journal of African Languages and Literature* 12.2 (1985): 19–25.

———. *Kehinde*. Oxford: Heinemann, 1994.

Erikson, Erik H. *Childhood and Society*. 2nd ed. 1950. New York: W.W. Norton, 1963.

———. *Gandhi's Truth*. New York: W.W. Norton, 1969.

———. *Identity, Youth and Crisis*. New York: W.W. Norton, 1968.

———. *The Life Cycle Completed*. Extended Version with new chapters by Joan M. Erikson. New York: W.W. Norton, 1997.

———. "Report to Vikram." *Identity and Adulthood*. Ed. Sudhir Kakar. 1979. Delhi: Oxford University Press, 1992. 13–34.

Erikson, Erik, Joan M. Erikson, and Helen Q. Kivnick. *Vital Involvement in Old Age*. New York: W.W. Norton, 1986.

Erikson, Joan M. "Preface to the Extended Version." *The Life Cycle Completed*. By Erik H. Erikson. Extended ed. New York: W.W. Norton, 1997. 1–9.

Falwell, Marilyn. *Heterosexual Plots and Lesbian Narratives*. New York: New York University Press, 1996.

Fanon, Franz. *The Wretched of the Earth*. Trans. Constance Farrington. New York: Grove Press, 1963.

Fee, Margery. "Why C.K. Stead Didn't Like Keri Hulme's *The Bone People*: Who Can Write as Other?" *Australian and New Zealand Studies in Canada* 1 (Spring 1989): 11–32.

Felski, Rita. "The Doxa of Difference." *Signs: Journal of Women in Culture and Society* 23.1 (Autumn 1997): 1–21.

———. *The Gender of Modernity*. Cambridge: Harvard University Press, 1995.

Fishburn, Katherine. *Reading Buchi Emecheta: Cross-Cultural Conversations*. Westport, CT: Greenwood Press, 1995.

Flockemann, Miki. "'Not-Quite Insiders and Not-Quite Outsiders': The 'Process of Womanhood' in *Beka Lamb*, *Nervous Conditions* and *Daughters of Twilight*." *Journal of Commonwealth Literature* 27.1 (1992): 37–47.

Friedman, Lawrence J. *Identity's Architect: A Biography of Erik Erikson*. New York: Scribner, 1999.

Friedman, Susan Stanford. *Mappings: Feminism and the Cultural Geographies of Encounter*. Princeton, NJ: Princeton University Press, 1998.

Gallagher, Donat. "Tirra Lirra by the Brisbane River." *Literature in North Queensland* 10.1 (1981): 101–10.

Gardiner, Judith Kegan. *Rhys, Stead, Lessing and the Politics of Empathy*. Bloomington: Indiana University Press, 1989.

George, Rosemary Marangoly. *The Politics of Home: Postcolonial Relocations and Twentieth-Century Fiction*. Cambridge: Camridge University Press, 1996.

Gilbert, Pam. *Coming Out from Under: Contemporary Australian Women Writers*. London: Pandora Press, 1988.

Gilligan, Carol. *In a Different Voice: Psychological Theory and Women's Development*. Cambridge: Harvard University Press, 1982.

Gilligan, Carol, N. Lyons, and T. Hanmer, eds. *Making Connections: The Relational Worlds of Adolescent Girls at Emma Willard School*. Cambridge: Harvard University Press, 1990.

Gilroy, Paul. *The Black Atlantic: Modernity and Double Consciousness*. Cambridge: Harvard University Press, 1993.

Gordimer, Nadine. "An Interview with Nadine Gordimer." By Nancy Topping Bazin. *Contemporary Literature* 36.4 (Winter 1995): 571–87.

——. "Living in the Interregnum." *The Essential Gesture: Writing, Politics and Places.* Ed. Stephen Clingman. New York: Alfred A. Knopf, 1988. 261–84.

——. *The Lying Days.* 1953. New York: Penguin, 1994.

——. "My New South African Identity." *New York Times Magazine* 30 May 1999: 40–43.

——. *My Son's Story.* 1990. New York: Penguin, 1991.

——. *None to Accompany Me.* New York: Penguin Books, 1994.

——. *Writing and Being.* Cambridge: Harvard University Press, 1995.

Gordimer, Nadine, and David Goldblatt. *Lifetimes under Apartheid.* New York: Alfred A. Knopf, 1986.

Green, Robert. "From *The Lying Days* to *July's People*: The Novels of Nadine Gordimer." *Journal of Modern Literature* 14.4 (Spring 1988): 543–63.

Greene, Gayle. "Bleak Houses: Doris Lessing, Margaret Drabble and the Condition of England." *Forum for Modern Language Studies* 28.4 (Oct. 1992): 304–19.

——. *Doris Lessing: The Poetics of Change.* Ann Arbor: University of Michigan Press, 1994.

Greenstein, Susan M. "Apologia Pro Vita Sua? Nadine Gordimer's *Writing and Being.*" *Research in African Literatures* 28.2 (1997): 145–53.

——. "*My Son's Story*: Drenching the Censors—the Dilemma of White Writing." *The Later Fiction of Nadine Gordimer.* Ed. Bruce King. New York: Macmillan, 1993. 191–209.

Grewel, Inderpal, and Caren Kaplan, eds. *Scattered Hegemonies: Postmodernity and Transnational Feminist Practices.* Minneapolis: University of Minnesota Press, 1994.

Griffin, Gabriele. "'Writing the Body': Reading Joan Riley, Grace Nichols and Ntozake Shange." *Black Women's Writing.* Ed. Gina Wisker. New York: St. Martin's Press, 1993. 19–42.

Gutmann, David L. "Psychoanalysis and Aging: A Developmental View." *The Course of Life: Adulthood and the Aging Process.* Ed. Stanley E. Greenspan and George H. Pollack. Vol. 3 Washington: DC: NIMH, 1980. 489–517.

Hall, Stuart. "Cultural Identity and Diaspora." *Colonial Discourse and Post-Colonial Theory: A Reader.* Eds. Patrick Williams and Laura Chrisman. New York: Columbia University Press, 1994. 392–403.

——. "Minimal Selves." *Black British Cultural Studies: A Reader.* Eds. Houston Baker, Manthia Diawara, and Ruth Lindeborg. Chicago: University of Chicago Press, 1996. 114–19.

——. "When Was 'The Post-Colonial'? Thinking at the Limit." *The Post-Colonial Questions: Common Skies, Divided Horizons.* Ed. Iain Chambers and Lidia Curti. London: Routledge, 1996. 242–60.

Hamelin, Christine. "*Fitted to his own Web of Music*: Art as Renaming in the bone people." *Australian and New Zealand Studies in Canada* 10 (1993): 106–20.

Harne, Lynn. "Beyond Sex and Romance? Lesbian Relationships in Contemporary Fiction." *Beyond Sex and Romance? The Politics of Contemporary Lesbian Fiction.* Ed. Elaine Hutton. London: Women's Press, 1998. 124–51.

Hawley, John C. "Coming to Terms: Buchi Emecheta's *Kehinde* and the Birth of a 'Nation.'" *Emerging Perspectives on Buchi Emecheta.* Ed. Marie Umeh. Trenton, NJ: Africa World Press, 1996. 333–48.

Haynes, Roslynn D. "Art as Reflection in Jessica Anderson's *Tirra Lirra by the River.*" *Australian Literary Studies* 12.3 (May 1986): 316–23.

Head, Dominic. "Gordimer's *None to Accompany Me*: Revisionism and Interregnum." *Research in African Literatures* 26.4 (1995): 46–57.

———. *Nadine Gordimer.* Cambridge Studies in African and Caribbean Literature. Cambridge: Cambridge University Press, 1994.

Hecq, Dominique. "*Tirra Lirra!* Tales of Purloined Letters and Edited Destinies." *The Contact and the Culmination: Essays in Honour of Hena Maes-Jelinek.* Eds. Marc Delrez and Benedicte Ledent. Liege, Belgium: L3—Liege Language and Literature, 1996. 171–82.

Heilbrun, Carolyn G. *Writing a Woman's Life.* New York: Ballantine, 1988.

Henke, Suzette. "Constructing the Female Hero: Keri Hulme's *The Bone People.*" *Myths, Heroes and Anti-Heroes: Essays on the Literature and Culture of the Asia-Pacific Region.* Eds. Bruce Bennet and Dennis Haskell. Nedlands: Centre for Studies in Australian Literature, 1992, 89–97.

Hite, Molly. "Optics and Autobiography in Margaret Atwood's *Cat's Eye.*" *Twentieth Century Literature* 41.2 (Summer 1995): 135–59.

Holloway, Karla F.C. *Moorings and Metaphors: Figures of Culture and Gender in Black Women's Literature.* New Brunswick, NJ: Rutgers University Press, 1992.

Holm, Antoinette. "'. . . of indeterminate sex': Escaping Androgyny in Keri Hulme's *the bone people.*" *New Literatures Review* 30 (Winter 1995): 83–96.

Howells, Coral. "*Cat's Eye*: Elaine Risley's Retrospective Art." *Margaret Atwood: Writing and Subjectivity: New Critical Essays.* Ed. Colin Nicholson. New York: St. Martin's Press, 1994. 204–18.

Huggan, Graham. "Philomela's Retold Story: Silence, Music, and the Postcolonial Text." *Journal of Commonwealth Literature* 25.1 (1990): 12–23.

Hughes, Mary Ann. "Transgressing Boundaries." *Span: Journal of the South Pacific Association for Commonwealth Literature* 39 (1994): 55–68.

Hulme, Keri. *The Bone People.* 1983. New York: Penguin, 1986.

———. "An Interview with Keri Hulme." By Andrew Peek. *New Literatures Review* 20 (Winter 1990): 1–11.

Hulme, Keri, and Gerry Turcotte. "Reconsidering *the bone people*." *Australian and New Zealand Studies in Canada* 12 (1994): 135–54.

Ingersoll, Earl G. "Margaret Atwood's *Cat's Eye*: Re-Viewing Women in a Postmodern World." *Ariel: A Review of International English Literature* 22.4 (Oct. 1991): 17–27.

James, Adeola. "Buchi Emecheta." *In Their Own Voices: African Women Writers Talk*. Oxford: Heinemann, 1990. 34–45.

JanMohamed, Abdul R. *Manichaean Aesthetics: The Politics of Literature in Colonial Africa*. Amherst: University of Massachusetts Press, 1983.

Jayakar, Kushalata. "Women of the Indian Subcontinent." *Women of Color: Integrating Ethnic and Gender Identities in Psychotherapy*. Eds. Lillian Comas-Díaz and Beverly Greene. New York: Guilford Press, 1994. 161–81.

Jones, Dorothy. "Post-Colonial Families Reconfigured: A Discussion of *The Bone People* and *Miss Smilla's Feeling for Snow*." *Kunapipi: Journal of Post-Colonial Writing* 19.2 (1997): 36–48.

Jussawalla, Feroza. "South Asian Diaspora Writers in Britain: 'Home' versus 'Hybridity.'" *Ideas of Home: Literature of Asian Migration*. Ed. Geoffrey Kain. East Lansing: Michigan State University Press, 1997. 17–37.

Jussawalla, Feroza, and Reed Way Dasenbrock, eds. *Interviews with Writers of the Post-Colonial World*. Jackson: University Press of Mississippi, 1992.

Kain, Geoffrey, ed. *Ideas of Home: Literature of Asian Migration*. East Lansing: Michigan State University Press, 1997.

Kakar, Sudhir. *The Inner World: A Psychoanalytic Study of Childhood and Society in India*. Delhi: Oxford University Press, 1978.

———, ed. *Identity and Adulthood*. 1979. Delhi: Oxford University Press, 1992.

Kanwar, Asha. *Virginia Woolf and Anita Desai: A Comparative Study*. New Delhi: Prestige Books, 1989.

Kaplan, Carey. "Britain's Imperialist Past in Doris Lessing's Futuristic Fiction." *Doris Lessing: The Alchemy of Survival*. Ed. Carey Kaplan and Ellen Cronan Rose. Athens: Ohio University Press, 1988. 149–58.

Kaplan, E. Ann. "Trauma and Aging: Marlene Dietrich, Melanie Klein, and Marguerite Duras." *Figuring Age: Women, Bodies, Generations*. Ed. Kathleen Woodward. Bloomington: Indiana University Press, 1999. 171–94.

Karamcheti, Indira. "The Geographics of Marginality: Place and Textuality in Simone Schwarz-Bart and Anita Desai." *Feminist Explorations of Literary Space*. Ed. Margaret Higonnet and Joan Templeton. Amherst: University of Massachusetts Press, 1994. 125–46.

Katak, Ketu H. "Post-Colonial Women Writers and Feminisms." *New National and Post-Colonial Literatures: An Introduction*. Ed. Bruce King. Oxford: Clarendon Press, 1996. 230–44.

King, Bruce, ed. *New National and Post-Colonial Literatures: An Introduction*. Oxford: Clarendon Press, 1996.

Le Cam, Georges-Goulven. "The Quest for Archetypal Self-Truth in Keri Hulme's *The Bone People*: Towards a Western Re-Definition of Maori Culture?" *Commonwealth Essays and Studies* 15.2 (Spring 1983): 66–79.

Lessing, Doris. *African Laughter: Four Visits to Zimbabwe*. New York: HarperCollins, 1992.

———. "Afterward." *The Making of the Representative for Planet 8*. New York: Knopf, 1982. 123–45.

———. *The Diaries of Jane Somers*. New York: Random House, 1984.

———. "Doris Lessing Talks About Jane Somers." A Transcription of a Radio Talk broadcast over KPKA, San Francisco, 19 Mar. 1985. *Doris Lessing Newsletter* 10.1 (Spring 1986):3–5, 14.

———. *Walking in the Shade: Volume Two of My Autobiography, 1949–1962*. New York: HarperCollins, 1997.

Levinson, Daniel J. *The Seasons of a Woman's Life*. New York: Knopf, 1996.

Liddle, Joanna, and Rama Joshi. *Daughters of Independence: Gender, Caste and Class in India*. London: Zed Books, 1986.

Lock, Helen. "'Building Up from Fragments': The Oral Memory Process in Some Recent African-American Written Narratives." *Race-ing Representation: Voice, History, and Sexuality*. Eds. Kostas Myrsiades and Linda Myrsiades. New York: Rowman and Littlefield, 1998. 200–212.

Loomba, Ania. *Colonialism/Postcolonialism*. New York: Routledge, 1998.

Lorde, Audre. "Uses of the Erotic: The Erotic as Power." *Sister Outsider*. Freedom, CA: Crossing Press, 1984. 53–59.

Marshall, Paule. *Praisesong for the Widow*. New York: NAL, 1983.

———. "To Be in the World: An Interview with Paule Marshall." By Angela Elam. *New Letters* 62.4 (1995): 97–105.

Martin, Biddy, and Chandra Talpade Mohanty. "Feminist Politics: What's Home Got to Do with It?" *Feminist Studies/Critical Studies*. Ed. Teresa de Lauretis. Bloomington: Indiana University Press, 1986. 191–212.

Mason-John, Valerie, ed. *Talking Black: Lesbians of African and Asian Descent Speak Out*. London: Cassell, 1995.

McClintock, Anne. "The Angel of Progress: Pitfalls of the Term Post-Colonialism." *Colonial Discourse and Post-Colonial Theory: A Reader*. Eds. Patrick Williams and Laura Chrisman. New York: Columbia University Press, 1994. 291–304.

———. *Imperial Leather: Race, Gender and Sexuality in the Colonial Conquest*. New York: Routledge, 1995.

McClintock, Anne, Aamir Mufti, and Ella Shohat, eds. *Dangerous Liaisons: Gender, Nation and Postcolonial Perspectives*. Minneapolis: University of Minnesota Press, 1997.

McCombs, Judith. "Contrary Re-Memberings: The Creating Self and Feminism in 'Cat's Eye.'" *Canadian Literature* no. 129 (Summer 1991): 9–23.

McRobbie, Angela. "Different, Youthful, Subjectivities." *The Post-Colonial Question: Common Skies, Divided Horizons*. Eds. Iain Chambers and Lidia Curti. London: Routledge, 1996. 30–46.

McWilliams, Sally. "Tsitsi Dangarembga's *Nervous Conditions*: At the Crossroads of Feminism and Post-Colonialism." *World Literature Written in English* 31.1 (1991): 103–12.

Mercer, Ramona T., Elizabeth G. Nichols, and Glen Caspers Doyle. *Transitions in a Woman's Life: Major Life Events in Developmental Context*. New York: Springer, 1989.

Mirza, Heidi Safia, ed. *Black British Feminism: A Reader*. London: Routledge, 1997.

Mishra, Vijay, and Bob Hodge. "What is Post(-)Colonialism?" *Colonial Discourse and Post-Colonial Theory: A Reader*. Eds. Patrick Williams and Laura Chrisman. New York: Columbia University Press, 1994. 276–90.

Mohan, Rajeswari. "The Forked Tongue of Lyric in Anita Desai's *Clear Light of Day*." *Journal of Commonwealth Literature* 32.1 (1997): 47–66.

Mohanram, Radhika, and Gita Rajan, eds. *English Postcoloniality: Literatures from Around the World*. Westport, CT: Greenwood Press, 1996.

Mohanty, Chandra Talpade. "Feminist Encounters: Locating the Politics of Experience." *Social Postmodernism: Beyond Identity Politics*. Ed. Linda Nicholson and Steven Seidman. Cambridge: Cambridge University Press, 1995. 68–86.

———. "Introduction: Cartographies of Struggle." *Third World Women and the Politics of Feminism*. Ed. Chandra Talpade Mohanty, Anne Russo, and Lourdes Torres. Bloomington: Indiana University Press, 1987. 1–47.

———. "Under Western Eyes: Feminist Scholarship and Colonial Discourses." *Dangerous Liaisons: Gender, Nation and Postcolonial Perspective*. Eds. Anne McClintock, Aamir Mufti, and Ella Shohat. Minneapolis: University of Minnesota Press, 1997. 255–77. Also *Third World Women and the Politics of Feminism*. Eds. Chandra Talpade Mohanty, Anne Russo, and Lourdes Torres. Bloomington: Indiana University Press, 1987. 51–80.

Moore-Gilbert, Bart. *Postcolonial Theory: Contexts, Practices, Politics.* London: Verso, 1997.

Morrow, Patrick. "Disappearance through Integration: Three Maori Writers Retaliate." *Journal of Commonwealth and Postcolonial Studies* 1.1 (Fall 1993): 92–99.

Mukerjee, Arun P. "Other Worlds, Other Texts: Teaching Anita Desai's *Clear Light of Day* to Canadian Students." *Order and Partialities: Theory, Pedagogy and the "Postcolonial."* Ed. Kostas Myrsiades and Jerry McGuire. Albany: State University of New York Press, 1995. 341–57.

———. "Whose Post-Colonialism and Whose Postmodernism?" *World Literature Written in English* 30.2 (Autumn 1990): 1–9.

Myer, Valerie G. *Margaret Drabble: A Reader's Guide.* New York: St. Martin's Press, 1991.

Nabar, Vrinda. "The Image of India in Anita Desai's *Clear Light of Day.*" *Recent Commonwealth Literature.* Ed. R.K. Dhawan, P.V. Dhamija, and A.K. Shrivastava. New Delhi: Prestige Books, 1989. 227–36.

Nair, Supriya. "Melancholic Women: The Intellectual Hysteric(s) in *Nervous Conditions.*" *Research in African Literatures* 26.2 (Summer 1995): 129–39.

Nandy, Ashis. *The Intimate Enemy: Loss and Recovery of Self under Colonialism.* Delhi: Oxford University Press, 1983.

———. "Woman versus Womanliness in India: An Essay in Social and Political Psychology." *Psychoanalytic Review* 63.2 (1976): 301–15.

Newman, Judie. *Nadine Gordimer.* London: Routledge, 1988.

Nfah-Abbenyi, Juliana Makuchi. *Gender in African Women's Writing: Identity, Sexuality and Difference.* Bloomington: Indiana University Press, 1997.

Ngcobo, Lauretta. "African Motherhood—Myth and Reality." *Criticism and Ideology: Second African Writers Conference, Stockholm 1986.* Ed. Kirsten Holst Petersen. Uppsala, Sweden: Scandinavian Institute of African Studies, 1988. 141–54.

Nicolson, Colin. "Introduction." *Margaret Atwood: Writing and Subjectivity: New Critical Essays.* Ed. Colin Nicholson. New York: St. Martin's Press, 1994. 1–10.

O'Brien, Susie. "Raising Silent Voices: The Role of the Silent Child in *An Imaginary Life* and *The Bone People.*" *Span: Journal of the South Pacific Association for Commonwealth Literature* 30 (Apr. 1990): 79–91.

Ogundele, Oladipo Joseph. "A Conversation with Dr. Buchi Emecheta, July 22, 1994." *Emerging Perspectives on Buchi Emecheta.* Ed. Marie Umeh. Trenton, NJ: Africa World Press, 1996. 445–56.

Ogundipe-Leslie, 'Molara. "'Re-Creating Ourselves All Over the World.'

A Conversation with Paule Marshall." *Moving Beyond Boundaries. Volume II: Black Women's Diasporas.* Ed. Carole Boyce Davies. New York: New York University Press, 1995. 19–26.

Ogunyemi, Chikwenye Okonjo. *Africa Wo/man Palava: The Nigerian Novel by Women.* Chicago: University of Chicago Press, 1996.

———. "Womanism: The Dynamics of the Contemporary Black Female Novel in English." *Signs: Journal of Women in Culture and Society* 11.1 (1985): 63–85.

Osborne, Carol. "Constructing the Self through Memory: *Cat's Eye* as a Novel of Female Development." *Frontiers* 14.3 (1994): 95–112.

Panigrahi, Bipin B. "Self-Apprehension and Self-Identity in *Clear Light of Day.*" *The New Indian Novel in English: A Study of the 1980's.* Ed. Viney Kirpal. New Delhi: Allied Publishers Ltd., 1990. 73–81.

Papalia, Diane E., and Sally Wendlos Olds. *Human Development.* 8th ed. Boston: McGraw-Hill, 1998.

Parekh, Pushpa Naidu. "Redefining the Postcolonial Female Self: Women in Anita Desai's *Clear Light of Day.*" *Between the Lines: South Asians and Postcoloniality.* Ed. Deepika Bahri and Mary Vasudeva. Philadelphia: Temple University Press, 1996. 270–83.

Petersen, Kirsten Holst, ed. *Criticism and Ideology: Second African Writers Conference, Stockholm 1986.* Uppsala, Sweden: Scandinavian Institute of African Studies, 1988.

Pettis, Joyce. *Toward Wholeness in Paule Marshall's Fiction.* Charlottesville: University of Virginia Press, 1995.

Pickering, Jean. "Margaret Drabble's Sense of the Middle Problem." *Twentieth Century Literature* 30.4 (Winter 1984): 475–83.

Pilgrim, Anita Naoko. "A Literary Movement." *Talking Back: Lesbians of African and Asian Descent Speak Out.* Ed. Valerie Mason-John. London: Cassell, 1995. 151–85.

Plasa, Carl. "Reading 'The Geography of Hunger' in Tsitsi Dangarembga's *Nervous Conditions*: From Franz Fanon to Charlotte Bronte." *Journal of Commonwealth Literature* 33.1 (1998): 35–45.

Prentice, Chris. "Re-writing Their Stories, Renaming Themselves: Postcolonialism and Feminism in the Fictions of Keri Hulme and Audrey Thomas." *Span: Journal of the South Pacific Association for Commonwealth Literature* 23 (Sept. 1986): 68–80.

Quayson, Ato. *Postcolonialism: Theory, Practice or Process?* Cambridge, United Kingdom: Polity Press in association with Blackwell Publishers, 2000.

Ramanujam, B.K. "Toward Maturity: Problems of Identity Seen in the Clinical Setting." *Identity and Adulthood.* Ed. Sudhir Kakar. 1979. Delhi: Oxford University Press, 1992. 37–55.

Ravel-Pinto, Thelma. "Buchi Emecheta at Spelman College." *Sage* 2.1 (Spring 1985): 50–51.

Ray, Sangeeta. "Gender and the Discourse of Nationalism in Anita Desai's *Clear Light of Day*." *Genders* 20 (1994): 96–119.

Reyes, Angelita. "Politics and Metaphors of Materialism in Paule Marshall's *Praisesong for the Widow* and Toni Morrison's *Tar Baby*." *Politics and the Muse: Studies in the Politics of Recent American Literature*. Ed. Adam Sorkin. Bowling Green, OH: Bowling Green State University Popular Press, 1989. 179–205.

Riley, Joan. "Interview." *Backtalk: Women Writers Speak Out*. Interviews by Donna Perry. New Brunswick, NJ: Rutgers University Press, 1993. 261–86.

———. *Waiting in the Twilight*. London: Women's Press, 1987.

Roof, Judith. *The Lure of Knowledge: Lesbian Sexuality and Theory*. New York: Columbia University Press, 1991.

Roy, Anindyo. "Postcoloniality and the Politics of Identity in the Diaspora: Figuring 'Home,' Locating Histories." *Postcolonial Discourse and Changing Cultural Contexts: Theory and Criticism*. Eds. Gita Rajan and Radhika Mohanram. Westport, CT: Greenwood Press, 1995. 101–115.

Rubenstein, Roberta. "Fixing the Past: Yearning and Nostalgia in Woolf and Lessing." *Woolf and Lessing: Breaking the Mold*. Eds. Ruth O. Saxton and Jean Tobin. New York: St. Martin's Press, 1994. 15–38.

———. "Sexuality and Intertextuality: Margaret Drabble's *The Radiant Way*." *Contemporary Literature* 30.1 (Spring 1989): 95–112.

Rushdie, Salman. *Imaginary Homelands: Essays and Criticism 1981–91*. New York: Viking, 1991.

Russo, Mary. "Aging and the Scandal of Anachronism." *Figuring the Body: Women, Bodies, Generations*. Ed. Kathleen Woodward. Bloomington: Indiana University Press, 1999. 20–33.

Said, Edward W. *Culture and Imperialism*. New York: Vintage, 1993.

Sarton, May. *As We Are Now*. New York: W.W. Norton, 1973.

Saxton, Ruth O. "The Female Body Veiled: From Crocus to Clitoris." *Woolf and Lessing: Breaking the Mold*. Eds. Ruth O. Saxton and Jean Tobin. New York: St. Martin's Press, 1994. 95–122.

———, ed. *The Girl: Constructions of the Girl in Contemporary Fiction by Women*. New York: St. Martin's Press, 1998.

Schmidt, Elizabeth. "Patriarchy, Capitalism and the Colonial State in Zimbabwe." *Signs: Journal of Women in Culture and Society* 16.4 (Summer 1991): 732–56.

Sharpe, Martha. "Margaret Atwood and Julia Kristeva: Space-Time, the Dissident Woman Artist, and the Pursuit of Female Solidarity in *Cat's Eye*." *Essays on Canadian Writing* 50 (Fall 1993): 174–89.

Sharpley-Whiting, T. Denean. "Anti-black Femininity and Mixed Race Identity: Engaging Fanon to Reread Capécia." *Fanon: A Critical Reader*.

Ed. Lewis R. Gordon, T. Denean Sharpley-Whiting, and Renée T. White. Cambridge, MA: Blackwell, 1996. 155–162.

Shohat, Ella. "Notes on the 'Post-Colonial.'" *Social Text 31/32* 10 (1992): 99–113.

Shohat, Ella, and Robert Stam. *Unthinking Eurocentrism: Multiculturalism and the Media*. New York: Routledge, 1994.

Sizemore, Christine Wick. *A Female Vision of the City: London in the Novels of Five British Women*. Knoxville: University of Tennessee Press, 1989.

———. "The London Novels of Buchi Emecheta." *Emerging Perspectives on Buchi Emecheta*. Ed. Marie Umeh. Trenton, NJ: Africa World Press, 1996. 367–85.

———. "Negotiating between Ideologies: The Search for Identity in Tsitsi Dangarembga's *Nervous Conditions* and Margaret Atwood's *Cat's Eye*." *Women's Studies Quarterly* 25.3–4 (Fall–Winter 1997): 68–82.

Skerrett, Joseph T., Jr. "Paule Marshall and the Crisis of Middle Years: *The Chosen Place, The Timeless People*." *Callaloo #18* 6.2 (1983): 68–73.

Smith, Rowland. Introduction. *Critical Essays on Nadine Gordimer*. Ed. Rowland Smith. Boston: G.K. Hall, 1990. 1–21.

Spillers, Hortense. "'All the Things You Could Be by Now If Sigmund Freud's Wife Was Your Mother': Psychoanalysis and Race." *Critical Inquiry* 22.4 (Summer 1996): 710–63.

Spivak, Gayatri Chakravorty. "Imperialism and Sexual Difference." *Oxford Literary Review* 8.1–2 (1986): 225–40.

———. *Outside the Teaching Machine*. New York: Routledge, 1993.

Sprague, Claire. *Rereading Doris Lessing: Narrative Patterns of Doubling and Repetition*. Chapel Hill: University of North Carolina Press, 1987.

Stimpson, Catherine R. "Zero Degree Deviancy: The Lesbian Novel in English." *Writing and Sexual Difference*. Ed. Elizabeth Abel. Chicago: University of Chicago Press, 1981. 243–59.

Strehle, Susan. *Fiction in the Quantum Universe*. Chapel Hill: University of North Carolina Press, 1992.

Suárez, Isabel Carrera. "Absent Mother(Land)s: Joan Riley's Fiction." *Motherlands: Black Women's Writing from Africa, the Caribbean and South Asia*. Ed. Susheila Nasta. New Brunswick: Rutgers University Press, 1992. 290–309.

Sugnet, Charles. "*Nervous Conditions*: Dangarembga's Feminist Reinvention of Fanon." *The Poetics of (M)othering: Womanhood Identity and Resistance in African Literature*. Ed. Obioma Nnaimeka. London: Routledge, 1997. 33–49.

Suleri, Sara. "Woman Skin Deep: Feminism and the Postcolonial Condition." *Critical Inquiry* Identities. Eds. Kwame Anthony Appiah and Henry Louis Gates, Jr. 18.4 (Summer 1993): 756–69.

Sykes, Arlene. "Jessica Anderson: Arrivals and Places." *Southerly: Magazine of the Australian English Association* 46.1 (Mar. 1986): 57–71.

Taylor, Jill, Carol Gilligan, and Amy Sullivan. *Between Voice and Silence: Women and Girls, Race and Relationship.* Cambridge: Harvard University Press, 1995.

Temple-Thurston, Barbara. *Nadine Gordimer Revisited.* New York: Twayne, 1999.

Thomas, Sue. "Killing the Hysteric in the Colonized's House: Tsitsi Dangarembga's *Nervous Conditions.*" *Journal of Commonwealth Literature* 27.1 (1992): 26–36.

Tiffin, Helen. "The Body in the Library: Identity, Opposition and the Settler-Invader Woman." *The Contact and the Culmination: Essays in Honour of Hena Maes-Jelinek.* Ed. Marc Delrez and Benedicte Ledent. Liege, Belgium: L3—Liege Language and Literature, 1996. 213–28.

———. "Plato's Cave: Educational and Critical Practice." *New National and Post-Colonial Literatures: An Introduction.* Ed. Bruce King. Oxford: Clarendon Press, 1996. 143–63.

———. "Post-Colonialism, Post-Modernism and the Rehabilitation of Post-Colonial History." *Journal of Commonwealth Literature* 23.1 (1988): 169–81.

Tuan, Li-Fu. *Space and Place: The Perspective of Experience.* Minneapolis: University of Minnesota Press, 1977.

Umeh, Marie, ed. *Emerging Perspectives on Buchi Emecheta.* Trenton, NJ: Africa World Press, 1996.

Uwakweh, Pauline Ada. "The Liberational Quality of Voicing in Tsitsi Dangarembga's *Nervous Conditions.*" *Research in African Literatures* 26.1 (Spring 1995): 75–84.

———. "To Ground the Wandering Muse: A Critique of Buchi Emecheta's Feminism." *Emerging Perspectives on Buchi Emecheta.* Ed. Marie Umeh. Trenton, NJ: Africa World Press, 1996. 395–406.

Vizzard, Michelle. "'Of Mimicry and Women': Hysteria and Anticolonial Feminism in Tsitsi Dangarembga's *Nervous Conditions.*" *Span: Journal of the South Pacific Association for Commonwealth Literature* 36 (Oct. 1993): 202–10.

Ward, Cynthia. "What They Told Buchi Emecheta: Oral Subjectivity and the Joys of Otherhood." *PMLA* 105.1 (Jan. 1990): 83–97.

Waxman, Barbara Frey. *From the Hearth to the Open Road: A Feminist Study of Aging in Contemporary Literature.* New York: Greenwood Press, 1990.

Wilentz, Gay. *Binding Cultures: Black Women Writers in Africa and the Diaspora.* Bloomington: Indiana University Press, 1992.

Willbanks, Ray. "The Strength to Be Me: The Protagonist in the Fiction of Jessica Anderson." *Span: Journal of the South Pacific Association for Commonwealth Literature and Language* 27 (Oct. 1988): 58–63.

Williams, Patrick, and Laura Chrisman, eds. *Colonial Discourse and and Post-Colonial Theory: A Reader*. New York: Columbia University Press, 1994.

Willis, Susan. *Specifying: Black Women Writing the American Experience*. Madison: University of Wisconsin Press, 1987.

Wilson, Lucy. "Aging and Ageism in Paule Marshall's *Praisesong for the Widow* and Beryl Gilroy's *Frangipani House*." *Journal of Caribbean Studies* 7.2–3 (1989–90): 189–99.

Wolff, Cynthia Griffin. "Erikson's 'Inner Space' Reconsidered." *Massachusetts Review* 20 (1979): 355–68.

Woodward, Kathleen. *Aging and Its Discontents: Freud and Other Fictions*. Bloomington: University of Indiana Press, 1991.

———, ed. *Figuring Age: Women, Bodies, Generations*. Bloomington: Indiana University Press, 1999.

Woolf, Virginia. *Three Guineas*. New York: Harcourt Brace Jovanovich, 1938.

Wyatt-Brown, Anne M. "Journeys of Late-Life Redemption in the Novels of Sarton, L'Engle, and Morrison." Paper presented at the South Atlantic Modern Language Assoc. Atlanta, Nov. 1993.

Wyatt-Brown, Anne M., and Janice Rossen, eds. *Aging and Gender in Literature: Studies in Creativity*. Charlottesville: University Press of Virginia, 1993.

Yaeger, Patricia. *Honey-Mad Women: Emancipatory Strategies in Women's Writing*. New York: Columbia University Press, 1988.

Yelin, Louise. "Decolonizing the Novel: Nadine Gordimer's *A Sport of Nature* and British Literary Traditions." *Decolonizing Tradition: New Views of Twentieth-Century "British" Literary Canons*. Ed. Karen R. Lawrence. Chicago: University of Illinois Press, 1992. 191–211.

Young, Robert. *Colonial Desire: Hybridity in Theory, Culture and Race*. London: Routledge, 1995.

———. *White Mythologies: Writing History and the West*. London: Routledge, 1990.

Index

About the Author

CHRISTINE WICK SIZEMORE is Professor of English at Spelman College. She has published journal articles and essays on such contemporary women writers as Doris Lessing, Margaret Atwood, Buchi Emecheta, Maureen Duffy, and Marge Piercy, and on various British and European modernists, including Joseph Conrad, Virginia Woolf, and Franz Kafka. She is the author of *A Female Vision of the City: London in the Novels of Five British Women* (1989).